COMING UP FOR AIR INSIDE THE SOUL OF A MEXICAN DANCER

BRUCE EVEN

ISBN: 979-8-3305-3746-4

DEDICATION

This book is dedicated to people who, with unbridled passion, give their body and soul to the people and pets they love.

CONTENTS

ACKNOWLEDGMENTS

I would like to acknowledge how challenging it was to write this, my first book. The completion of this fictional story involved dedication, passion, love, tears, patience, persistence and exhaustion. It took a lot out of me, but it was well worth the effort. I hope you all enjoy it.

1 CONTEMPLATING A NEW LIFE

Today, I woke up in a haze. As I, Socrates Chamberlain, attempted to make sense of my brain fog, a state of inertia set in, preventing me from unfurling my body and getting out of bed. My body felt heavy. My life's drudgery had been weighing me down for some time now, but I had been ignoring it. I couldn't ignore it now. The pipeline representing my life had become so clogged up with sludge that extra strength Drano and a plumber's snake would be insufficient to restore it to its normal flow. No longer could I bide my time by wading or marinating in the sludge. If I didn't act soon, I feared that I might be mired in this mess forever.

I eventually forced myself to get up and follow my usual morning routine before dragging myself out the door to go to work. As the trolley arrived at the station and its doors opened, I spotted an empty seat and sat, slumped over. I immediately fixed a hypnotic gaze on the back of the seat in front of me for the duration of the trip, mostly oblivious to the passengers getting on and off.

When the trolley arrived at my stop, I struggled to shake my lethargy as I slowly stood up. I opened my eyes wider in an attempt to find my bearings as I stepped off the trolley to take the short walk over to my workplace. I decided that I needed a moment to gather my thoughts and break out of my funk, so I sat down on a nearby bench. While seated, I observed what I usually ignored: my fellow San Diegans. I watched them as they scurried about, mindlessly, like lemmings, caught up in their own thoughts, as they hastily marched off to buses that connected them to their work destinations. My yearning to witness some sign of excitement was left wanting. Mostly dressed in dark, drab clothing, the commuters were mostly void of expression or emotion. Where was the laughing, the singing, the pretending to balance on the sidewalk curbs as if on a balance beam, like I did as a child? I wondered whether I was now one of them too. I briefly glanced skyward. A grey marine layer above me accentuated the dreary ambiance of the cold February morning. It rained a light mist of misery over us all. It was a Prozac type of day. I stood up and followed my fellow lemmings.

As I neared the windowless building where I worked, I caught a glimpse of the barbed wire atop the parking lot fencing. It made me question whether I was indeed walking to work or instead to an incarceration facility. The dilapidated, unappealing structure had seen better days. As I approached the main door, outside of it stood a rusted, twisted, tentacle-like sculpture. Usually innocuous, the grotesque piece of modern artwork now seemed to be reaching out to strangle me. I side-stepped it as I entered the building.

I settled into my cubicle, turned on my computer and checked my emails. It appeared to be a normal workday, with no new emergencies. Seated near the backdoor, I greeted my fellow co-workers as they arrived. When my boss came in, she made some sardonic quip about wondering what mayhem awaited us this morning. I faked a smile and continued reviewing emails.

When my break time finally arrived, it was time to step outside to go get some coffee. I began my walk by dodging several cars circling around the parking lot, as exasperated clients and employees futilely searched for a place to park. After solving the parking lot puzzle, I hightailed it through the next-door car repair shop, arriving at the sidewalk. As heavy traffic blew by me, I passed a fast-food joint, where the usual gathering of homeless people was loitering in its parking area. As I continued walking, I stopped abruptly as a car drove in front of me, nearly running me over. I looked for an apology from the driver as he hurriedly entered the strip mall, but there was none. I gathered myself, let out a large sigh and marched on.

I now had arrived at the huge intersection that I'd crossed thousands of times before, where traffic decibel levels were always high, and pedestrians were often viewed as an afterthought. Two people stood next to me as we waited for the light to change. A guy holding a skateboard casually smiled at me, then turned away. The other person, a frail and disheveled woman in her 40s, was having an agitated conversation with herself. A strong breeze blew open my jacket as our turn came to cross the street.

After finally arriving at my destination, I silently praised myself for once again successfully navigating the concrete-filled, motorway maze. After picking up my chai tea latte, I sat down at a table and let out a sigh. I casually glanced at my beverage, which usually had a leaf design of steamed milk. This time though, it had formed itself into what seemed to be a dragon's head. Taken aback for an instant, I ignored Monday's dragon and dove right in anyway, taking my first, satisfying sip. I pulled out my cell phone, but then I stopped myself. Instead of my usual doomscrolling or viewing photos of what my friends had for dinner last night, I stuffed the phone back into my pants pocket. I declared to myself it was a "contemplate the universe" break time. I closed my eyes and asked myself why I was continuing to choose to live this cog-like, stressful lifestyle. No immediate answer appeared, but the caffeine was having its desired effect. I was more awake now and ready to tackle whatever work awaited me.

Once I got back to the office, I put on my work game face, eager to make my bosses happy. I was by now very accustomed to grinding out workdays. But the grinder part of me was now being interrupted more and more by the part of me that longed to do something else. These vexing, internal battles were now becoming more frequent. They involved two sides of me—one clinging to security and the other saying you are secure enough now, that it's time to let go and move on. The thoughts dancing in my head were now more dissatisfied ones, with more urgency attached to them to take some type of action to escape this madness. Still, I did nothing. I remained frozen at 37 years of age. If someone would just help me thaw out, I would be forever grateful. I knew though that it would ultimately have to be me to take out the blowtorch to melt the ice away.

It's an easy cop-out for me to put the blame on my parents for how I am today, especially since I am now free to do whatever I want. Still, remnants of my past most likely have influenced my thinking today, especially my failure to act. I grew up a shy kid, with a military father who always told me what to do, as if I was one of his subordinates. In the military, you aren't allowed to challenge orders and at our house, it wasn't any different. It made life simple, but also induced the lemming syndrome. Have someone else think for you while you blindly follow orders. I was afraid to stand up to or disagree with my father because I knew if I did, I would be severely punished. I grew up in fear. But it wasn't just my dad. I also paid too much attention to what other authority figures told me to do, even if it was in my best interest to do otherwise.

When my mom told me to get a secure job and when my dad said go for a high paying one, I did it. Not that either one was horrible advice. But neither said what I wanted to hear—'Son, go for a job that makes you happy, no matter the security or salary.' The job I eventually settled on wasn't what I really dreamed of doing, but it was a decent one, doing graphic design work. It's the job I'm still doing today. I work for a non-profit agency dedicated to helping the public, especially low-income people, live healthier lives. The pay is good and it's a mostly secure job with a good employee benefits package. I do my job well. I'm almost always very professional. I'm accustomed to giving others the typical fake business smile. I hate it, but I do it. And it isn't that big of a deal. The constant deadlines, the stress, the meetings I don't want to go to were never a big deal either. Until now anyway. Now the accumulation of it all was wearing on me.

I've had moments to ponder whether I should indeed go in another direction in my life, like at the coffeehouse, but I was often too tired or lazy to make any effort. Or I would begin to make a half-hearted effort one day to change and then forget about it. For example, I don't know how many times I've stopped and started to write a book. Instead, what I usually did was go home and distract myself with what took minimal energy---watching reruns of *The Big Bang Theory* or sports on the television, or the latest social media videos. They are harmless habits until you are inside their vortex and don't even realize it.

When I began my job several years ago, my boss gave me lots of assignments I enjoyed doing—mostly writing and designing. But today, they have morphed into something entirely different. Those assignments have been slowly overtaken by administrative and mind-numbing work. To be fair, most jobs involve work people don't want to do. I get that. And I am good at it too, because I pride myself in doing a good job, no matter but it is. But once I showed I was good at performing the boring stuff, my boss kept giving me more of the same. When I complained, she said there was no one else available to do it. Which of course was a bunch of baloney because if I left, amazingly they would find someone else to do it. Imagine that. But I digress.

A few years ago, to better deal with the stress and doing work I loathed, I started popping the occasional Xanax, Benadryl or whatever prescription drug I could find that helped relax me. But now the popping isn't occasional. I drink more wine at night and more coffee in the morning. I need to call on my favorite co-worker friends more and more to provide me with short therapy sessions on my breaks. Insomnia has become an issue, with my mind refusing to stop ruminating over life's problems. Even my dog, a scruffy Tibetan

Terrier I named Rafie, has started to sigh at me because I hug him for longer stretches in my attempts to relieve chronic stress. The latest evidence of the effects of stress on my body is my burning skin. It is causing inflammation inside of me, sapping my energy and vitality. More red flags were now waving at me than at a Russian military parade at Red Square.

Don't get me wrong. I am very grateful for the opportunity to do my job. When I was younger, very little bothered me. But today is different. I certainly don't want to die at my desk. What I really want to do is to have more time to finish my book, paint, work out more, develop deep and meaningful relationships and have more time to spend with Rafie. Unfortunately, the albatrosses of money and security are still comfortably in the front seat, driving my metaphorical car. I was now urging myself to be more brazen in my attempts at moving them to the back seat, where they always belonged anyway.

I wish I'd left my job at various times in the past. But each time I seriously considered it, I gave in to my boss's opinions and advice. Are you all sensing a theme now? Be a team player, she told me. Make sacrifices for the business. I've secretly spent years hating myself for placing too much attention on what others, especially my boss, said was best to do. I am now overly fixated about trying to please her. This fixation, combined with my belief in the exaggerated importance my boss places on our work, have sent my stress levels through the roof.

I managed to survive the work week, with no major work issues to deal with. As Saturday morning arrived, I again struggled to get out of bed. One of my eye lids temporarily refused to open as I meandered over to the bathroom in my jogging pants and tank top. I stared at my tousled hair and cowlick in the mirror as I brushed my teeth. Too lazy to shower, I put on deodorant and cologne and changed my clothes to make myself more presentable. Rafie walked over to where I was, with a look of condemnation in his eyes.

---Okay, Rafie, okay, I know I slept too late.

Soon we were on our way from my downtown condominium to our favorite French cafe to hang out for a while. Next, I headed back home to do some chores before I took off in my Countrymen Mini Cooper to my favorite temporary oasis from the madness of the world---a quaint family-owned bookstore. It was where I liked to unwind with other like-minded souls, perusing the vast knowledge of the universe. As my eyes scrolled through the bookshelves, what caught my eye today was a self-help book. I am usually loath to read these types of books, but I decided to throw my preconceived viewpoint aside. I found a comfy chair in the store, and opened the book, in search of whatever pearls of wisdom I could glean from it. While reading it, one particular chapter hit home. The author explained that each person we meet forms a distinct opinion of us, but just because they do, doesn't mean we should accept it as the truth.

By the end of my time at the store, I had read enough of it to make an impact on me. I started to seriously question why I was so overly influenced by others' views of me. It made me question the power I gave to others over my life. Instead of questioning their validity, I almost always seem to accept and cling to others' view of me. Sort of like how I cling to my clothing items. My crowded closet of old clothes is a testament to this. Much of my wardrobe is made up of worn-out clothes long passed their usefulness or almost new clothes I have barely worn. Yet there they are, still in my closet. Give us away to charity please, my clothes seemed to tell me. But I refused to listen.

Before you all start referring me to a therapist for talking to my clothes, I only do it occasionally, okay? And you'd be right to wonder that if I can't throw out my old, unused clothes, how can I possibly step out of my robotic comfort zone and leave my longtime job? At some point, I got hypnotized into performing the same activities in the same city, in the same way, most of the time, without thinking about whether I was truly happy.

As I arrived home and was ironing my clothes to wear to work on Monday, another sign urging me to change appeared in the form of a *YouTube* music video. An artist I'd never heard of was singing a song about how well she was doing in life, but she still wasn't happy. I know life's experiences and complexities can't be summed up by a song, or worse, a sanctimonious quote from the internet. But hearing a song at the right time when you need it most can be inspiring. I played back the song several times until the words became impregnated in my brain. So now, as you all can see, instead of ignoring the subtle signs of desired change, I was now paying them some attention. Will being more conscious of them lead me to taking larger strides, eventually jumping over my psychological hurdles and crossing the finish line? That remained to be seen. At least I could draw from a few past life experiences where I have crossed similar finish lines. There were previous times where I seized the moment, acted on my desires, believing in myself and my talents.

One such time when I dipped my feet in the risk-taking pool was when I had just turned 22 years of age. After graduating from San Diego State University with a journalism degree, I headed off to the massive metropolis of Mexico City. At the time, I was still enamored with the memories of a vacation I took the year before to the Mexican capital. I did this by myself, to the disbelief of my family and friends. My reasoning was to get experience at what I thought at the time would be a career as a newspaper reporter, as well as learn some Spanish. I had little money, except for a few thousand dollars I had saved up from selling my baseball cards. Not everyone can or wants to live without their first-world comforts, but I thought I would at least try for a while. I remember my mom cried as she dropped me off at the Tijuana International Airport, saying I would die in Mexico. Thanks, mom, I thought to myself at the time. What was the big deal? If it didn't work out, it would be a nice vacation. So off I went. I managed to not only survive my three years living there, but I also thrived.

Well, okay, I wasn't always thriving. There were some moments of survival as well. I walked or took public transportation everywhere I went, which kept me in shape but often left me exhausted at the end of the day. I got lost several times. I washed my own clothes by hand and made milk from powder. I lived in a room meant to house pigs for a few months on a mountain where goats roamed freely. I moved to a neighborhood in the state of Mexico that was perceived to be so dangerous that taxi drivers would not drive into it. They let me out at the main road as I walked to my house. I once was briefly kidnapped and taken to a Weight Watchers party. I also jammed into the metro daily with thousands of others, nearly suffocating twice as a wave of bodies engulfed me, lifting me off my feet.

The lack of my usual comforts from the U.S. was usually tolerable however, since, as I said before, I always knew that I could go back home if I wanted to. I eventually did go back, but the experience left an indelible mark on me. This is when I settled into a comfortable, secure life as an office worker. Years went by, bringing us to the present. Despite the occasional discomforts of living in Mexico, I often felt more alive there than in the U.S. I never forgot that.

With the self-help book's ideas still fresh in my mind, I did what any introvert pondering his existence does—I isolated myself. During my free time, I shut out the noise and focused. For once, I didn't let myself be influenced by the views of others. So, I began to research and discover how to best go beyond my limitations. After thinking my situation over, I realized that I wasn't quite ready to leave my job yet. But I was committed to doing so very soon.

When this departure eventually happens, I assume some of my co-workers will miss me or even accuse me of being selfish. But so be it.

I now desired to finally be free, truly in the flow of what I most loved doing. To me, the end result of being truly happy is less selfishness. I knew deep inside that if I felt better, I'd give off more positive energy, which would help others as well. And I would attract others with the same energy, fulfilling my goal of spending more time building close relationships with people who inspire me. This slow buildup of momentum towards breaking out of my shell and doing what I truly wanted to do led to what happened to me next.

2 NEW INSPIRATIONAL FRIEND

"When you are inspired by some great purpose, some extraordinary project, all your thoughts break their bonds: your mind transcends limitations, your consciousness expands in every direction, and you find yourself in a new, great and wonderful world. Dormant forces, faculties and talents become alive, and you discover yourself to be a greater person by far than you ever dreamed yourself to be." ---Hindu author, mystic and philosopher Patanjali

My intense desire for change was leading me to meet new people, especially those associated with the arts scene, which was where I felt most comfortable. As I was scrolling through suggestions of friends on social media on my cell phone, I came across the profile of a guy who had the same name as my dog. The longer I stared at his profile, the more my intuition was telling me to communicate with this person. I'm not sure why. An inexplicable energy started stirring inside of me. My imagination began to run wild, thinking of the possibilities. Without even knowing who he was, I was already envisioning him being a part of my life team, a special person to assist me towards reaching my goals and living a more fulfilled life.

It sounds crazy, but before even meeting or texting this guy, I could already imagine his potential growth in his career and how I might assist him. I told myself, Socrates, your natural tendency is to get carried away, so slow down. Did that self-talk work? No. My intensity sometimes had a life of its own and stopping or slowly it down was always a constant challenge for me. After I finished reading his profile, I continued to be intrigued. I should probably first explain that the people with my Myers-Briggs personality type, INFJ-T—meaning introversion, intuition, feeling and judging–turbulent---are the rarest on the planet, and the type most likely to say they have psychic powers. After viewing his photos and videos, my powers were telling me he was a generally calm, confident, non-conventional person, very determined, resilient, uninhibited, at one with the world, but also with some crazy, Tasmanian Devil qualities. While my powers weren't perfect, it was uncanny how accurate they often turned out to be. I wasn't picking up that I should be fearful of him. I didn't sense that he was superman either. Just someone to inspire me to work towards my goals, as well as be a better person.

He was from Mexico, which endeared me to him even more. The love and warmth I received from the people there felt right after growing up in a family where hugs were given infrequently. I also envisioned the young man could help me improve on my already very good Spanish.

Just judging from his photos, which can be deceiving, he was handsome, around 5 feet, 8 or so inches tall, with a slender build. He had soft, smooth, light brown skin, short, black, matted hair and bushy eyebrows. His eyes were beautiful, large and brown. He had a pug nose, and big, wide, full lips, with a glowing smile. His photos showed off some muscular definition in his flexible, supple and long legs. His body appeared to be light and delicate. All combined, he checked off a lot of boxes for what I considered attractive. I hoped that he was just as attractive inside as well. I had the sense that he was gay too. As a gay man, I learned to develop a "gaydar" sensibility, an ability to pick up clues as to one's sexual orientation. It was honed after years of needing to be discrete about my intentions with other guys.

He was a 24-year-old dancer. I'd never met a dancer before, at least not that I could remember. But as I mentioned before, I felt a special energy towards him, but not necessarily 100 percent positive. Instead of being afraid of this energy, I stepped forward and gave in to it. I requested to be added to his long list of social media friends. I was disappointed when I received no response. I went about my life. Soon afterwards though, he finally got around to accepting my request.

Before texting this young man, I thought I'd prepare myself and learn a little about his field of interest, dancing. I looked up information on my laptop about contemporary dance, which was the style of dance he performed in his videos. I learned that it is a form of expressive movement that sprung up in the middle of the 1900s, coming from an adverse reaction by some in the dance field to the highly structured classical ballet. Contemporary dance techniques are very fluid, with dancers using their entire bodies to express emotions. It can also include the typical aspects of traditional dance.

What really interested me about the dance style was its emphasis on creativity. As I looked at *YouTube* videos of the dance style, I loved the improvisation of it all. Choreographers seemed to be attempting to outdo one another regarding their experimentation with new, thought-provoking presentations and wardrobes. I loved how they pushed the boundaries of what was created in more traditional dance settings. And dancers were often encouraged to show off their own, unique skill sets. I also learned about the history of contemporary dance and its most famous dancers and choreographers, including Charles Weidman, Eric Hawkins, Elizabeth Dalman, Katherine Dunham, Twyla Tharp, and of course, Martha Graham, often called the "mother of contemporary dance."

Next, I took some time to view the young man's online videos. They showed him dancing with grace and precision. He definitely was a talented dancer. I decided to send him a text message and this time, there was no delay. To my surprise, he messaged me back immediately. He later told me he almost never texts people he doesn't know on social media. I took it as a sign that he too felt we were being drawn together by each of our desires.

—Hi. I don't want to disturb you. I am just a gringo who admires you from a distance.

—Hi. You aren't disturbing me at all. At least not yet. Hahahaha.

—Hahahaha. Thanks for accepting me as your friend.

—You are welcome.

—May I ask you why you accepted me as a friend?

—I don't know. Why did you request to be my friend?

—I guess it was because I can see your potential as a dancer. I'm drawn to people, in part, because I see their possibilities. I genuinely like to help others grow. It is fulfilling to me. Sounds weird, doesn't it?

—No, not at all.

—Cool. I am also looking for a friend to talk to, depend on, trust, enjoy and have fun chatting with. I want someone who will bear witness to my existence, so my life will not go unnoticed. You know what I mean? Someone who vows to care every day about everything I do, even if it's boring. That's probably too intense for you, right? Have I scared you away yet?

—No, and that's nice. Usually, guys that text me are just looking to have sex. Hahahaha.

—Hahahaha. Well, I'm a gentleman. I'll need you to take me out to

dinner and tell me your name before that happens. Hahahaha.
—Hahahaha.
—*Soy Sócrates. Vivo en San Diego.* (I'm Socrates. I live in San Diego.)
—Is your name really Socrates?
—*Si, jajajaja* (Spanish laughter). *Mis padres pensaron si me dieron el nombre de un filósofo griego, me inspiraría a aprender. ¿Cuál es tu nombre?* (My parents thought if they gave me a Greek philosopher's name, it would inspire me to learn. What is your name?)
—Archimedes, but you can call me Archie. Hahahahaha. Just kidding. My name is Rafael, but everyone calls me Rafa. Rafael Coria Galarín is my full name. I don't like my name. I like my mother's last name because it isn't common.
—*Jajajaja! Me gusta tu sentido de humor.* (Hahahaha! I like your sense of humor) It's nice to meet you by text message. I noticed you answered me in English. *¿En serio, hablas inglés? Está bien si no lo haces. Aprendí español viviendo en la Ciudad de México, pero me falta aprender más.* (Do you really speak English? It is fine if you don't. I learned Spanish living in Mexico City, but I still need to learn more.)
—Yes, I do. But I need to practice a little more because my family doesn't speak English.
—Well, I'm here to practice with you, if you want, Rafa. By the way, up until now, your written English has been excellent.
—Thanks.
---Can I ask you some more questions?
---Of course.
—How's the weather where you live?
—It's hot and windy. Last night the wind was blowing very hard. I thought the roof of my house was going to fly off.
—Wow.
—How about in San Diego?
—The weather is perfect as usual. Have you been to San Diego?
—No, I've never crossed the border, but I really want to.
—I live in downtown San Diego with my dog, a Tibetan Terrier. His name is Rafa too. I call him Rafie.
—That's cool. I have a lot of cats and some dogs.
I sent Rafa a photo of my dog.
—He is so cute.

   At this point, more boxes are being checked off. He is polite, learning English and an animal lover.
—I'm sorry. I've been chatting with you, and I don't even know where you live.

—Monterrey, Nuevo Leon. *Soy un Regiomontano.* That's means I am a person from Monterrey.
—Okay cool. Your profile says you live in Palm Springs, although your online photos seem to be places in Mexico.
—I posted that due to security issues.
—Are you hiding from the police?
—Hahahaha. No.
—I've never been to Monterrey. How is it to live there?
—It's okay. It's the capital of the state. There are lots of *maquiladoras* (factories) here. Lots of people too.
—Very cool. Maybe I'll get a chance to visit one day.
—You should, Socrates. Although where I live, it isn't that great. My family and I live at the base of a mountain in a poor section of the city.
—Have you ever climbed the mountain?
—Yes, a couple of times.
—Cool. Speaking of climbing, I saw a video on your Instagram profile where you are climbing a rope with only your hands, without using your feet. I was impressed with that and your other videos.
—Yeah, I just posted that video today after my class. Aerial acrobatics is only one of the disciplines that I practice. Contemporary dance is my favorite, but I also do ballet, jazz, tap, and gymnastics.
—Nice. Contemporary dance is my favorite as well, although I'm not a dancer.
—Cool. Seems like we have a few things in common, Socrates.
—I agree. So, tell me. Your body must be feeling good and strong with all your dancing workouts.
—Pain is the only thing I am feeling right now. Hahahahaha. But I love to feel this pain. As a dancer, being tired, being in a little pain, that's just the process. I like to challenge my body to do the impossible. I search for the limits my body can reach, and then I try to go beyond that. I like to see what I am capable of. I want to allow myself the possibility of surprising even myself. The discipline of hard work helps me in my life outside of dancing as well. I enjoy it. It makes me feel productive.
—I love that. They say the harder you work, the luckier you get.
—I'm still waiting for that luck to arrive for me.
—Be patient. It will. You seem to be very athletic and flexible. Do you play any sports?
—No. I'm not into sports. I took some karate classes when I was a little boy. They were free, government-funded classes. That's about it.
—Okay. Another thing that caught my attention was your smile. I love

it. Your smile really lights up your face in your photos.

—Thanks, but I don't. I don't like my teeth. That is why I don't smile much in photos.

—Maybe you should try to learn to love your imperfections. That is kind of what Mexicans do anyway, right? For example, if the bus doesn't have air conditioning, you learn to live with it, even if you don't like it.

I continued to ask Rafa questions. He rarely asked me any, so I was left to guess whether it was due to shyness, disinterest or distraction. When he did answer my questions, they were short and to the point, sometimes just a word or two. But as a former journalist, I felt like I had a knack for getting people to open up during interviews. Even though I worked as a graphic designer, I also wrote our non-profit organization's newsletter, which often involved interviewing people to promote health in newspapers and magazines. Texting Rafa wasn't an interview per se, but when you first meet someone, it sort of is. I was also naturally curious about people. I love learning about who they are and what motivations they have in life.

3 RAFA DEALING WITH HARDSHIP

The following day, we continued our text conversation. Rafa explained that he started dancing seriously relatively late in life, at 21 years of age. Traditionally, professional dancers begin taking classes as young children. I asked Rafa why he started so late.

—My mother nor I could pay for my dance classes, due to economic problems. These obstacles motivated me to fight to move towards my goals. Even though it is a lot of work, I keep trying.

—Sometimes when you work harder to achieve something, you appreciate it more, don't you?

—Totally, Socrates.

I sent him a photo of my rustic dining room table, which I had spent my entire day off staining. It was an example of what we were talking about—working hard on something and thus caring for it and valuing it more.

—Nice table. I don't even own one.

I began to better understand Rafa's economic hardships the more we texted each other. As with many of us, the environment he grew up in played a significant part in how he saw life. He lived without the basic commodities most middle-class people living in first world countries take for granted.

The worse one's economic situation is, the more rewarding overcoming the hardship can be. But overcoming them was extremely challenging in Rafa's situation. In Mexico City, I witnessed how poverty could sometimes slowly beat down a person until he or she no longer cared. This reality was brought home to me once after reading a question presented to an online group of Mexicans. The question was

"What is your motivation for getting up each day to go to work?" The majority of the answers were debts, hunger and being poor. I imagined that it must have been tempting for Rafa to deal with the constant exasperation of economic difficulties by turning to alcohol, hard drugs, or cigarettes.

After a few marathon texting sessions, I began to sense that he was starting to show early signs of being beaten down by the weight of the challenges that faced him. As the evening arrived, he texted me from his job at the 768 Downtown Club in downtown Monterrey.

—Hi Socrates. How are you? I'm so tired. I frequently am these days.

—I'm fine, thanks. Sorry about that. What is your job at the club?

—I bus tables, do cleaning, and work as a waiter too. I often come home late, because my mom's house where I live is a long way from the club. So, I take a bus or maybe a Didi (a rideshare taxi), if I have extra money.

The next morning, Rafa was supposed to go to school, where he was attempting to obtain a certificate of high school completion. He texted me saying he was still too exhausted from work the night before, so he ended up staying home. His route home from work involved boarding a bus for an hour-long ride, then walking 20 minutes in pitch black darkness on a dirt road to his small house. Despite the difficulties involved in getting to and from work, school and dance class, he tried not to let them get him down. I asked him about his life goals.

—I want to be a professional dancer and actor. I want to go to the University of Monterrey and eventually be an exchange student in the U.S. I want to travel. I want to own my own business. The sacrifices I endure along the way are part of the process.

—That's cool. I admire your determination. But you can't do everything, Rafa.

—I know, but I want to. Hahaha!

—Well, good luck! Are you able to save enough money to help get all the instructional assistance you'll need to be a professional dancer?

—Not really, Socrates.

—I imagine transportation costs drain your savings too.

—Yes, very much so.

---Well, rest up. I'm heading off to the gym.

---Have a good workout.

---Thanks.

4 WHO WE ARE

Perhaps I was being selfish by texting Rafa so much, knowing how tired and busy he was. But my excitement of meeting someone new got the best of me. Although I continued to text him a lot, I figured he could respond to my questions and comments at his leisure, whenever that was. Later Rafa would say to me *Me estás haciendo bolas,* meaning that I was overwhelming him with my texts. I could already tell he had the tendency to get distracted very easily. Maintaining his attention for a long period of time often proved difficult. I, on the other hand, could handle lots of information at once, even with distractions around me. To appease him, I would try to temper my tendency to write a lot, but just like Rafa's efforts to stay focused, it was often a futile exercise. Distraction and written expression were ingrained in each of our personalities.

Getting to know someone without spending in person time with him or her can be difficult, and often impossible for some people. It takes a lot of patience and persistence to keep the interest up. But with Rafa and me, for the moment, it wasn't an issue. In fact, there was an advantage to our long-distance friendship. Via text messages, Rafa often revealed his intimate side in a way he might be reluctant to do in person.

In a relatively short period of texting, I learned many facts about Rafa. One of them was that he didn't know how to cook, nor did he want to learn. He was happy having others do it for him. His mother cooked and washed the dishes, and often would do many other tasks to keep him happy. Despite living in poverty, Rafa was treated as if he was a spoiled prince. My mother stopped doing those tasks for me once

I became an adult, but many Mexican mothers often continue to do them for their grown-up children. It was an enduring act of love, which explained in part why Mexicans' love for their mothers often was stronger than for any other spouse, partner, lover or friend in their lives. *Mamitis*, a slang word in Spanish meaning a child who is overly attached to his mother, was very common in Mexico. My experience was that Mexican mothers would sometimes complain about their children's or husband's lack of help around the house, but they also often preferred to help or spoil them, even if they didn't feel appreciated. Today, after exchanging a few niceties, I asked Rafa to describe himself.

—Well, I am very serious and quiet, but I have moments when I can be silly around my girlfriends. I've always been a person who forgets things. I am usually very reserved. I don't really mind screaming, loud people, but I am not one of them. Sometimes it is hard for me to maintain a conversation. I often don't know what to say. I am not a person of many words.

—Yeah, I am already figuring that out.

—I am also not a fan of everyone knowing about my life. Just don't try to change the way that I am, and everything will be okay.

---Got it. What other aspects of you should I know?

---I grew up without being affectionate and expressive. You'll never see me cry.

—So, you are the typical macho man? You don't show your emotions?

—I do. I've been a *llorón* (crier) since I was a child. I do cry a lot, just not in front of others. Only a few people have seen me that way.

—Okay. Can you give me some examples of when you cried?

—I cried in pain when I got my tattoos. I've cried when I've gotten sick many times. Sometimes I've cried when someone has done something nice for me. Recently, I cried watching the movie *Un Camino Largo a Casa* (A Long Way Home). It's about a five-year old who gets lost on a train thousands of miles from his home, learns to survive alone, then gets adopted. Decades later, he sets out to find his lost family and finally finds them.

---I saw that movie too. It was a tearjerker.

---I remember when I was a child, I went with my father to Ensenada and while I was feeding the seals, a pelican came over and stole the food, so I began to cry. That was a typical reaction of mine growing up. So, I guess I can be dramatic. I suppose it is ironic that I don't like soap operas because they are so dramatic, like me. I don't like that side of me. Maybe that's why I hide my tears from others now.

—Okay, got it. You don't like drama in others because it's a part of you that you hate.

---Yeah, I suppose.

---Continue on. What else?

—Let's see. I'm single and live with my family in a small house with few luxuries. I pay for the internet, but they pay for the rest. I don't know how to drive and don't want to learn. I love to make funny faces. All my friends know that.

—Do you have a lot of friends?

—Well, lots of people know me through my dancing and school.

—How about a best friend?

—No, not really. I'm always so busy.

—Okay, what else? Tell me some more random things about you.

—Let's see. Random things. My waist size is 28 inches, and my shoe size is 8 1/2 inches or 27 in Mexican size.

—Oh wow. You have a small waist. Can I ask a more personal question?

—Sure, go ahead.

—Do you have any health problems? Are you suffering in any way?

—Physically, I suffer a little, due to a surgery I had a few years ago. If I eat too fast, I make unwanted indigestion noises. Other than that, I'm fine. If you are asking about money, I have always had what I need to live but it doesn't mean that I don't want more money to buy things that would make my life better. I know how to live with the basics and be happy.

Later, when I visited Rafa's neighborhood on the outskirts of the city, I found the government-built, low-income homes there had the basics---water, electricity and internet access, but lacked infrastructure. There were only a few sidewalks and paved streets, and these few were in various stages of disrepair, as were road signs. Trash-filled dirt roads and lots were common, mixed in among a few small businesses. There were little to no streetlights. Dogs and cats wandered the streets in herds, playing, fighting, searching for food and procreating. There was little to no privacy, with homes built right next to each other. No curfews existed regarding noise. On windy days, the internet and electricity service would easily be knocked out. If this wasn't enough to deal with, dirt and dust were everywhere—in the air, in the street, on food and clothes, inside and outside of homes.

The house of Rafa's mother was in the middle of a row of houses. The green-colored, cylinder-block structure was very small and cozy, with two bedrooms and one bathroom. A dirt yard and chicken-wire fencing stapled to wooden posts surrounded the front, back and side yards. Two barred windows faced the front yard, where two mesquite trees shaded the family from the hot Monterrey sun. At the base of one of the trees lay a small garden of succulent plants Rafa had planted. On the left side of the house stood a decaying brick wall. On the opposite side sat an old, rusted washing machine from the 1950's that violently shook when in operation. A clothesline hung in the back. On all sides of the house, dust-covered discarded or unused items were strewn about or embedded in dry mud.

Upon entering the cement-floored home was a small living room area filled with two dusty couches that had seen better days, a small television, and a boom box sitting on top of two cinder blocks. The family often ate on a hastily made wooden bench between the two couches. Framed photos of family and a religious calendar hung on the wall. In the same room was a small kitchen, with a sink, refrigerator and small portable burner sitting on the counter. There was little space for storage, so dishes and other items were left stacked up high on the counter. A rancid smell of mold emanated from the one small bathroom, which also served as a storage room where clothes and boxes were scattered about. The sink had only one faucet from which only cold water barely trickled out. A small piece of a cracked mirror hung sideways on the wall above it. The cramped shower was filled with buckets. Its flimsy door served as a towel rack. Rafa's bedroom was adjacent to his mother's, and consisted of an old mattress on the floor, a dresser, a few shelves, a closet and a rack of shoes covered in dust. I asked Rafa about how it is for him growing up in these conditions.

—No matter how bad it gets, I have a home for me and that is all that matters.

—Okay. Can you tell me a little about your family?

—I have a mom, who is originally from the state of Sinaloa, two sisters and a brother. These days, I don't see them much because we all have different schedules. I have one grandparent alive who lives in Baja California, who I don't see much. I have two uncles and three aunts on my mom's side of the family, but I don't see them much either. I am closest to my mom and youngest sister.

—And your dad?

—He died when I was 16 years old. He was born and raised in the state of Tamaulipas.

—That's too bad. How did you deal with that loss?

—I remember that after his death, everything made me feel mad and I used to stay in my room and lock the door.

—I'm sorry. Do you remember him often?

—Sometimes. I have a photo of him in my room. I remember our trips together. How he cared for all of us. Things he used to do. The food he ate. For example, there are these cookies called *Marias* he always used to eat. I remember him when I eat them. I remember his politeness. He always used to wait for us kids to be served at the table before he would eat. I couldn't have asked for a better father.

—That's cool. Your poor mom. How did she survive his death?

—Well, we all supported her. She got a job as well.

—Did she remarry?

—No. She has a boyfriend now.

—I understand. Tell me, who do you most resemble most, your mother or your father?

—If you are asking about physical appearance, I would say mostly like my mom. I have more of her skin tone, and I have her eyes. And most of the family members on her side of the family are slender and I am a fairly skinny guy. My dad's side of the family tends to be a little bit larger. I do think I have my dad's lips though. My mom's lips are thin. But character wise, I seem to be more like my dad. My dad was a serious guy, like me.

Rafa then said something that didn't mean much at the time.

—Another aspect of my personality is that I am very friendly, but I can be a little uptight.

Rafa continued to describe himself. He started to open up with me, especially about his feelings of loneliness. He had a lot to say about the subject. He now read me a short poem that he had written.

—At times, I feel like a seed, growing in the shadow through the soil, struggling to reach the sunlight. I slowly but surely unravel, opening myself up to the world, to chase the wonders and unknowns of life. But I don't always feel comfortable doing so.

---Thanks for sharing that with me.

---You are welcome. I'm going to tell you something that I've never told anyone. I feel better when I am alone. I really do. Loneliness is my best company, my best friend. At times, I don't feel that I belong in any setting. I often talk to myself. I have imaginary friends.

—Interesting. I often feel the same. I stay home alone because it gives me a chance to recover from the exhaustion that is this world, because I get easily overwhelmed. I do like being alone because it gives me the chance to use my vivid imagination. But I don't necessarily feel better alone. I enjoy and need my alone time, but I'd equally enjoy being with a few friends.

—I guess we both are somewhat similar. Nighttime is my favorite time to use my imagination. It's my favorite part of the day where I like to think and reflect, even cry. I sometimes turn into a different person at night. More introspective and silly. I like to imagine situations in my life where they could be different. I imagine I change reality and that events start to work in my favor. I like to imagine a place where I have self-confidence and I'm not depressed or have insecurity issues. A place where no one can see me so I can walk around without being judged. A place where I can be myself, where I don't have to put on a fake smile, pretending that everything is fine. A refuge that I can go to anytime I need to. I like to imagine a portal where I can transport myself and see only darkness, except for the light of the moon. I imagine it as an eternal place where I can move around and unwind, where I feel secure, and I can express all that I need to.

—Wow, those are impactful and deep thoughts. It's great that you use your imagination like that, if only to make yourself feel better. It's also sort of sad that you don't see that special place here on Earth. I love nighttime too, especially late when everyone else is asleep. The quiet helps me come up with very creative and innovative ideas.

—Cool. Can you give me an example?

—Okay, let me think. I came up with a different way to hit a tennis ball after practicing by myself for weeks on a backboard. No one else hits the ball like I do. It's a cross handed, two-handed slice forehand. It helped me win a few tennis tournaments. It's effective because I can get a lot of power behind the shot.

—Really? Interesting.

—The issue for me though, is that, unlike you, I am alone almost all the time and that is too much time to think! Hahahaha. I tend to panic when alone so much. In the silence, I must also face myself. It's like my mind is entering a bad neighborhood. It's too scary to enter it alone. So, I turn on the television, computer, music, call friends, spend hours on *YouTube* or other social media. But slowly but surely, through meditation, I'm learning that it's okay to get to know the real me, not the Socrates the world has created in their minds.

—I feel that way too. If it's quiet for too long, I can't deal with it. I'd rather stay home alone, but with noise, watching television, eating snacks. I'm not much of a partier, although I do go out from time to time.

—I mostly party alone in my bedroom, singing songs, pretending I'm a famous artist. Ha! Thanks though for sharing those intimate thoughts with me. Feel free to express them with me whenever you want. Maybe you should do it more often.

—Thanks, Socrates. And you are right. I need to do it more. I'm glad that I have you, someone with whom I can express myself. I trust you already.

—Don't get carried away. I just met you. Hahahahaha.

—Hahahaha. True.

I'm glad Rafa had a place to go to, if only in his mind, to sort out his feelings. And I believe he needed such a place. He lived with several dogs and cats, and his mother and her boyfriend. His brother and his sisters, their husbands and their children frequently stopped by his mom's house. He was working, going to school and dancing. He was taking public transportation. He was rarely physically alone, except in his small bedroom and walking to and from public transportation. You can, however, be lonely in a crowded room and maybe that is how Rafa often felt. Although he said his best friend was his loneliness, I later learned that his real best friend was his cell phone. That inanimate object spent way more time with him than his loneliness ever did. Rafa continued his description.

—Let's see. Another thing about me is I have a sensitive body.

—Interesting. Yeah, I can be like that too. For example, when a hair stylist is putting the paper white collar around my neck or even the bib, sometimes it will take him or her a few minutes to do it, because I start giggling and can't stop.

—Hahahaha.

—What about sleep, Rafa? Do you sleep well?

—I can fall asleep at anytime, anywhere. Sometimes it takes me a little while to fall asleep but usually sleeping is not a problem for me. I sleep well, but often not for many hours. I didn't have my own room until just recently, so I am used to noise and people. I can sleep with the television on, but I don't like to, because it wastes energy. I don't like waste, period, whether it is energy, food or anything else. I like to stay up late doing stuff on my cell phone and watching movies or series on television. Often, I have homework to do.

—Thanks for sharing. You've provided me with some great insight into who you are.

—You are welcome.

—I'll give you a rest. You get to read about me now. Hopefully you won't get too bored and distracted while I'm describing myself. I am a 37-year-old white guy. I'm not very hairy, mainly because I shave my body hair. I don't consider myself handsome or unattractive. Wait, let me rephrase that. It's more like some days I think I am attractive, and others not so much.

—Yeah, that is normal for most people.

—I am clean shaven, have blue eyes and short brown hair. I am athletic, generally happy, affectionate, passionate and empathetic. While I believe every human is creative, I enjoy taking my abilities to higher and higher levels. If you look close enough, you can probably see creative juices coming out of my pores. Hahaha! My imagination is almost limitless. I work as a graphic designer. I am in the process of writing my first book. I'm a passionate painter. And I love reading.

---Nice. I love all that. What about your negative aspects, if you don't mind me asking?

---I have anxiety issues and I tend to get carried away with anything I am passionate about, including people. Don't say I didn't warn you. Also, I don't have a great relationship with my family. I wish they loved me unconditionally, but you can't choose your family. They don't like my politics either. In U.S. culture, that can be a problem.

—You don't need them, Socrates.

—Yeah, I know. But the people who say that to me, like yourself, have close relationships with their families. You all take being with your families for granted. It's not easy to form a family of friends, although I've managed to do that to some extent. I do love my mom a lot and I maintain frequent contact with her, but I keep my distance too.

—I understand.

—Okay, back to my description. I have the rarest of all personality types on the planet. And my unusualness doesn't stop with my personality. I believe that I was born with the ability to feel the emotions of those around me, which is often overwhelming. Actually, it goes beyond feeling them. I have an ability to unconsciously absorb other people's emotions without even knowing them. While I do help others with this ability, which I like to call a superpower, it's something I need to be careful about. After all, other people's emotions can be pretty strong sometimes, right?

—Wow, that's amazing.

—Yeah. It's amazing, but it makes life very difficult. Absorbing people's emotions goes hand and hand with being extremely sensitive. I take in more information from my environment than most people do. For example, you and I can be walking down the street and I'll be hyper aware of all that we are passing around us. I will pick up on the smallest details. My brain is wired to process it all more deeply. I see details others miss and make connections that others don't. When I am talking to another person, I often don't just listen to their words. I pick up on their use of words, their tone of voice, how the person moves their body, what his or her eyes and facial expressions are telling me, as well as their silence. I hear what people aren't saying. I am very observative. I observe myself too. I pay attention to small habits. How I talk to myself. What I read and watch. I know all humans process non-verbal cues, so I know what I am saying isn't that unusual. I guess I'm just very good at doing it.

—You do sound like a sensitive person. How do you deal with all that?

—Often, not very well. I was seemingly born without the protection others possess, so I am more affected by such things as emotions, medicines, stimulants, and violent movies. Because of this, I often take long periods of rest to recover and regain my energy, because I can quickly become exhausted. My sensitive brain can easily get over-stimulated, so I attempt to avoid loud and busy places. I do my best in calm, quiet settings. I enjoy being around people, just not a lot of them. I'm picky about with whom I spend my energy. For my closest friends, I will do almost anything. As I mentioned before, I am very empathetic and caring. I love creating almost anything, especially with my writing and painting. I'm also very intuitive. I can often read people's minds.

—Interesting. I don't think I've met anyone like you. You definitely seem very unique, and I think special too. By only texting you, I can tell that you are very detailed with your words and descriptions.

—Yeah, I am, but not everyone appreciates or likes how I am. I often keep my thoughts to myself out of fear of people judging me. But judge me they do anyway. I've been called weird, obsessed and disillusioned. My mom called me a lost soul. In her defense, I was never easy to understand.

I sent Rafa some photos of my condominium. He was impressed. Next, I sent some photos of myself I had taken during a modeling session that were very artistic and sexy.

—I can honestly say that you are very hot, Socrates. And polite. And you speak Spanglish. I do too, often without realizing it.

—You are very handsome as well, Rafa.

—Thanks so much.

—Before we start sexting, maybe I should change the subject. Hahahaha.

—Hahahaha. Okay.

—So, what does dancing mean to you in your life right now?

—Almost everything. Dancing is how I most like to express myself. As I said before, if you want to be a dancer, you must love the pain and as you know, I do. I enjoy the process, the stretching, and how I feel when I dance.

—Do you think you were born to be a dancer?

—Yes. I'm not an amazing dancer, but I do my best. I have good technique but I'm always trying to improve it. I am a perfectionist and often I feel that my technique is never good enough.

—But being a good dancer is much more than technique, right?

—True, but learning the proper technique is like the foundation for building a house. It must be there first.

—What are your technical issues?

—Oh gosh. If we discuss them, we'll be up all night. Hahahaha. I tend to lose my focus. I need to focus on what I am doing but I can't because I'm just thinking about all the people around me and what they are saying and thinking about me while I am dancing.

—I understand. Lots of my tennis friends have the same problem when playing in tournaments. What gives you the most problems?

—My mind. I need to feel the song I am performing, yet I am not always in the mood to do so.

—Do you hang out with your fellow dancers a lot?

—After dance practice, we sometimes go out to eat and talk about it. But really, I don't have much free time, because I always have things to do.

I think many of us can relate to how busy Rafa's life is. Life gets in the way of a lot of what we plan on doing in our lives. I've always thought about how much of life involves mundane tasks, such as preparing food, eating, washing clothes and the dishes, cleaning the house, buying food, and paying bills. There is also the responsibility of taking care of friends, family and pets, staying in shape by working out, fixing household items, dealing with family emergencies, etc. I decided to change the subject and discuss his job.

---Do you like working at the club?

---Yes, I do, for the moment anyway. The customers aren't always nice to me.

---It's too bad you don't dedicate more time to dancing, but I suppose we all make sacrifices at times to get to where we want to go.

---True.

—I hope soon you can spend more time dancing. I'd love for you to dance just for me, but the truth is that your talent should be shared with the world. There is a famous quote by Pablo Picasso that says "The meaning of life is to find your gift. The purpose of life is to give it away." Well, you've found your gift—dancing. You should be sharing it as much as possible with others.

—I don't know what to say.

—Say whatever you want to.

The next night, he texted me saying he was working at the club again and that he couldn't text for a long time since there was no texting allowed after 10 p.m.

—What time do you get off work, Rafa?

—5 a.m. That's why I told you that sometimes it's very hard to be me. I come home exhausted but then I must get up and do it all over again and again.

Our conversation turned to our likes and dislikes. Rafa started.

—I like hot, summer days much more than winter, but summers here can be dangerous. My body starts to ache in the cold. I can't stretch very well. I do love cloudy days. Maybe a hot cloudy day is best. Hahaha! The one exception is I love to work out when it is cloudy and cold.

---I am the opposite. I enjoy cold, cloudy days. Of course, San Diego's cold never gets extreme. It's just the right amount of cold. Do you ever use the weather app on your phone?

---No, never. I also never bring anything to protect me from the rain, like an umbrella. If it rains on me, so be it.

—I look at the weather report daily. I want to know if the pollution is bad, if I need a coat to wear or an umbrella. I can't walk around work or be at a meeting with my clothes soaking wet. I need to know if I need sunblock, or if I should bring sunglasses. I also need to know if it is going to rain because it is hard to walk Rafie and he hates the rain.

—I understand.

—So, what else? What do you like to watch on television, Rafa?

—I like comedy and horror movies, and series on *Netflix* and *YouTube*. I love the movie *Amelie*. It's about a girl who grows up lonely. She imagines life in a magical way, and then uses her imagination to do lots of good deeds for others. These efforts help her overcome her being so timid. I see a lot of me in her. Right now, I'm watching the series *Dancing Moms*. It shows me how hard being a dancer in the U.S. is. I just finished watching the third season of the series *The Rain*. It's about a virus in the rain. When it touches your skin, you die. I am not a big fan of Mexican cinema, history or superhero movies. However, I do like the animated movie *Nacho Libre* (A play on words with the character's name and wrestling). It's on *Netflix* right now if you want to watch it.

—Let's see. I just now pulled it up. I am watching the preview, and I am already laughing! Another question. Do you watch *RuPaul's Drag Race?*

—No. I don't like drag queens that much. Do you?

—I love it. It's interesting to me that you don't like drag queens. In your dance practice videos, you sometimes seem so effeminate, even acting like a woman.

—Well, I guess in a small group, I enjoy it. In public or at a bar, not so much.

—Okay. What about bad habits? I think you mentioned that you smoke cigarettes.

—Yeah. I smoke them on the weekends, although it is often now during the week as well. I drink some, but not much.

—Can I ask you why you smoke? It's like one of the worst things for your health. And for someone who dances, that really seems to be like you are intentionally attempting to make it harder on yourself, since breathing is so critical to any athlete's performance.

—I know. Smoking relaxes me when I am upset, sad, stressed, etc. Or simply for pleasure.

Our streak of having things in common has ended. Smoking is disgusting. We decided to move on the subjects of music and food. I asked Rafa who his favorite singer was.

---Without a doubt, it's Lady Gaga. She is above and beyond my favorite singer and entertainer. Her album *The Fame Monster* is my favorite. I follow her on social media and know almost everything about her.

—Very cool. I love her too. And not just because of her music. I love how she promotes kindness. You never know how being kind to someone might turn someone's life around. You never know how much someone might need a hug or someone to listen to. She made me realize that I shouldn't wait to be kind. And I love how she supports the Lesbian, Gay, Bisexual, Transgender and Queer Plus (LGBTQ+) community.

—I love that about her too. I relate to her in other ways as well, such as her determination, creativity and life experiences.

—It's great that you have someone who inspires you so much, Rafa. What about other artists and music that interest you?

—I love many varieties of music, especially electronic and pop. I seem to have a new favorite song every week. For right now, my favorites include *E-25* by Nebuloza, which is a song in Spanish, *Zero Gravity* by of Verona, an indie rock group, and Bobby Bacala's song *Miss Kenichi*, which includes the phrase "life as a punishment. I kind of wonder if it is. I'd say Max Richter is one of my favorite musicians. I also love the French song *Le Terre Vie du Ciel* by Armand Amar. It means Earth Seen from The Sky. Have you heard of it?

—No.

—You need to listen to it, Socrates. It carries me off into another world. It's long, over 10 minutes. I turn up my headphones and I become transformed when I listen to it. I feel like I've left my body. It's sort of a sad song. I like sad songs. Maybe that is why I love being Mexican. There are so many sad songs sung here.

—Yeah, I'm familiar with the tradition of sad songs in Mexico. They are often very beautifully sung, and I love them too, depending on the moment. But I try not to listen to them repeatedly since that could negatively affect who I am.

—I don't listen to them much. Two songs I love from Mexican artists are *La Chona* (an attractive woman full of life) by El Caballo Dorado (The Golden Horse) and *Tucanazo* by Los Tucanes de Tijuana (The Toucans from Tijuana). These aren't sad, but very famous songs most Mexicans know and love.

—Nice. I've heard both before. They even play them at American baseball games sometimes. Is there a type of music you don't like?

—I never sing *Norteño* (a style of Mexican music related to polka and corridos) songs.

—Other tastes?

—I love ice skating, especially the skaters Yulia Lipnitskaya and Bruno Massot. I love the dancer Travis Wall.

Next, I asked Rafa about his food tastes.

—I love pasta dishes, especially fettuccine alfredo. I like most Mexican dishes---*enchiladas, quesadillas, tostadas, sopes, chicharrones, chilaquiles* with cream, *guacamole* and *tortilla* chips. I also love potatoes, teriyaki sauce, and all types of fruits, especially grapes and bananas. I love all nuts except for peanuts. I'll eat salads and broccoli sometimes. I usually eat other vegetables mixed into other foods. I eat a lot of junk food too, such as *Doritos* and *Rice Krispies Treats*.

—I find it interesting that you usually eat vegetables mixed into other foods. It's like what a mother does to get her child to eat veggies.

—Yeah, I do.

—Hahahaha. So, you never left the baby stage?

—Hahaha. I guess not. I want to be a child forever.

—Anything else?

—To drink, I love water, *Coca-Cola, Arizona* fruit drinks, vodka, wine coolers and natural juices. I don't like beer, but I drink it sometimes. I drink coffee late at night without it affecting my sleep.

---And food dislikes?

---It's a long list. It includes all fish. Even the smell of it makes me want to vomit. The exception is tuna. I also don't like ketchup, gelatin, onions, sushi, raisins, liver, mole, black beans, olives, hot salsa, mustard, blueberries. low-fat milk and most milk substitutes. I can't drink much whole milk, but I like it.

—Wow, such a specific list. It will take me a while to memorize all of them or maybe I should make a list, in case someday I cook for you. Anything else?

—Not related to music or food, I don't like to compare myself to anyone. We are all unique in our own ways. My social and personal worth isn't based on how I compare to others. For me, comparing creates anxiety, guilt and lowers my self-esteem.

---I can see that. We are each on our own journeys. If it causes you problems, definitely avoid doing it. But if you are honest with yourself, you, me and everyone else spend a large amount of our lives comparing ourselves to other people and in many other aspects. It's almost unavoidable and there are lots of positives to doing it. You compare your current dance skill set to skills you see in a video of another dancer to improve. You compare when you choose friends and lovers. I compared my condo to others I wanted to buy. I compare the quality of fruits and vegetables at the supermarket, which stock options or health insurance to choose, what hair style I like, and what clothes I wear.

---Yeah, that's true. But sometimes comparing is bad because I'll never be as handsome or as talented as other people and I'll never be them.

---Well, attractiveness can be subjective. And even if someone is better than you in something, you can still use the comparison to improve your abilities as much as you can. But yeah, it is futile to try to be 100 percent like anyone.

---Okay, so what about your likes and dislikes, Socrates?

—I love watching movies where I can learn something or be inspired. I like silly comedies too, where you learn nothing. Hahaha. I enjoy watching *YouTube* music videos, news and sports on the television. Regarding food I love, those include French fries, pumpkin pie, peanut *M&Ms*, Italian and Mexican food, salads, and most vegetables and fruits, especially blueberries. To drink, I mostly drink water, water with electrolytes, a variety of coffee drinks and aloe vera juice. I like an occasional glass of wine and *Coca Cola* with popcorn. Regarding my favorite music, like you, I have a wide variety of types of music that I like. And there is no one I enjoy listening to more than Barbra Streisand. I guess you and I are typically gay, liking Lady Gaga and Barbra Streisand. Oh, and to throw in something I don't like, I'd I don't like fake behavior in people.

---I'll never remember all that.

---I don't expect you to. Just try to remember me, at least occasionally.

---I'm already sensing that won't be a problem.

---It is true that I am unforgettable. Hahahaha.

---True, but maybe not in a good way. Hahahaha.

---Sheesh. Your first bitchy comment towards me. You broke your long streak of politeness. I feel honored.

---You should be.

5 RAFA'S TRAUMAS

Today was a new day and somehow the subject of our texts turned to life traumas. I mentioned a few that I had experienced, including the roof collapsing over my desk at work and a car crash. This led to Rafa opening up about his own traumas.

—I'm going to tell you another thing about me that very few people know, Socrates. You know Lady Gaga's song *911*? She describes the song as a poetry of pain. I relate a lot to that because a few years ago, I was raped. Two men took me into a room during a party, tied me down and took turns abusing me. They hit me too.

—Oh my gosh, that's awful. I'm so sorry that happened to you. Thanks for confiding in me to tell me that. Are you still traumatized by that? Maybe that's a stupid question. I'm sure it's hard to forget.

—With the passage of time, the trauma has subsided. Thinking about it now, it was partly my fault, since I was a little drunk.

—No, it wasn't your fault at all. Even though you were drunk, what they did was very wrong. Don't blame yourself.

—Another traumatic event for me was getting pulled out of school. I was encouraged by a psychologist, who is a friend of our family, to journal about it. So that's what I did. I still have the short story.

—Cool. I'd love to read it sometime.

—I just now emailed it to you.

(Rafa's short story translated into English)

A dry wind whipped around my long, curly black hair as I squinted to shield my eyes from the swirling dirt coming up from the dirt road. During my walk back home from school, I stopped to rest in the shade of a nearby mesquite tree to briefly escape from the blistering hot

Monterrey sun. I stood there in my sweat-stained blue school uniform for a few moments before starting on my journey again. I decided to cut through an empty lot, dodging broken beer bottles, as well as an empty *Dorito's* bag that flew past me. Two abandoned tires sat among a patch of weeds and a condom wrapper. As I looked up, I saw a frail-looking, white-haired hound dog venture towards me.

—*¿Qué tal, flaquito? Ven por acá.* (How is it going, skinny? Come over here.)

As my slender-framed body bent over, the dog licked my face and wagged his tail. I spent a few minutes petting him. Not sure why, but I'd always felt a special kinship with animals that I didn't always feel with humans. I looked around but could see no human looking for their dog.

—I like you, *flaquito* (skinny dog). You are coming home with me.

I reached down, lifted the stray dog to my chest, and headed home. Once we arrived, I opened the chicken-wire entrance gate and searched to find my mother to tell her my news. I eventually found her in the side yard, wringing dry an article of clothing she was washing by hand.

—*Mamá, mamá, ¿adivina que?* (Mom, mom, guess what?)

She didn't pause to look up as she responded.

—*¿Qué pasó, mi hijo?* (What is it, my son?)

—*Mira lo que encontré. ¿Podemos quedarnos con él?* (Look who I found. Can we keep him?)

Mrs. Galarín glanced up to see me, her 13-year-old son, holding a panting dog.

—*Ay hijo, otro perro callejero. Ya tenemos tres gatos que trajiste a la casa el otro día. Ya sabes que no somos un albergue de mascotas.* (Oh no, another stray dog. We already have three cats you brought home the other day. You know that we aren't an animal shelter.)

—*Por favor. Creo que puede ser el destino.* (Please. I think it could be destiny.)

—*Definitivamente no, Rafa.* (Definitely not, Rafa.)

As I heard my mother's response, I slouched my shoulders in disappointment. A few seconds later, she let out a big sigh.

—*Está bien, pero nada más por un rato.* (Okay, it's fine, but only for a while.)

I screamed out a "yes" as I excitedly jumped up and down, caressing and kissing the newest member of the family. The reality was that there wasn't enough food to feed our family of six, let alone a dog and three cats. Until now, we managed to scrape by on my dad's trucker's salary and what my mom could save from a part-time, entry-level job at a nearby *maquiladora* factory. My mother turned off the water trickling out of the facet above the wash bin and dried her hands.

—*Rafa, vamos adentro por unos minutos. Necesitamos hablar.* (Rafa, let's go inside for a few minutes. We need to talk.)

I let the dog down and swatted at a mosquito that was buzzing around my face as we entered the house and sat down on the couch.

—*¿Qué quieres decirme, mamá?* (What do you want to tell me, mom?)

—*Hijo, tengo malas noticias para ti. Han cortado mis horas en la fábrica y hay una huelga de camioneros pasando ahora. Por eso, tu papá no está trabajando. Necesitamos cortar gastos. Eso quiere decir que, por el momento, no tenemos los fondos suficientes para mandarte a la escuela. Los gastos de inscripción, los libros, los uniformes, y los costos de transporte son muy caros para pagar.* (Son, I have some bad news for you. They've cut my work hours at the plant and there's a trucker's strike going on right now. That's why your dad isn't working. We need to cut expenses. This means, for the moment, we can no longer afford to send you to school. The costs of enrollment, books, uniforms and the transportation costs are too much to pay.)

—*¿Cómo? Noooo mamá. No. ¿No puedes pedir un préstamo de alguien? ¿Qué tal tía Eugenia? ¿Tal vez mi abuelo?* (What? Nooooo mom. No. Can't you ask someone for a loan? What about Aunt Eugenia? Maybe grandpa?)

—*Lo siento. Ellos tienen sus propias deudas. Ya he decidido. Pues, tu padre y yo decidimos.* (I'm sorry. They have their own debts. I've already decided. Well, your dad and I did.)

—*¿Qué voy a decir a mis amigos? Favor de decirme que esto es una broma.* (What will I tell my friends? Please tell me this is a joke.)

—*Cuando acabe el paro, pensamos que podrías viajar con tu papá en el trailer, repartiendo mercancia en diferentes puntos del país. Sé que esto es un shock para ti. Es para mí también y para toda la familia. Es nada más un cambio temporal en nuestras vidas hasta que ahorremos más dinero.* (When the strike is over, we thought that you could travel with your dad in the semi-truck, delivering merchandise to different locations in the country. I know this is a shock to you. It is for me as well and for the whole family. It's just a temporary change in our lives until we save more money.)

I wasn't satisfied with my mother's explanation. Suddenly, an overwhelming feeling of anger swept over me. I jumped up from the couch, picked up my new furry friend from the floor and ran to my room, locking the door behind me. I collapsed on the dusty blankets sprawled out on the floor. Curling up into a ball, I laid there in stunned silence as I tried to come to terms with my mother's news. I had long ago adapted to the harsh realities of growing up poor, but this was a new low. My aching intestines were a reminder to me that I hadn't eaten all day, but I was too distraught to heed their calling. My new companion, sensing my sorrow, began licking away the tears streaming down my face. The End.

—Wow, I just read it. Great job, Rafa! Fantastic. Very descriptive. Writing that must have been very cathartic for you. I can only imagine the frustration your entire family must have felt at that moment. You told me dancing is how you express yourself, but when you want to, you can be just as expressive with your writing.

—Thanks. Just like with my dancing, I am a perfectionist. I did lots of rewrites on it to get it just right. If I could go back and change one thing in my life, it would have been to stay in school. That and to begin to take dance classes as a young boy.

6 RAFA'S OBSESSION

Now that we were feeling a little more comfortable with each other, I decided to send Rafa my first audio message.

—What do you think of my voice, Rafa?

—I can tell you are a gringo. *Jajajajaja.*

----*Jajajajaja.* I don't really like hearing my voice recorded.

—Same here.

—Hey, I read your *jajajaja.* As you know, I use it now too. Can you please describe the different written Mexican laugh meanings for me?

—Sure. *Jajaja* and *jejejeje* are the usual Mexican text laughs. Most people type *jajajaja.* Some do *jejejeje,* which is more sarcastic. And *jijijiji* is laughing like a child.

—Thanks. That is very helpful.

—You are welcome.

As our texting continued, sometimes I would write as many as eight texts to his one. His responses, despite knowing each other a little better now, continued to be concise. He continued to say that he didn't always know what to say. Frustrating indeed. I, on the other hand, always seemed to know what to text or say in an audio message. I always had plenty to talk about. At least I thought I did. Rafa began to admonish me for being so wordy. I would only half-jokingly say that I got excited when he responded with more than an "ok," "oh," "yes," or "oooo." We were mostly two opposites regarding verbal and written expression. We were both introverts, but I could change into an extrovert if I was close to someone. He, on the other hand, stayed the same. Rafa often would keep his emotions deep inside. But occasionally, me expressing my feelings openly and freely inspired him to do the same.

I wished Rafa would lengthen his texts and he wished I would shorten mine, but neither was going to happen. It was who we were or who we wanted to be. I suppose the advantage was that I wasn't interrupted much and Rafa wasn't pressured to carry the conversation. Rafa later would tell me that I texted so much that it didn't give him a chance to initiate a text. Of course, he could have sent two texts, one to answer and the other to initiate another conversation. But he said he normally never did that. He also said that he preferred that another person start the texting, which was more believable. I guess in some relationships, some people prefer the other person to dominate the conversation. I had some experience with this before. My mother almost never called me. I always had to call.

The text conversations Rafa and I had were often random. I would change the subject abruptly and he would have a hard time catching up. After a couple of hours had passed, naturally, I texted first.

—How was school today, Rafa?

—It was fine.

—Did you learn anything new?

—I guess I did. Hahahaha.

—What does that mean?

—I don't know. I did a lot of math today.

—Oh gosh, I hate math. A grade of "C" is an "A" for me.

—Me too. I'm horrible at it.

—I guess numbers aren't our forte. Forte means something we excel at. However, I did notice one subject that you do excel at, which is posting silly memes and comments on your Facebook and Instagram pages. You really posted a lot today. Can I ask you why you do that?

—I don't know. I get bored and they make me laugh. I post memes for fun. They usually aren't personal or have anything to do with me.

—Ah, okay. You also post a lot of photos of yourself on Instagram. What is that all about?

—I enjoy modeling or pretending to model. It's why I love mirrors too. *No soy presumido.* (I'm not conceited.) I know it might seem strange, me admiring how I look.

—I'll give you the benefit of the doubt regarding you not being conceited. Obviously, if you enjoy posting so many photos of yourself, go for it. But in my opinion, it all seems superfluous and unnecessary. I have another related question for you. Do you have any concerns about posting naked photos of yourself?

—No. They are tasteful and artistic. When I post naked photos of me,

I think a lot about it before I do it. I don't like to show my body as much as I would like to, because I'm so thin.
---Your body looks fine to me.
---Thanks.

Rafa told me he was never far away from his cell phone. This habit wasn't any different 24-year-olds in this regard, but his was an extreme case. His waking leisure hours were often exclusively spent on it, often ignoring friends and family who were present. He just didn't care how rude his actions were. He was happy in his own world. His all-consuming habit kept him up until the wee hours of the night and morning. To his credit, he was very talented at including graphics and music with his photo and video posts. And for a person always lacking money, he always managed to find money to pay for his phone bills.

Another habit of Rafa's that went hand and hand with his cell phone usage was his being constantly distracted. When Rafa texted me that he was born distracted, I didn't think much of it. Later, I learned his "I was born distracted" comment was a good excuse to justify ignoring those of us around him while he was using his phone. He refused to believe that distractedness could also be a learned behavior. His mother said it was a convenient excuse for him to ignore others while he did what he wanted to. On the record, I'd say attending to the needs of others wasn't a priority of Rafa's, Off the record, I'd say he often behaved like a brazen asshole.

Maybe Rafa really did have Attention Deficit Hyperactivity Disorder (ADHD) or some form of it. But if he did, it might be helpful to seek help for it, which he said he never did. Rafa wasn't hyperactive, but he certainly had problems concentrating on anything for more than a few seconds or minutes. The exception was his dancing. This led me to believe he could turn the distraction button on or off if he wanted to.

ADHD often begins in childhood and can persist into adulthood. Available evidence suggests that it is genetic, although the cause and risk factors are unknown. I was torn between skepticism and empathy. Rafa could be forgetful as well. Often, he would repeat what he had told me many times before, as if we had just met each other. It was like he had some form of amnesia. It was okay though. At this point, I was still trying to get to know the young man and was open to letting it be. As Rafa's friend, I unconditionally supported him, despite his faults or health issues. I wish I could say Rafa supported me in the same way. He didn't. It was another red flag that I ignored. I changed the subject again.

—Would you like to go to dinner with me sometime, Rafa?

—Yes, it would be a pleasure.

—Besides going out for dinner, I was wondering what else we could do if I visited you. I googled well-known mountains in Monterrey and the *Cerro de la Silla* (Hill of the Chair) came up. I was thinking that it might be cool to go there one night and watch the stars.

—I love being in nature staring at the stars. That would be amazing.

Rafa was continuing to text me in a formal way, even now after having chatted with him so much. Half the time, I had no idea whether he was being formal because that is what he thought he should be saying to be polite or whether he really meant it. I often played the game with him too, mainly because even a formal text comment was better than no text reply at all. Regardless, we set a date to meet each other. I was excited and I hoped he was too.

7 A RAFA ARCHAEOLOGICAL EXPEDITION

It was around Christmas time, so I texted Rafa and asked him if he celebrated it, like most Mexicans. I guess I should have known he wasn't like the rest of his compatriots.

—I liked Christmas when I was a child, but now it is used as a reason to get drunk in my family. Christmas isn't about celebrating. It is about being kind to each other. I think beer is for going out with friends to a club, not getting drunk at home during holidays.

—I assume the excessive alcohol has something to do with the Christmas being celebrated late at night in Mexico. My family is fast asleep when you guys are celebrating. My Christmas' involved happiness, gifts, good food and some alcohol. They were some of the happiest memories of my family life. My dad said for Christmas, everyone had to be on their best behavior, and we were.

—It's nice without the alcohol ruining it.

---Rafa, do you at least participate in the posadas (holiday parties) before Christmas? I assume you enjoy eating *tamales*, *bacalao* (salted cod) and other holiday food.

---I do sometimes. It depends on my mood.

---What about holiday music?

---I hate Christmas songs. When they sing the songs, I feel as if it is a witches' sabbath.

—Hmmm. I don't get that at all. What are you doing right now?

—I am wrapping some gifts.

—Cool. So, you are getting in the holiday spirit a little bit. May I ask for whom are the gifts?

—I'm heading to an orphanage to give gifts to the children there.

—Nice. That is so thoughtful of you. Can I ask you why you are doing this?

—I know what it feels like to have nothing. And I value what little I have.

—Cool. I think too that when you help someone, you become a little part of that person somehow. It helps us feel connected with each other.

—Yes, I believe that too.

—So, with the holidays upon us, I'd like to ask you something. Do you celebrate them for religious purposes? Can I assume that you are Catholic, like most Mexicans?

—No, I don't. I'm not religious. But there is something you don't know about me.

—And what is that?

—I used to be a Jehovah's Witness. I still have the suit and tie I wore when I was out talking to others about it.

—Interesting. Can I ask why you chose to be part of that group?

—Just kind of exploring to see what it was all about. I'm over that now.

I loved learning these little tidbits about Rafa. Sometimes I felt like a Rafa archeologist, going on expeditions to see if I could find hidden artifacts. One part of Rafa that I uncovered during these expeditions is that despite being overly focused on himself, there were also rare times when he showed that he really cared about others. In particular, he very much cared about the LGBTQ+ community, as well as the impact he and others had on climate change and our planet.

These expeditions also revealed more than once that empathy and caring were not Rafa's default mode of apparatus. Often, he buried his feelings deep inside of him. Expressing them didn't come naturally and he lacked the social skills to process them. He was also narcissistic. I was shocked at learning how vicious he could be at times and not feel any remorse. Sometimes he appeared to enjoy making people suffer. Sometimes, this ugly side of Rafa made me question whether he was worthy of my friendship.

If Rafa had wanted to do some archeological expeditions in search of artifacts about me, he wouldn't have had to dig very far. I didn't hide my artifacts very well. One of them was that I had the tendency to be overzealous about sharing advice. Today I was trying to motivate Rafa to achieve his goals. He never asked me to do this and in retrospect, maybe I should have waited until he asked me. But he seemed to be very appreciative of my advice, so I kept giving it.

—Rafa, I think it's important to create the world you want in your imagination, repeating positive thoughts, and paying attention to the constant chatter in your mind. Try your best to block out the noise around you. I also strongly believe that forming a team that unconditionally supports you is imperative for success in whatever you want to do in life.

—Thanks, Socrates. It is important to me that you share your knowledge with me. I've been waiting for someone like you to come into my life.

—You are welcome. You have a lot of things going for you, so try to focus on those. You obviously have a tremendous talent for dancing. You are determined, with a good work ethic. You speak two languages, so that tends to make you more flexible and open-minded.

—Thank you for taking the time to write all these beautiful words.

—You are welcome, Rafa. Thanks for reading it all. I know you are busy, but I will be happy to spend whatever time you have available for me on my visit where I can elaborate on my comments.

—I will make time to be with you.

We hadn't been texting for very long at this point, but due to its intensity, it seemed like we knew each other a lot longer. We exchanged additional contact information. I shared with him some paintings I had created. He loved them. I told him about the book I was writing.

—It would be a pleasure for me to read it. In fact, I want to be the first to read it and get your sign on it.

—I will make sure you are the first. And I think you mean signature.

—Yes, signature. Thank you.

I sent him a newsletter that I designed and wrote for work, as well as some articles I had published. He said he would read them when he got home, but he admitted later that he never did. I believe he sincerely wanted to read them, but he didn't have the time or got distracted. Reading a book or even a magazine was too much for him to concentrate on. He did read a lot, but that reading was usually restricted to texts, memes, social media posts, something short and quick. The few books he owned sat on a shelf in his small room, gathering dust. If he read them at all, it was a page or two at most. What was surprising though, was that he seemed to value them enough to not throw them away.

Today, I noticed Rafa posted photos of himself on Instagram dancing on the beach in Tijuana. Later the same day, he posted artistic dancing photos of himself taken by a professional photographer on the top of *El Cerro El Potosi* (El Potosi Mountain). They were beautiful and very artistic. It was pure Rafa. He was constantly searching for beauty,

whether it was in himself, his dancing or a landscape in Europe.
—You are very photogenic.
—I don't think so.
—Why don't you like the photos? They are beautiful.
—Because I know I can do better. The poses are okay. It's my face that I don't like.
—I like your face.
—Thank you.

What I found interesting was Rafa often would post unattractive photos of himself as well. He did it to express his feelings about what was going on in his life at that moment. Some had an artistic side to them. Others were more of a flirty or sexual type, while others showed him as being bored, sick or sad.

While he shared the physical part of himself to the world, it was rare that anyone got to see his extensive inner world. But Rafa allowed me to peek inside this world via text. I wasn't quite sure why I had such exclusive rights. After all, we'd not yet met in person. But he'd answer almost every question I asked him. I took full advantage of my journalism skills and my desire to know him profoundly. Inevitably, as time passed, his dark side emerged. It was a side of him that he desperately attempted to hide from everyone else. This dark side would, not surprisingly, be revealed at night, when he often was tired and let his guard down.

He used a few strategies to keep his personal information, especially negative information, from spreading beyond myself and his family members. One was to keep us, his close friends, isolated from each other. This prevented us from talking about him amongst ourselves.

He was also strategic regarding his flaws. When one of his was mentioned, he often would ignore it and instead judge and attack the person for the same flaw or attempt to invent one that doesn't exist. He did this to extricate himself from saying he was sorry or admitting he made a mistake.

Strategies were also employed if anyone got too close to Rafa. When someone began to violate this, he would say subtle comments to distance the person. But later, if ignored, he would be more direct. Eventually, as I got to know Rafa better, he became my metaphorical guitar. I learned which strings to strum lightly and which ones to strum harder to get my desired result, which was a harmonious Rafa who felt comfortable with the amount of time we spent together.

Of course, there were moments when the guitar seemed to play a melody out of tune all by itself, without me touching the strings at all.

Rafa told me that at times, even he didn't understand why he behaved the way he did. His instability gave me a foreboding feeling that one day our friendship could easily fall victim to his ever-changing world. Because of this, I tried my best to take advantage of the time I had with him. I voluntarily mounted the wild, bucking bull that is Rafa. Whether I can ride him longer than the few who dared to mount him previously remains to be seen. I have no doubt that I will inevitably be thrown off. The question is whether I have the patience or the desire to keep getting back on this bull.

Honestly, there was a part of me that was attracted to his unpredictable and heterogeneous personality. These personality traits were attractive, fascinating, frustrating, intriguing and mystifying to me. He was a never-ending *rompecabezas* (puzzle). With most of my friends, I generally knew how they would react and behave in a given situation. Not so with the inscrutable Rafa. In a relatively short time span, his emotions could run the gamut between excitement and apathy, and childlike happiness to explosive anger. He could be aloof and distracted, then minutes later, explain why he was depressed and crying a few hours before. As we continued texting, I asked him about his mixed bag of feelings.

---My life is a constant emotional roller coaster ride, Socrates.

---That is obvious. Hahahaha. You take instability to a whole new level. If I haven't texted you in a few days, usually I have missed several occurrences in your ever-changing, soap opera-like life. One day you are sick and the next fine. One day you are injured and the next fully recovered. One day you are working out at a gym and a few days later you have stopped. One day you apply and are accepted for a job and a few days later, you decide not to do it.

---I know. Sometimes I am all over the place.

---Sometimes? Abrupt changes also occur in your appearance as well. Out of nowhere, you'll shave all your hair off, then grow a beard, wear heavy makeup, add a tattoo, pose in a dress, or change to an androgynous look.

---I guess I get bored a lot. Hahahahaha.

8 A SHARED LOVE OF LANGUAGES

Rafa's strong desire to learn not only English, but other languages as well, was one of our mutual interests that endeared me to him. We both were looking to improve our knowledge of each other's native language, so it was a perfect fit. Today, I wanted to learn a little more about why this desire of his even existed.

---Hi Rafa. Hey, I would you like to do an English class video chat with me today?

---Okay, sounds good.

---Great. You know, we've spent all this texting each other and I don't think I've asked you how you've learned to write English so well.

---To this day, I've never taken a formal English class. Ever since I was a kid, without even trying very hard, I have picked up a little English here and there, on my own, watching *YouTube* music videos. But that all changed in my teenage years, when I moved in with my sister. It was during this period when a lot of kids of Mexican illegals in the U.S. were getting deported to Mexico. Many had lived in the U.S. their entire lives and did not speak Spanish very well. Several of them moved into my sister's neighborhood and we became friends. I couldn't speak English and they couldn't speak Spanish. Slowly but surely, we taught each other. It was frustrating for all of us, but I improved my English so fast. I still need to learn a lot. I write well, but my speaking isn't that great.

---That's fantastic that you got that opportunity! Is there another reason, other than wanting to understand your friends, that you wanted to learn English?

---My friends certainly, how do you say it, piqued my interest. Did I say that right? I also consider myself a naturally curious person. I've always enjoyed learning about different cultures and their languages. And then there are the more practical reasons, such as helping me to get a better job. English obviously is a global language, so speaking it well will be helpful when I travel. And I get to meet more friends like you.

---Those are all good reasons. What are you doing now to improve your English?

---I participate in an international online group video chat. I watch *The Simpsons* learning English program. And by continuing what I've always done---watching movies and videos on *YouTube* and social media.

---Nice.

—Socrates, this is going to sound weird, but I like your Spanish mistakes.

—Really? Why? I know I need practice.

—Not much. It's just that listening to you, I see where non-Spanish speakers have problems, like with the future tense.

—That and whether something is feminine or masculine. Sometimes I know the gender of the word, but to remember it and say it quickly isn't easy. And Rafa, please don't ask me to pronounce Indian words like that volcano *Popocatepetl*.

—That is hard for Mexicans to pronounce too.

—To get away with not knowing how to say a word or pronounce it correctly, I sometimes will fake it by pronouncing the first part of it, then running all the rest of the letters together. Hahahaha.

—Hahaha. Sometimes I do that too.

---And speaking of how to pronounce a word, for me, one often overlooked benefit of being bilingual is the increased ability to understand the accents of native Spanish speakers speaking in English. I've had so much practice listening to these people speak. The other day in San Diego, I was hanging out with a couple I knew who had been together for less than a year. One was from Panama and the other was a Mexican-American who doesn't speak Spanish very well. The Mexican-American frequently didn't understand his boyfriend's heavy English accent. I was able to step in to explain to him what he was trying to say.

---I never thought about it much, but you are right.

—By the way, I really appreciate all your help with my Spanish. You are a good teacher, Mr. Coria.

—Thanks. You are too.

Rafa explained that he wished to be a polyglot someday. In addition to English, he knew some sign language and could speak a little

German too. We both agreed to be strict with each other regarding each other's mistakes while texting and during our video chats. We also patiently took the time to translate words or phrases we didn't know. When either of us read or heard a word or phrase we didn't know, we'd stop what we were doing and look it up. This included slang or off-color phrases and words, since speaking like natives was very important to us.

Like Rafa, I used as many ways as I could to learn Spanish. These included forcing myself to speak to my bilingual friends in San Diego in Spanish only. I used the traditional cue cards to memorize new words and sentences. Other methods included listening to Spanish music and radio apps on my phone, watching television and social media videos, as well as read books. I also asked a lot of questions. I was motivated and I made learning Spanish a priority. As a result, I was rapidly advancing in my Spanish language skills. While improving English was a priority for Rafa as well, he had many more competing priorities than I did and as a result, our video chat language classes soon ended. I was disappointed but very much understood why he couldn't continue. He has plenty of time in the future to rededicate himself to learning languages.

I woke up the next day to learn that Rafa had gone to work sick the previous night. I asked him why he didn't stay home to recover.

—Money doesn't fall from the sky, Socrates. At my job, there are no paid sick leave days.

A few days later, after he had recovered, he informed me he was just now waking up at 2 p.m.

—I was at an after-work Christmas party, got drunk and had to be helped to a friend's car and taken home. I mixed whiskey with wine and threw up several times afterwards. I lost count of how many drinks I had. I knew I shouldn't mix them, but I didn't care.

—Wow! It must have been some party. It's nice to unwind like that every now and then. But it sounds like you unwound too much. Hahahaha.

—I did. There is a saying in Spanish that goes like this: *"Una vez al año no te hace daño."* It means doing something once a year isn't going to hurt you. Of course, sometimes we say that for bad habits we do all the time as well. Hahahaha.

—Hahahaha. You were a bad boy, Socrates. If you do it again, I will have to come over there and spank you.

—Then I will have to be bad again. Hahahaha!

He sent me a photo of himself with his work shirt on.

—You look sexy.

—Hahahahaha. Thanks, but no, not at all. I'm not being modest. I look like a nerd.

Upon my request, Rafa sent me his first audio message:

—Hi, I am Rafa, and this is my voice in English and *esta es mi voz en Español* (this is my voice in Spanish). I hope you like it. I really need to practice speaking more, because I'm not really that good at it.

—I like your voice.

Rafa's voice sounded effeminate yet not over the top, which maybe described my voice as well. We kept texting each day, with me continuing to initiate the conversations. Today, December 20th, two weeks into our friendship, he agreed to meet me in person in his hometown. Later that evening, I texted him.

---Hey, guess what, Rafa? My hotel reservations in Monterrey have now been made. I'm coming to visit you!

---That's dope. That is the correct slang word to say great, right?

—It is, but I never say that. I'm too old. Hahaha! But I think you can, so yeah, well said.

---Why do you say you are too old to say "dope"?

---I don't know. It sort of sounds stupid when an older person says it.

---Come on. Socrates, you aren't that old.

---I guess not.

---I also heard a woman saying I'm looking snatched. That means looking very attractive or goodlooking, right?

---Correct again, Rafa. I'm surprised I even know that. Hey, back to the trip. Would it be alright if I brought you a gift?

—You can bring me whatever you'd like to or something you think I would like. I'll let you take a guess. Hahahaha.

—Maybe I'll bring you a jockstrap.

—What is that?

—It's called a *suspensorio* in Spanish.

—Oh okay, nice. I could wear it during my dance performances. Is it comfortable?

—You can tell me. Some are, some aren't so much. I like to wear them for workouts. They give you more freedom, are sexy and keep your junk from moving around.

—Nice.

—Hey, did you know that we first chatted on December 6?

—Wow, you are counting the days since we met.

—I am. That probably scares you, right? I promise that I'm not too obsessed with you. At least not yet. I promise not to stalk you.

—A little. I wouldn't mind if you were stalking me. It will be a pleasure to meet you.

Rafa's politeness was adorable, but at the same time, it felt like an impediment for us to get to know each other even better than we already have. I had made some inroads towards getting him to be more informal with me. I will just need to be patient. I reminded myself that formal language for Mexicans is also a form of respect and an eventual gateway to getting to know someone better.

9 MY FIRST VISIT TO MONTERREY

The week passed quickly. Finally, the day came for me to head out to visit this whirlwind friend of mine. I crossed the border and took a taxi to Tijuana International Airport to catch a flight to Monterrey. The plane ride was a little bumpy, but I arrived safely. I took a rideshare directly to Real Inn and settled into my room. The anticipation of meeting Rafa for the first time wasn't the only reason why I was excited. It was my first time ever in Monterrey and I was planning to visit some of its attractions during my five-day trip. I plopped down on the bed and googled a few facts about the city. The search results showed that it is the third-largest city in Mexico, after Mexico City and Guadalajara. It is known for being a major player of industry and business, as well as its modern architecture, nightlife, food, and culture. I was hoping Rafa could fill me in on the specifics. After a quick shower, I texted Rafa, but he didn't reply for an hour. Finally, I got a response.

—Welcome to Monterey. It's been a busy day for me. I'm sorry that I didn't respond sooner to your text. I hope to see you soon. Have a nice day.

—Thanks. During these vacation trips, I like to think about life questions that I ordinarily don't have the time to think about. For example, why am I doing what I'm doing now? Hahahaha! I'm crazy.

—Nice, I like that. And I like your craziness.

—Thanks. My experiences in life have taught me that when I really want something, if I see it clearly enough with a lot of passion and energy, it magically happens. I've also seen the opposite happen. I've hypnotized myself into believing that I am not worthy or deserving of being happy.

—I admire how confident you are in yourself, Socrates.

Rafa had told me beforehand that despite very much wanting to see me, he would be too busy to meet until near the end of my short trip. The wait to see Rafa was unbearable, but I managed to keep myself busy for a few days, hanging out at restaurants, and doing sightseeing. I walked around the *Macroplaza*, one of the largest public squares in the world. For the second day, I went up to the top of the *Cerro de la Silla* (Chair Mountain), which offered a breathtaking view of the city. The third day was museum trip day. I visited the Museum of Mexican History, the Museum of Contemporary Art, and the Museum of Steel. I was also enjoying the rich, culinary delights the city had to offer. I'm not much of a meat eater, but I read time and time again that Monterrey was famous for its delicious meats, so on three consecutive nights, I ate *cabrito* (roasted goat), *carne asada* (grilled beef), and *machaca*, a type of dried beef. The third night, my overindulgence caught up to me. I wasn't feeling well after coming back to the hotel. It turned out that I had a severe type of food poisoning. I texted Rafa right away about my getting sick.

—Oh my gosh, I'm so sorry. I'm worried about you. Hopefully you will feel better tomorrow.

—I hope so too. I've been to the bathroom like 10 times. Any suggestions?

—Maybe eat an orange. Those work for me. Make sure you drink a lot of water and electrolytes to stay hydrated. Sounds like you've lost a lot of fluids.

—I'm drinking chamomile tea.

—Chamomile? What is that?

—It is *té de manzanilla*.

—Today, I learned how to say *manzanilla* in English.

—I'm sure you can teach me too.

—Of course. Take care and I'll text you later to see how you are doing.

I started to vomit at four in the morning. When I woke up, I texted him, writing that, despite not feeling well, I was still excited to meet him. Later, I finally started to feel better.

—Good luck tonight at work, Rafa. It's nice to know someone cares about me.

—Now I do.

—It's no fun being away from home and being sick.

—Yes, I know. It happened to me a few years ago.

—I miss my dog too. I have been doing some light yoga stretches in my hotel room.

—That's great. It will help you to relax your body.

A few hours later, Rafa texted me with some not so good news.

—You know what? I am sick to my stomach as well. I don't know why. Of course, we are going to have dinner. Or at least we can eat some fruit if our stomachs can't digest a whole meal.

A few hours later when Rafa was off work, he texted me.

—Socrates, what are you doing tomorrow? I have a headache.

I told him I was free, so we made the date for tomorrow, New Year's Eve. After a decent night's sleep, I woke up still not feeling better, but at least I wasn't throwing up anymore. I couldn't do any sightseeing, so I spent the day recovering in my room. I texted Rafa in the evening.

—Hi. Hope you are better, Rafa. Right now, I am coughing a lot and have no energy.

—Last night, I felt bad the whole night and was going to the bathroom to vomit. Maybe I could go to the lobby at your hotel before I go to my sister's house. I really don't know why I am still sick. I went to see the doctor and he gave me some pills. I think I got sick due to the change of climate. I will go to see you "*en un rato*" (in a while). By the way, "*un rato*" can mean a few minutes or a few hours. Ha! By the way, I'm in the toilet again.

—Sorry you haven't gotten better. And I think you meant to say you are on the toilet. In the toilet means you are inside of it. Ha!

—Hahahaha! Okay, *gracias* (thanks). Both of us on the toilet is not the best way to start out the new year. My mom gave me a penicillin injection a while ago, so hopefully I will start to feel better soon.

An hour later, Rafa arrived at the lobby of the hotel. I went down the elevator, still not well, hoping I wouldn't have a coughing attack or blow my nose too much. I wore a tight, light blue sweater and jeans, attempting to look as handsome as a sick guy could. I still felt weak and dizzy, but I was not going to come all the way here without meeting Rafa. When I first saw him, the first thing I noticed was his brown, piercing eyes as he stood up from the lobby couch to greet me. I gave him a big smile and he gave me one too as we shook hands. He was dressed in a heavy, brown coat with a black tee shirt. My first impression was that he looked younger than his age. I liked his voice, but it was seldom used during our three-hour conversation. I did most of the talking, which was somewhat uncomfortable. He looked away from me frequently, seldom making eye contact. When he did, his facial expression shifted between contemplation and indifference. It took me off guard. He wasn't exaggerating when he had previously said he was better at writing English than speaking it. When I attempted to speak to him in English, he barely understood me, so I gave up on that and only spoke in Spanish.

I used my interviewing skills with him, hoping to extract more than a few words out of Rafa, but they weren't working. He started to look at his cell phone a lot, which I took as a sign that he really wasn't into me or maybe just bored, but it was hard to tell. I am usually good at picking up a person's body language, but this time, I was lost. At times, I wasn't communicating well either. He was so handsome, which made me feel nervous talking to him.

I felt a connection with him via our texts, so I knew there was a lot more to him than what I was seeing now. Those text messages saved our friendship, because in person, I was not impressed. Meeting him was uneventful and I felt a little sad. It was like the person texting and the person I met were two different people. As it got closer to midnight, Rafa said he had to leave for his family's New Year's celebration. As we said goodbye, he stuck out his hand and I shook it, but then instinctively, I hugged him. He gave me a big hug back and didn't let go for a while. I didn't know what to think about that.

I went back to my hotel room alone. I looked at my phone. It was a few minutes before midnight, almost time to celebrate the new year. When it arrived, I looked out my hotel room window and saw fireworks going off at an amusement park 20 or so blocks away. I texted Rafa about it and he responded immediately.
—Really? Nice. I wish we could go, Socrates. Hey. Happy New Year!
—Happy New Year to you too, Rafa.
I wish we could go. That comment comforted me.
—So, what did you think of my Spanish, Rafa?
—Well, it is obvious that you are a North American, but it is really good.
—Thanks! You definitely need to speak more English.
—I know.
—Not sure how you are going to do that.
—Nor me.
—Maybe send me more audio messages of you speaking English and I can review them and make any necessary corrections.
—Okay. I am willing to learn everything there is about American culture. By the way, I liked you a lot. You are very friendly and cool. I felt comfortable with you.
—Really? You seemed like you weren't that interested in me or what I was saying.
---I was interested. It's just that I'm very shy and I was nervous.

---Okay.

There was hope that Rafa wanted to see me again but no comments about if he thought I was handsome or not. I took that to mean he wasn't interested in me as a boyfriend. But maybe he was and was too shy to say it.

Later, on New Year's Day afternoon, we continued texting and sending each other audio messages. He mentioned how Mexicans speak in *doble sentido* (double meaning) and that to learn Mexican Spanish, I'd have to figure out what the double meanings meant. Either that or I'd have to use my intuition. Later, we discussed our experiences with understanding jokes in each other's language and how difficult it was. I stopped texting Rafa for a few minutes to pack up my belongings. As I was finishing, I heard a buzz from my cell phone.

—Hey Socrates, I know that you'll be heading back home today, so I wish you a nice trip back. I really want to thank you so much. I promise that one day when I have a visa, I will come to San Diego. I know we're going to be very good friends. I have a good feeling about you.

The word "friends" stayed in my head for a long time. Not boyfriends, but friends. Ugh. But still, how can Rafa be so confident that we are going to be good friends? Up to this point, we'd only known each other for less than a month. It got me thinking about destiny. I believe we all made our own destiny, but also that we attract certain people into our lives according to our desires. But life is mysterious too. Like when you meet someone, and you feel you've met them before. Where does that come from? Sometimes, I felt like I had met Rafa before.

During the flight back to Tijuana, I had a lot to think about regarding the future of our friendship. When I arrived and took a taxi to the border, I texted him about the long wait at the border. Eventually, I made it back home to my condo in downtown San Diego. We both finally recovered from being sick.

10 DANCING AND GRATEFULNESS

After my trip, our conversations turned to Rafa's dancing. I told him how fascinated I was with how dancers were able to contort their bodies. Today, I wanted to learn as much as I could from Rafa about what he loved the most.

---Rafa, tell me, how did you become so flexible?

---It was lots of hard work.

---I can only imagine. Later, please teach me how you did it, okay? You must keep practicing daily or you might lose some of that flexibility, right?

---Yes. It's been helpful for me to have others to work with on my stretching. I love to see the expressions on their faces. Hahaha!

—You've inspired me to stretch more too, Rafa. I am getting closer to doing the splits.

—Great! I want to see that. It isn't easy in the beginning. But it comes with time.

—Yes, patience and practice.

—Exactly, Socrates. If you want to be a dancer, you must endure the physical grind. It's been many hours of training, pain and passion. I am not an amazing dancer, but I do my best. I have good technique, but as you know, I am a perfectionist, and because of that, in my mind, I am never good enough regarding technique.

—Can you describe some of your technical problems?

—Socrates, if I did, we'd be up all night long.

—Hahahahaaha.

—When I am dancing, my biggest problem is my mind. I need to focus, and I cannot because I'm often thinking about the people around me and what they're saying about me while I'm dancing.

—Wow Rafa, you are really caught up in what people think about you. Anyway, back to your dancing. What are some of your career goals regarding contemporary dance?

—I see myself dancing for a major dance company.

—Well, keep the faith, no matter what. Take things a step at a time and with persistence and confidence, who knows where you might end up if you believe in yourself.

—I'm trying my best. One advantage I have is my body. A dance teacher told me that I have a dancer body so I can do many things that others can't. Regarding my belief in myself, dancing has built up my confidence, helping me in so many ways. Hey, I'm off to work. I will text you later.

—Are you working as a waiter or a busboy tonight?

—As a helper. I guess that is a busboy. I'm in charge of cleaning up all the mess the people leave behind. I also help the waiters to deliver food and drinks to the tables.

My texts to Rafa started to get longer and longer. I began to realize how involved I was getting with Rafa, and he did too. He was busy working late, studying and taking dance classes, but he continued to answer all my texts. I sent him a text the next day.

—Hi Rafa. Today, I thought about giving you a break from my texts but then I thought why should I waste an opportunity to share a little love with you? Hahahahaha. It's your fault anyway for being so unforgettable. Ha! I promise you that I will sign up for a stalkers anonymous class soon. I hope your dance class goes well today.

—Thanks so much. I'm not as sweet as you. I usually don't say those sweet comments. And don't worry about texting me too much. You never brother me. You make me feel useful and I thank you for that.

—Okay cool. You'll probably regret telling me that! Hahaha. By the way, it is you never bother me. What you said doesn't make sense.

—Thanks for correcting me. Please continue being strict with me. I want to learn to speak and write correctly.

—No problem. I'm here to help you. Hey, guess what, Rafa?

—What?

—I had my first dream about you. I'm very good at remembering my dreams.

—Really?

—Yeah. I had a dream that you were pulling out a *Pall Mall Tokio* brand of cigarette to smoke it.

—OMG! That is the brand that I smoke! That is amazing.

—*¿En serio?* (Seriously?) I'm not completely surprised. I have some psychic abilities.

—You are incredible, Socrates. You really are.

As we continued to text each other each day, I continued to work out, hang out with Rafie and do graphic design work. Rafa kept texting me, saying how much he wanted to be with me in San Diego. I think though that it might have been more about him wanting to be in San Diego than with me. I also began to wonder whether he really meant what he was saying. Sometimes, I dominated the conversations and maybe he was only reacting to what I said to have something to say or be polite.

—You know Rafa, it would be nice sometimes if you took the initiative and texted me first sometimes. I guess maybe that is how you are, wanting me to start the conversation. But it can't just be me supporting you all the time. You need to support me too.

—Of course, we will support each other.

—Cool. I like that.

—What are you doing right now, Socrates?

—I'm writing my book.

—And how is that going?

—It's a slow process. I come home tired from work and often am too tired to write. Often, if I have energy, I'm busy working out or playing with Rafie.

—What is your book about? I want to be the first person to read it.

—Of course, you will be the first to read it. It's a fictional story about a young man searching for himself. You will see that the main character has some similarities to me, but most are made up.

I texted Rafa a more in-depth summary of the book. This time, instead of politely saying the long texts didn't bother him, he commented on it.

—You love to make me read, right? It sounds interesting.

After I passed along several bits of wisdom, Rafa surprised me with some comments that I took to heart. What he said was too long for him to write, so he sent me an audio message.

—Socrates, I want to say thank you so much for taking the time to share your thoughts with me. Truly, I appreciate it. It is amazing to me that you would do this. I really feel like you are pushing me to be less shy, and more confident about my feelings. Often, I can't express myself when I feel tired or sad or angry, or even happy. Because I can't, I often explode or cry. It is nice to have a friend like you who I can talk with. It is important to me that you share your knowledge with me. I really like you and I know we will be very good friends. I know I said that before, but I mean it. We are friends now, but I feel we can really be close. I am so honored to have a friend like you. You also have a friend in me, and you should know that.

—You are welcome. I'm very happy to have met you and look forward to more meetings.

It was one of the rare moments that Rafa said more than a few words or sentences. A small breakthrough. It was a nice feeling to know that I was having a positive influence on him. One of my strengths I learned from a work survey was that I love to assist others close to me with their goals and desires in life. I enjoy focusing on only a few people and really making a difference. But since I can get carried away with that, I also need to set boundaries.

As our texting continued, some misunderstandings were bound to occur, due to the different languages. That's what ended up happening this afternoon.

—Hey Rafa, how are your mood swings today?

—Mood swings? Are you saying that I have multiple personalities?

—Oh, not at all.

—For a moment, I thought you were saying that I was like Billy Milligan, the guy who had 24 personalities inside of him.

—Mood swings are different from multiple personalities. They are fluctuations of emotions you might feel for long periods of time.

—I understand now. It's really amazing how the brain can alter its functioning when it isn't working well, like what was going on with Billy.

—So true. It's also amazing what it can remember when it is working well. Like mine. For example, I remembered that today is our one-month anniversary of texting.

—Wow, your brain is functioning well. I wish I could remember as well as you.

—You do okay. Anyway, guess what? I may soon be right in front of you more often. I applied for my SENTRI card to be able to cross the border quickly. I have already received preliminary approval as a person to be trusted by the U.S. Immigration and Customs Office.

—*¿En serio?* (Really?) Does that mean that you will come regularly to Mexico?

—Yes, regularly. I must wait for the interview. Be prepared to see me again.

—Nice.

11 WITCH POWERS AND CUSS WORDS

My text messages weren't always random ones. Sometimes they were strategic as well, but not in a manipulative way. Such as my texts with photos of meals I prepared. I enjoyed cooking and I was proud of my cooking abilities. It was another way I expressed my creativity. I was over a month into texting with Rafa, and I was already thinking about what skills I could offer him. I didn't dare tell him that though. I probably already put enough pressure on him as it is. As you grow older, you learn that it is important not to always reveal what you are thinking. It's also important to know when to overlook comments that aren't that important. Yay for wisdom.

When you get older, you hopefully also get smarter because of more life experience. For example, younger people in their 20's and 30's who fall in love usually aren't thinking about convenience or practicality when choosing a mate. Knowing how to cook though is a very practical skill that brings people together. I have great memories of a close friend who, for many years, cooked Mexican food and other types of meals for me. I also always remember my grandmother's cooking. Sometimes I even cry when I think about it, mostly due to all the tender, loving care and effort she put into preparing our meals. Food can most definitely be an emotional experience, and I hoped with Rafa, it would be too. Today, I sent him a photo of some chilaquiles that I cooked.

—Oh wow, it looks delicious. You are making me hungry, Socrates.

Later I sent Rafa photos of spaghetti, raviolis, Spanish rice, pizza, chicken, stews, desserts and other dishes that I made. By now, I had memorized his food tastes and customized my photos to fit them. I changed the subject and asked him about any fears he might have.

—My biggest fear is that an earthquake happens when I am taking a shit.

---Hahahaha. Come on. Seriously.

---Well, I am afraid of spiders. You might not know that.

—I didn't know that. Be ready later for me to scare you with fake spiders.

—Hahahahaha. There are many things that you don't know about me, Socrates, beyond what I like or don't like.

—Hopefully, you'll give me the opportunity to learn more about you.

I started sending Rafa more text and audio messages in English to help him learn. It started to pay off. His speaking skills began to improve. He agreed that we should start up our English class video chats again, so his verbal skills could match his written ones.

—Rafa, if I haven't told you already, I love the way you speak English. I feel like hugging you every time I hear you speaking it. Hahahaha.

—You as well. What are you up to right now? I am really enjoying this series called *The Chilling Adventures of Sabrina*, about a dark story of a woman who was dealing with being half witch, half mortal. Sometimes I wish I could be a witch to have all that power. What would you do, Socrates, if you had witch-like powers?

—Hmmm....well, I would for sure use my powers to help mankind. I would help people who are suffering and take power away from people who are using it in a cruel way. And I would most definitely fly to work. Hahaha! And you could fly to San Diego! And imagine the show you could put on as a dancer.

—That would be awesome!

—You know, I think some of us have some latent witch powers. We just need to practice them a little. What do you think?

—What do you mean?

—For example, a few years ago, I played a drawing game where I was paired up with a friend against other paired up teams. A word clue was given to one player and then he or she had to draw the word clue on a piece of paper as fast as he or she could and the other had to guess the clue correctly before the other teams did. My partner and I were losing by a lot of points, and it was getting close to the end of the game, so we concentrated harder and then like magic, we started guessing correctly each other's clues very quickly. We became in sync with each other's thoughts on some level. On the last clue to win the game, I had barely drawn the clue before my partner guessed it correctly. He leaped into my arms in ecstasy.

—Wow, that's amazing.

—It's a skill to mentally connect with another. Thoughts can travel like electricity. That is one of the aspects of life that makes it fun. When you realize all the amazing things that can be achieved using thoughts and your body. The possibilities seem endless.

—Yeah, I fucking love that.

Rafa's connection to me was indeed growing stronger, to the point where he even felt comfortable saying a cuss word or two in English. I wasn't sure how I felt about that.

—Sometimes Rafa, I think I've taught you too much English with you texting me cuss words.

—Hahahaha.

—Just promise me you'll use discretion when using them. And if anyone asks, you did not learn those from me.

—Hahaha. Okay, I promise. I already knew many of them before I met you.

Besides teaching Rafa new words, I sometimes sent him photos of San Diego to show him to the city where I lived. The next day I sent a video of me walking to a beautiful restaurant on Shelter Island, on San Diego Bay.

—Someday, I will walk on those sidewalks, Socrates. I just woke up from a nap. I'll cock something for myself before going to work.

—I think you meant cook. Cock means penis. Hahaha!

—Oh my gosh, I don't know what happened. I know the correct spelling is cook. I didn't realize that I wrote that. Sorry. Socrates, you must think that I am rude and nasty.

—Don't worry. Believe me, I type too quickly sometimes and misspell words. I forgive you.

—Thanks.

—Besides, cock also has other meanings. It can mean a male bird or to raise a gun to make it ready for firing it.

—Okay, I don't feel so bad now.

—We are closer friends now. You are allowed to say those words every now and then. I want you to be yourself with me, Rafa. You are very formal and that is nice, but please be authentic too. As you know, I don't like fake people.

—Thanks, but I don't like to say cuss words often around you, since you don't use them. I will try to be more authentic. I don't like fake people either.

12 SELF IMPROVEMENT ADVICE

Today, Rafa was busy running around Monterrey, exhausted once again. It seemed to be a common occurrence for him. I thought he might benefit from some of the pearls of wisdom I was writing about in my book pertaining to that subject. He didn't ask for the advice, but as usual, I offered it anyway.

—Hey, Rafa.

—*¿Que onda?* (What's up?)

—I found some time to write my book.

—Nice.

—Yeah, and I thought about you when I was writing this one section. The main character gets so busy with projects that he neglects many areas of his life he thinks he can put off until later in his life. He became convinced that running from one place to another was necessary for him to get ahead in his career. His bad habits became so ingrained in his life that they later became difficult to undo. Opportunities to take small breaks, to exercise and to socialize with friends were considered wasted time, so he passed on them. As he got older, health problems began to appear, due to his unbalanced lifestyle.

—Ooooh. I never thought about that. Thanks. Maybe that is something happening to me right now. I'm thinking of giving up my job.

—Really?

—Yes. I'm not earning as much as I used to. I need more money to pay for my school and dance classes. I can't wait until they decide to pay me more. The job involves lots of hours of stressful work and criticism from my boss and club patrons. It's not worth it. I don't have time to rest properly, like you were saying about the guy in your book. I know I can overcome all of this by myself.

—I see. You are very independent in your way of thinking too. Maybe a job where you have more control would be better.

—Definitely. I don't like people ordering me around.

—Good luck in searching for a better suited job. Keep in mind though that almost every job involves others telling you how they want a particular task done.

—That is difficult for me to do.

—I know, but the sooner you understand this give and take, the easier life will be for you.

—I suppose.

—I'm not saying you should stay if you are unhappy, underappreciated and not being paid enough.

—I know.

—When I want to make a big change in my life, I often create a mantra and repeat it over and over again in my head, until it becomes a reality. Henry Ford, the famous car maker, once said, "Whether you think you can, or you think you can't, you're right. That means your experiences will often match your thoughts. In other words, you will attract whatever you strongly believe. Because of that, it is important to choose your thoughts well. People rarely examine their daily thoughts. Rafa's response to my text was a few hours later.

—I'm not at home. I am still working, but I read some of what you wrote. Thank you so much for your suggestion. You make me feel like nobody else does. I don't send you a kiss. I send you many kisses. Rest up. I will text you tomorrow.

—Okay. Good night, Rafa. Hopefully I will see you again soon.

—I hope so.

He answered me the next day after I told him that I found some dance videos on *YouTube* that he might like.

—Thanks. I search for dance videos that inspire me as well.

—I really admire you for the effort you put into your dance training. There is the mental part, learning the movements. Then there is the physical part, executing the memorized movements without having to think about them, due to constant practice. There is the use of your flexibility and strength. And of course, the flow and artistry. And coordinating it with others. I love it.

—Thanks, Socrates.

I sent him a photo of a book of mine on how athletes today use mental training for peak performance. I asked him if he thought it would be useful for him.

—Yes. Please bring that book when I see you next for me to read.

Because I knew I was competing with others for his spare time and due to my strong desire to get to know him and help him, I would often suddenly change the subject of our conversations to get in all I could before he texted others.

—I think you are a fascinating person, Rafa. I really do! I have so many questions for you. I love how you reveal so much about yourself via text.

—Thanks for taking the time to get to know me. You are such an amazing man. Now I feel things for you. I needed someone like you in my life. Thanks for that.

I decided to change the subject and I asked him about his tattoos.

—I have four of them, each representing different aspects of me.

—Very cool, Rafa. How about getting another one representing your new English word for the day?

—What is that?

—Equanimity. It means being calm, especially when dealing with difficult situations. That's what meditating has taught me. When I sit or am lying still meditating, I'm in better touch with my body and mind. It helps me feel at one with everything and feel interconnected with the world. I forget the stress at work, the necessity of earning money, the bad things in the world, and my separation from my family, among other things.

—That's cool for you, Socrates. I don't have the patience to meditate.

—Yeah, lots of my friends say the same thing. I started doing it due to my anxiety issues. But as it turns out, it has so many other benefits, kind of like your dancing does for you. I believe the quietness helps me get closer to the people and events that I wish to be experiencing. That includes meeting people like you, Rafa. Ultimately, trying to be equanimous would hopefully lead you to a space to perform your best, whether at work, in school or dancing.

—Nice. When you describe it like that, I understand why you do it.

—I remember a female bodybuilder who used to work out in the same gym that I did in Tijuana who really exemplified equanimity for me. She blocked out all distractions, maintaining her focus, taking deep breaths and waiting until she was mentally and physically ready before performing each weight lift. Once I saw her bring in an oxygen tank. I remember thinking "holy cow." But she didn't care what others thought about her. She was quietly focused on the task at hand. She was equanimity personified.

—Wow, that's impressive. I wish I could do that with my dancing.

Rafa seemed to be absorbing the information I was texting him. He continued to politely say that he was grateful for it all. I wondered though if I was wasting my time. If he wasn't getting anything out of them, I was. My texts were reaffirming what I already believed, so they were good reminders for me. As for Rafa, I wished he was more direct with me. I wouldn't mind if he said to me "Hey thanks, but I'm too busy and I'm not really interested in your tidbits of wisdom. If I need help with something, I'll ask for it." I texted Rafa this afternoon.

—How is your Sunday going, Rafa?

—It is my only day off without school, dance classes or work so sleeping is the only thing I do. Hahahaha.

—I understand. My work isn't as physically taxing as what you do all day, but it can be equally exhausting. It's more of a mental grind. Sometimes I send or answer over a hundred emails a day.

—That's too much for me, Socrates.

—It's too much for me too, but it is part of my life. I try to eat well to have energy to do everything I do. What about you, Rafa? Do you eat specific foods to provide you optimum energy to dance?

—No, I eat anything I want.

—You've never experimented to see how food might affect your dancing, for better or worse?

—Never. I know vegetables are good for me, but I don't want to eat them.

—I would think that any dancer or other athlete who is serious about their career would want to focus on what he or she puts into their body.

---Socrates, I don't have much money, nor does my family, so eating well isn't easy.

---Yeah, true. I suppose you eat what's available a lot of the time.

---Yeah, like most of the time.

---*Tortillas*, beans, rice and *nopales* (cactus), the staples of the Mexican diet, are all healthy options. And I think most of those foods are subsidized, so they aren't that expensive. I also believe that the good habits you create at your age will serve you well later in life. Young people often say "I want to smoke, drink and eat what I want now, while I can." While there is some truth to that, habits, once established, sometimes are very difficult to change.

—Thanks Socrates, but I am who I am.

---Rafa, food tastes aren't the same as the color of your eyes. They can change. I can name a few foods that I didn't like as a child but now enjoy eating.

---Say what you want. I am not changing.

—Wow, you are stubborn.

—I knew you were going to say that.

—I love you anyway, Rafa.

—Love you more.

A few hours passed and he texted me again. He didn't wait for me to initiate the texting.

—Hi Socrates. How are you? I wanted to tell you that you are making me a better person. You may not believe it, but I really care about you. Why didn't I meet you before?

—You were a child before. Hahahaha.

—True. I want you to know that I've learned a lot from you already and I'm paying attention to everything you say and write.

---That's nice to know, Rafa. I hope you know that I'm not telling you to do anything. They are all suggestions or things to think about.

---I know. Thanks, Socrates. Your suggestions and your efforts to get to know me have affected me. I've surprised myself by how I am so open with you. I usually don't talk about how I am feeling with others. You know me so well already. I wanted to tell you that I was thinking about you when you messaged me earlier. *Te invoque. Jajajaja.* (I summoned you. Hahahaha.)

—Hahaha. Wow. Our energies connected. That seems to happen a lot for us.

What Rafa said seemed to come out of the blue. It surprised me. Maybe, just maybe, my texts weren't a waste of time after all.

13 SCHIZOPHRENIA AND NO MORE WORK

Tonight, Rafa and I are texting each other late. I loved the nighttime version of Rafa---looser, less serious, often more open to joking around.

—Rafa, here's a photo of my dinner. I made ravioli filled with spinach and cheese, with potatoes and broccoli.

—I'm going to live with you because I don't like cooking and it looks like you eat well!

---I try my best. What are you up to?

—I'm watching a film called *Voices*. It is about a guy with schizophrenia. He is totally crazy. I am watching it in English with English subtitles. This makes me think of the hell that people like him with that illness must go through to live. I recommend you watch it too.

—Okay, I found it. I'm starting to watch it now.

We ended our conversation at 3 a.m. It would become a common occurrence. Days later, we had another late night into the early morning textathon, even though I had to work early the next day. The movie Rafa recommended was indeed about a guy with schizophrenia. What he omitted to say was that he was also a killer who cut up his victims' body parts and put them in jars, with their blood spilling all over the floor.

—Hey Rafa, I'm still watching *Voices*. I can only watch it in parts.

—Really? Why?

—Because I am too sensitive. You know that. I often must look away from the screen. I absorb the violence and sadness as if I was actually in the movie with the people. I am glad that they didn't show the other two women being killed.

—I wanted to see that. All that blood gets me excited.

I paused for a moment or two, stunned by Rafa's text, before responding.

—Excited?

—Yesssss.

—Why? Should I be worried about you?

—When he killed the second girl and there was blood on his face, I thought, oh damn, I wanted to be there to put the blood all over my body parts.

—Is that a fetish you have?

—Why the question, Socrates?

—It's not normal.

There was a pause. Rafa finally sent a text.

—Hahahaha. Of course not. How disgusting. I am playing with you.

—You scared me, bitch. You have a sick sense of humor.

—Well, I did really want to see how he cut the meat but just because it looked so morbid. I guess it would have been interesting to see how he did it. This reminds me. I am planning to write a play some day. Guess what it will be called?

—I don't know. The Lady Gaga Chronicles?

—Yes, you guessed correctly. How did you know? No, it will be called Schizophrenia.

—That would have been my other guess, even though it's somewhat boring. Hey, you told me that you don't like to write. I am the writer. You are the dancer. You express yourself via dancing, not writing.

—I know, but this time, I am going to really try to express myself via writing. It would be about a youth who was recently diagnosed with the disease. He will be constantly attempting to fight the voices of people in his head. I envision that there will be the main character, a psychologist, and five imaginary people. The audience will interact with the characters. They will hear the voices of imaginary people. The voices will be torturing him, telling him to kill people. They will bother him when he is with others. He will see imaginary people dressed in black. I see myself playing a big role in the play as the imaginary person who tortures him the most. I also may play other parts as well. And I will be naked. I still need to create the rest of the story.

—Wow, that sounds like a great play. And you naked? Is Monterrey ready for that?

—You don't know the people here. I've seen them urinate on the stage.

—Oh wow.

—I think it would be a good idea to talk to a psychologist who treats people with schizophrenia to learn as much as you can.

—Yes, I will do that. I will investigate everything. I won't leave anything out. I am familiar with this disease because a friend of mine had it. We grew up together. He died three years ago. I would dedicate it to him, but his family is very sensitive about it. Obviously, I am going to invite them since they are like my other family. His sister Maria is my best friend.

—Wait a minute. Best friend? You told me you don't have a best friend. Anyway, I thought I was your best friend!!! Hahahahaha.

—Hahahaha. Well, I text with you more than anyone, that's for sure. Maria and I don't talk much anymore, but childhood friendships are special.

—True. I have a friend like that myself.

—Back to the play. It will most likely take a year to write it. I will need to get together with Maria and her mom. There won't be much dancing, but there will be lots of drama.

—Let me know if you want me to contribute.

We finally called it a night and went to bed. The next day, I learned that Rafa got sick from some food he ate from a street vendor. It was interesting that it happened so soon after our healthy food talk. A few days later, I received a text message from him, saying that he had indeed quit his job. The night he quit, he had worked a long night and had only received 100 pesos for his efforts. Without a job now, I wondered how he would pay for his bills, his school, his dance classes, etc.

14 REJECTION IN MONTERREY

In late January, Rafa and I decided to meet up again for a long weekend. I made a reservation for the same hotel, the Real Inn, that I stayed at when I first met Rafa. After a friend of mine dropped me off at the airport, I boarded my United Airlines flight to Monterrey, with a stopover in Houston. During the flight, I questioned myself about what I was doing, but was hopeful about what turn our relationship might take. After I arrived, I took a cab to my hotel and settled in as I waited for Rafa's school class to end. He eventually texted me, saying to meet him outside a Starbucks not far from the hotel in half an hour. I was a little late when I decided to walk over. By the time I arrived, I was already perspiring through the white striped dress shirt I was wearing. I spotted Rafa crossing the street to greet me.

—Hi there Rafa.

—Hola. *¿Que onda?* (Hi. How's it going?)

—I'm great. I'm so excited to see you.

—Me too. Thanks for coming, Socrates. Wow, you are really sweating.

—I know. I walked over from the hotel. I'd be lying if I said I wasn't a little nervous too.

—Let's go inside so we can relax, and so you can dry off.

I ordered a venti vanilla latte and Rafa ordered a fruity cold drink. After we had begun chatting for several minutes, he picked up his phone to call a girlfriend of his, which I thought was a little inconsiderate. But talking to her helped him relax a bit. Soon, we were all laughing. Everything seemed to be going fine. We left for the hotel a few hours later and went up to our room. He immediately flopped out onto the bed.

—Awww, this feels great, Socrates. I am so tired. I didn't sleep at all last night because I got home so late.

—Really? How are you even functioning?

—It's okay. I am accustomed to being tired.

—By the way, your socks and feet really smell bad, as well as your breath.

—Sorry. I'm still wearing my clothes from yesterday.

Some of the excitement I initially felt was slowly going away. I wondered why he didn't make the same effort I did to be rested in anticipation of our meeting. But then I remembered how he always seemed to live his life without much rest, always on the go. This was normal for him. He laid motionless on the bed, looking at me. I knew he was shy, so I wasn't expecting him to touch me first. I would have to make the first move. I leaned over and gave him a light kiss on the lips. I was hoping for a response from him, but there was no reaction. He had a blank stare. Ugh.

—Would you like a massage, Rafa?

—I give good massages, but I don't like to receive them. I think I mentioned to you before that I have a sensitive body.

His texts alluding to wanting more than friendship seemed to contradict his behavior now. At this point, I felt uncomfortable and confused, but I made the best of it and continued, talking to him as if nothing had happened. We walked over to a nearby *Sanborns*, a popular chain restaurant, and ate dinner. I attempted to strike up a conversation, but it was like our first meeting, with me doing most of the talking. He spent most of the time texting or looking at his phone, almost as if I wasn't there. I felt disappointed and uncomfortable. Whatever excitement he previously said he felt about seeing me again via text was gone. He acted like nothing was wrong. Being indifferent and uncaring seemed to be his 'go to' attitude around me. At this point, I didn't know being quiet was part of his personality.

We walked back to the hotel and sat down by the pool on the lounge chairs. There was no one there, so we were all alone to talk. He asked me if he could smoke a cigarette. He walked away from me to smoke it since he knew I didn't like the smell of smoke. We made some idle chat, which relaxed both of us a little. He finally said a couple of complete sentences.

—Socrates, I care about you, and I don't want to hurt you. I feel at my young age, I still want to be free and not be with any boyfriend. I need to just focus on my schoolwork.

I sat there for a few moments to gather myself and regroup before I responded. At this point, I expected his comment, but it didn't prevent my heart from falling into my lap.

—Rafa, did you just now figure this out after seeing me in person again? If you knew this already, why didn't you save my time and energy and tell me this when I was in San Diego?

—I know. I'm sorry.

—Sorry? That's it? This is infuriating. That's your new word of the day, in case you don't understand it. What you said is typical of someone who isn't attracted to someone. If you just said Socrates, I'm not attracted to you when I was in San Diego, I would have been fine with it.

There was no response from Rafa, so I continued.

---I've heard this speech before with other guys, only to find out that suddenly they are boyfriends with someone else when they meet someone who is hotter.

—Socrates, I'm not saying that you give up on being my boyfriend. I'm saying that it is too fast. For now, friendship is all I can offer you. You don't know me well. I'm not as sweet or as good as you. I want to be honest with you. You know that if I fall in love with you, it could be one of the best things to ever happen to me, but now I need you as my friend. I need my space. I just wanted to make things clear. Don't feel bad. You are super sweet and deserve the best from me. You are a super special friend. I want to concentrate on my studies and my dancing right now. Besides that, I fell in love a couple of times and they both ended badly.

—Well, I'm sorry about that, but I am different from them. How long were those relationships?

—One was two weeks and the other two months.

---You really think those count as relationships? They were like the duration of a short and long vacation.

---Also, to have a relationship, Socrates, you'd have to live here, and you don't. I never see you.

—There are long distance relationships that sometimes work, but you are mostly right. But I would move over here if you asked me to.

—No, don't do that.

—You just said to have a relationship, one must be physically together for you.

—You are going to make me cry. Let's get to know each other. That is why I am saying that it is very early. You've been very sweet to me, and you don't deserve that I fail. I don't want to make any mistakes with you. I already feel something very special for you. Let's get to know each other even more.

—You're saying this and then you'll find someone else.

—Don't worry. My heart is closed regarding the possibility of finding someone else.

—If it is closed, then that goes back to my first question of why did you invite me here? I still think you're still looking for someone. Why did you text me, saying that I was hot and that you loved me and cared about me and were excited to see me. You sexted me at times, saying you'd have to be bad again so I could spank you. I feel like you deceived me.

—Yes, I know. And I was wrong to do that.

—If what you are offering to me is the same as you offer to all your other friends, I don't want it. I want to be special to you. You know, I feel like crying. I think you've got your priorities mixed up. Personal relationships are just as important as work and school. No matter how busy we all get, it's as important to dedicate time for loved ones. It's not an added burden, as you suggest it is. It is just the opposite. We all need loved ones to support us. We think it's all about wanting to have sex, but it's not just that. It's the intimacy we look for. You know, to laugh, to smile, to be silly, to be touched, looked at, admired, to feel comfortable, to know someone really understands you and loves you unconditionally. That's what I can be for you.

Rafa didn't respond. He looked away and took a few more puffs of his cigarette. I stared out at the pool, lying in the lounge chair in silence as hotel guests walked by in the distance. I seriously pondered whether I should just go back to San Diego now. I felt horrible, ugly, deceived and lonely. I thought about telling him to go back to his house. But I also thought about how I had put so much effort into getting to know him, and he seemed like such a unique person. And the chances of me finding his doppelganger with his personality were way too low. I decided to hang out with him some more, at least for now. I told myself to calm down. Maybe I can make the best out of a bad situation. My logical side was attempting to take over the conversation in my head, but my broken heart was still very much ruling the moment. I wanted to curl up into a ball and get away from the world. Rafa finally said something.

—Socrates, let's do what good friends do. Let's go to a club. Let's talk about things friends talk about. I will start before we get there. I'll tell you some personal things about me. For example, regarding sex, I only have sex with my friends. I am both a top and a bottom. Sometimes I have group sex. What about you?

—Rafa, I'm not in the mood to talk about those things.

Rafa turned to his side in the lounge chair, smiling. He was now happy, relaxed, even loose, now that he'd finished saying he only wanted to be friends.

—Come on, Socrates. I'll tell you some more. I get excited wearing neck and harness gear. You know, leather gear. I like to be mildly mistreated a little, such as being tied to a bed. What about you? When was the last time you had sex?

I looked at Rafa and still didn't say anything. I hated this. I really did. I took a deep breath and let it out. I finally gave in.

—It was six months ago when I had a massage. Before that, I don't remember. I asked a guy to come over and draw sketches of me naked a few months ago. He ended up coming back a few more times. I also had some artistic black and white photos taken of me where I ended up having sex with the photographer. The photos were beautiful. But truthfully, I've probably had more sex with myself than with any guy. I have a large imagination that can take me anywhere I want to go. Anyway, my life doesn't revolve around sex.

—You surprised me by being so bold and posing for the nude photos.

—I surprised myself by posing nude. But life is about trying new things and sometimes getting out of one's comfort zone.

—Exactly.

—Have you had group sex, Socrates?

—Yes, I've tried that once. I didn't like it. I prefer to imagine it. That is the only way it appeals to me. While I am only interested in a monogamous relationship with someone special, I'm also not as "nice" as you might think I am. I've had anonymous sex several times in places you probably have never had it, but those days are over for me. Besides, it's too dangerous.

—I've had group sex many times, although I never had two dicks inside of me at the same time. My butthole isn't so stretched out. It is still tight. What about other types of sex?

—Like what?

—Like body part sex.

—No. For me, it is painful to watch videos of a guy sticking his entire arm in some guy's ass.

—Yeah. I tried it once and I didn't like it.

I didn't really feel like talking about this subject with Rafa anymore. He, on the other hand, seemed like he could go on and on. He continued to talk about his sex life, but I wasn't paying attention. All I could think about was his deceit.

Rafa seemed to be at ease with me, but I wondered if it was all a show. Was I just another stranger he spent time with at a hotel? I knew I was getting closer and closer to the sugar daddy age, but I detested that. I never had done that, and I never will. Granted, he wasn't receiving money from me in exchange for sex, but it seemed like another form of it. It felt like I was paying for the privilege of his presence. His indifference, despite a couple of months of texting and one previous visit, made me rethink whether I was indeed special to him.

After heading up to our room, we got dressed up and went out to a gay club called *La Golondrina* (The Swallow). We arrived early to get a good table to see their drag queen show, scheduled for later in the evening. Rafa had previously told me he didn't like drag queens, but I wasn't in the mood to point that out, so I didn't say anything. I continued to feel horrible and ask myself why I agreed to go out. I tried to put on a fake, happy face. I kept telling myself that maybe there was still a little hope that I could still eventually win him over.

As the night progressed and I'd downed a few alcoholic beverages, my mood lightened a bit. As I sat across the table from Rafa, I imagined how it would feel to kiss him. He looked so handsome sitting there. The loud noise and music in the club forced us to lean in closer to each other to speak. Every time I leaned in, the secretion of his pheromones, combined with the smell of his skin and his breath, intoxicated me, causing me to get an erection. Despite the disappointment of being rejected, I was hopelessly falling in love with him. He was happy showing me a good time. When we got back to the hotel, Rafa quickly fell asleep. I tried to sleep too, but his loud snoring didn't allow me to. I got out of bed and took a Xanax, which knocked me out for a few hours.

The next day, we had breakfast at the same *Sanborns*. We were still kind of sleepy when we arrived. I continued to struggle in my attempt to get more than a few words out of him.

---You know Rafa, you were snoring last night.

---I was?

---Yeah. It was partly the reason why I couldn't sleep well. I was thinking about putting a blanket over your head.

---You should have.

That's all Rafa said for the next few minutes. He was self-absorbed, engrossed in videos on his cell phone. I finally lost my patience and called him out for his phubbing.

---You know, it is rude to look at your phone the whole time you are out at a restaurant when you are with someone. Especially someone who came a long way to see you. You have all the time in the world to look at those videos later. Even if you aren't interested in me or I'm not your type of guy, at least for the moment, pretend that you care about me, or exchange some polite conversation with me until I go to the airport.

---Okay, just a minute. Check this out. It's very funny.

My words seemed to be wasted on him. He was oblivious to his bad manners. While I looked at him laughing at his video, I decided to let my annoyance with him go. I told myself to be patient and accept him the way he is, for better or worse. I said my peace. Who knows, maybe some of what I said sank in. We were eventually able to strike up a short conversation and we took some selfie photos. After checking out of the hotel, we started walking to a nearby downtown shopping mall. We both loved walking. It seemed to relax both of us.

—You should come to Monterrey more often, Socrates.

This comment surprised me and made me smile. Maybe someday we could have more than this awkward friendship. We enjoyed a coin-operated massage chair at the mall before we took a rideshare to the airport. He politely stood in the airport line with me before I got close to entering the gate for my flight. He wished me a safe and enjoyable flight home. I kissed him on the top of his head as we hugged goodbye.

—I love you, Rafa. Take care.

There was no response from the young man.

15 EXPLOSIVE OUTBURST

After Rafa's rejection, I fully understood where I was with him. Now back in San Diego, I continued texting him as if nothing had changed between us. But things had changed. He began pointing out that the frequency of my text messages was bothering him, despite saying before that it wasn't a problem. My text messages offering my learned wisdom were now no longer viewed by Rafa as me helping him become a better person. Each time he seemed upset about my texting, I politely asked him to forgive me. I asked him to try to see life through my eyes, but that now seemed more difficult for him to do. Even if we were going to be just friends, I love to thoroughly get to know people in my life, whether they are good friends or intimate relationships. Rafa didn't understand that this was normal behavior for me. I could understand that. He'd probably never met someone with my personality type. But I also needed to be respectful of his time and expectations of our friendship.

For the first time, Rafa said I was obsessed with him. Obsession seemed to be too strong of a word. Maybe I was excessive with texts but certainly not obsessive. At least in my view. Or was I? Rafa kept answering my texts. I don't recall him ever saying to me "No Socrates, I won't answer that question." He was mostly an open book. The times he didn't reveal himself, he just didn't comment on my text. And that was fine with me. Not every text deserved a response.

Slowly but surely, I began to feel that Rafa was pushing me away. Whatever I was to him, I still wanted to help him achieve his goals in whatever way I could. That's what true friends do. Okay, maybe Rafa wasn't helping me as much, but I enjoyed helping him out. If I was going to only be a friend, I wanted to be his best friend or one of them. I wanted to be an important part of his life, while at the same time, doing my own projects and working on my life goals too.

Today, Rafa's impatience with me finally reached a crescendo as we were talking again about the infamous Billy Milligan.

—Rafa, I would love to have different personalities to call on for certain things, like to speak French at a restaurant in France. Or be a plumber.

—Hahahaha. A plumber.

—You know, I said before that you had many different moods, but maybe you have several versions of yourself as well.

—Are you now saying I have different personalities too?

—No, but maybe if you did, one of them would want to have sex with me. Hahahaha.

—Hahahaha. That is never going to happen.

—Saying that hurt my feelings.

—Hahahahaha. You are too sensitive.

—Yes, I can be at times, but you recently rejected me. That wound is still open. Can't you understand that?

---Socrates, I want to be myself around you. I want to be able to joke around without worrying that you might be offended.

---I understand that, but I also want to be able to freely express how I feel without being judged for it. I'm being honest with you. I don't want to have to lie to you or hide my feelings. I didn't take it as a joke. I'd hope you'd at least show some empathy for how I am feeling.

What followed was Rafa sending me 28 angry audio messages. Some of it was street Spanish that I didn't understand. When people get mad, they tend to cuss in their native language and Rafa was no different. I started to cry in my audio messages back to him. That only seemed to make it worse. I continued to try and explain that being sensitive had its advantages, that it was who I am. But it was useless. Looking back on it all, it now seems like the incident was an excuse for Rafa to say he needed a break from me.

He could easily have diffused the situation by saying "I'm sorry. I wasn't trying to make you feel bad." I would have said 'I know,' and that would have been the end of it. Despite my pleas to let the disagreement go, he couldn't. He was too angry at the moment to think rationally.

—I think it's better now that we stop texting, Socrates. You'll find someone better than me. There is a world of people that you can get to know that are better than me.

—I think you are exaggerating. One day, if I say something that hurts your feelings, I will say I am sorry. But I'm not going to say our friendship is over because of it. We've joked around dozens of times already. I am not, nor are you, obliged to laugh at every joke we say. It doesn't mean we can't still joke around.

—I've made my decision. I wish you good luck with your life, Socrates.

—It's funny how you turned this around to make me out like the bad guy. And maybe you're right. If you are going to run away every time we disagree, maybe it is best to say goodbye.

I couldn't sleep for days after Rafa's heinous explosion. I'd never experienced that side of him before. He removed me from all his social media accounts. It was now that I recalled when he said at times, he could be a little uptight. He mostly kept his temper bottled up inside of him in public. But in private, he could snap at any time and at anyone. It was impossible to reason with him when his tantrums started. Their aftereffects could last for months. And 'I'm sorry' was normally not in his vocabulary. His mother later told me it was one of his defects that she regretted that she didn't attempt to correct as a child.

Most people facing his explosions might be tempted to look for friendship elsewhere. I admit that it did cross my mind. If he was continuously abusive, I would have. But I felt what he brought to the table overall was worth dealing with this and other imperfections. The weight of his positive attributes outweighed his negatives, although at times, it wasn't always obvious. For now, the negative weight was too heavy to bear. I asked myself if it was goodbye forever?

16 REUNION

Two months passed without a text message between the two of us. I kept the faith that one day, he would text me again. As the weeks passed, I began to miss him, but I was respectful of his decision. I would think about him every now and then. The connection I felt with Rafa was too strong to just forget him. And sure enough, one day, he finally decided to text me.

—*Hola* (Hi), Socrates. *¿Cómo estás?* (How are you?)

—Hi. I'm fine. And you? Missing me yet?

—The truth is yes, I really missed you and our conversations. I thought about texting you at various times.

—I was thinking you might forget me.

—Socrates, I could never forget you, even if I tried. No one has ever texted me as much as you have. I also want to say I'm sorry. Not because I got upset, but because of all those audio messages I sent. I didn't mean them.

—Yes, that was rather impetuous of you. And they came without warning. Usually when a hurricane is heading one's way, there is time to prepare. But Hurricane Rafa arrived suddenly, unleashing an acidic downpour on me.

---Hold on. I'm looking up the meaning of the word impetuous. I see it now. Yeah, I did act quickly without thinking much about it. When I explode, I really explode.

---No kidding. Apparently, your wrath takes no prisoners. Its aftermath left a swath of destruction.

—Yeah, true. I grab hold and don't let go, even when it is in my best interest to do so. I know you are sensitive. I should respect that. It's part of who you are.

—Yes, it is, but it's obviously part of who you are too, or you wouldn't have exploded. You'll get along with me better if you focus on the positive qualities of my sensitivity instead of the negative ones. My sensitivity allows me to better understand and empathize with others, as well as take my creativity to greater heights. As I tried to tell you when you were mad, just because I am sensitive, doesn't mean you can't still joke around with me. I laughed at all your other jokes. Even though it was a joke, there is often something real behind it. I interpreted it as you saying I was ugly.

—I wasn't saying that at all, Socrates.

—Well, remember that not everyone interprets what you say the same way you do.

—Point well taken. You know, I was thinking that maybe this incident will make our friendship stronger.

—It could. I heard that the French sometimes say that any type of relationship, be that of spouses, lovers or friends, that can't survive a heated argument, wasn't worth it to begin with.

And so, the mending of hard feelings between us began. I promised to text less and give Rafa some days off from me. He even texted me first after I didn't text him for a few days. We were back to where we left off, except this time, we had a better understanding of each other. And the time away from each other gave us each a chance to share what was new in our lives. One of these was that Rafa would be in Tijuana during the upcoming weekend to spend it with two friends from Sinaloa visiting the city. On Fridy afternoon, he texted me.

—Hey, I'm now on the long bus ride to Tijuana. It's a day and a half trip, around 30-35 hours.

---Wow, so long.

---Yeah, it is. The biggest cities the bus goes to are Saltillo, Torreón, Durango, Mazatlan, Culiacán, Guasave, Los Mochis, Navojoa, Ciudad Obregón, Hermosillo, and Mexicali. There isn't much to see. It's mostly lots of desert, until we reach Baja California, where there are some coastal views. Maybe I'll have time to see you when I get to Tijuana. I'll let you know. I only got three hours of sleep last night, so if I stop texting, I probably fell asleep. I brought the book *La Tregua* (The Truce) by Mario Benedetti to read on the way over. I mention it because there is part of the book that reminded me of you and me. You are the character with the best memory, and I am the distracted one. Haha! The principal character appears so at ease with his life, but a lot of things happen to him.

—Very cool. I'm also currently reading a book. It's about the painter Frida Kahlo. Much of it is about her relationship with husband, Diego Rivera. One part of the book really spoke to me. Frida said that the exchange of comments about each other's paintings, their mutual trust and critical sense of the subject were some of the most beautiful moments in her life and in her relationship with him.

—Nice.

—Rafa, I think it would be cool if one day, you and I could do the same. You know, sit on a patio reviewing your latest dance performance, while you critique my paintings.

—Yeah, that would be cool.

—You know how intense I am sometimes? Well, I think that is how Frida and Diego felt about each other. The enormous passion they felt towards each other, as well as towards their craft, made them better painters and strengthened their relationship. I know that way of living might seem to be a little overboard. Some people want to do nothing more than eat, sleep, have sex, be entertained and survive their workdays. And there is nothing wrong with wanting all that. I enjoy those aspects of life too. But there must be more to life than all that, and I try to find it.

A half hour passed with no response, so I figured he didn't know how to respond to what I texted, was immersed in his book or he finally fell asleep. I texted him again.

—I'll let you go, Rafa. Have fun. Are you going to go to the beach and swim with your friends while there?

—I don't go in the ocean. I am afraid of it.

—Okay.

—I forgot to tell you that I figured out a way to dance in my backyard. I'm going to make my own stage.

—Nice. I love how inventive you are. Be safe.

Once Rafa arrived in Tijuana, he took a taxi to an inexpensive downtown hotel where he was going to stay with his friends. I waited to hear back from him, but there was no response. I figured he was having too much fun. Finally, I got a text message from him on the last day of his visit.

—Socrates, I'm busy with my friends and I'm not going to be able to see you. Sorry.

—Oh, shoot. It's not every day that you are so close to me, and I was hoping to take advantage of that.

—I know. Me too. How about if I make it up to you and we spend a weekend together at a hotel in Monterrey next weekend?

—That sounds nice, Rafa. I will search for a hotel.

—Great!

—What are you doing right now?

—I am taking a shit right now, Socrates. It's hot and I am sweating. I just wanted you to know that.

—Maybe you were right. We are getting too close to each other! Hahahaha! That is TMI, too much information. Hahahaha.

—Hahahahahahahahahahahahahahaha.

—You know, you don't have to always laugh at my comments just to be polite.

—I know. I don't fake my text laughs with you but with that comment you really did make me laugh hard.

A few minutes later, I heard back from him, saying that he was urgently attempting to contact his sister because he lost his money to pay for his bus trip back to Monterrey.

—Oh my gosh, Rafa. Don't worry. If you want, I'll send you money for your trip back home. You can pick it up at Oxxo and pay me back later.

—You would really do that? Thanks so much! Look at me. I said I'd never take money from you and now I am.

—Well, this is an emergency and that is what friends do for each other. Anyway, I am happy to help out.

In any relationship where there is a huge difference in income, there are times when it can cause friction. I had no intention of being Rafa's sugar daddy and he didn't want us to have that type of relationship either. I can, however, get carried away with my helpfulness. Sometimes, I need to set some boundaries for being helpful, but this assistance seemed reasonable.

17 AN UNUSUAL EVENING
AT THE HILTON

After a couple of days passed, I texted Rafa a photo of a hotel I liked in Monterrey.

—What do you think about this one? No more Real Inn.

—Nice. Whichever one you choose is fine with me. I'm not that demanding.

—You aren't, but I am. Hahahaha. Well, I'm not that demanding either, but I will not stay at a dirty hotel or one where I can't sleep.

—Hahahaha. Obviously. You are a gringo.

—Just so you know, gringos do stay at cheap hotels. There are lots of poor gringos.

—Okay, well I can sleep anywhere. Well, not on the street.

—Stay with me and your status as a diva will improve, Rafa. Hahahaha. Soon you will be demanding the best of everything.

—Hahahaha.

I showed him another one.

—How about this one?

—Wow. That is too luxurious for me.

—Great. The too luxurious one it is. Our reservation is now confirmed.

—Sounds good.

—Hey Rafa, if you don't mind, I'd like to take advantage of the time with you and learn some stretching exercises. In particular, I want to learn how to do the splits.

—Of course. We can do stretching exercises in the hotel room. Oh, and I won't smoke because I know that you don't like it.

—It's a no smoking hotel. You have no choice. Hahahaha.

I made my plane reservations, and a week later, my bags were packed for a short weekend trip. Early Friday morning, I took the San Diego Trolley to the U.S.-Mexico border, then a taxi to the Tijuana International Airport, where I boarded yet another flight to meet up with Rafa. After a two hour, 45-minute flight, the plane landed at the General Mariano Escobedo International Airport in Monterrey. I quickly grabbed a taxi that took me to the Hilton Monterrey Hotel. As I exited the taxi, I looked up to see Rafa already at the lobby door, waiting for me. I was so excited. I was hoping that this would be a fun weekend for both of us. There would be no sexual pressure, no misunderstandings on this trip. We checked in but had to wait in the lobby while they prepared our room.

—Socrates, did you notice the hotel attendant's eyes?

—Yeah, I did. Wow, so intensely blue. Beautiful.

When our room was finally ready for us, we took the elevator up to the 10th floor. As we opened the door, our jaws dropped as we gazed at the beautiful, panoramic city view.

—Wow, this is incredible, Socrates!

—Oh my gosh, it is. Which mountain is that in the background?

---*Cerro del Mirador.* I guess it would be called Viewpoint Hill in English. Although it's really a mountain.

We both hurried over to the large floor to ceiling windows to get a better view. I then turned around to take a closer look at our sleeping accommodations.

---I don't know what is more beautiful, the view or the bed. Watch me! Rafa turned to look at me as I jumped backwards into the king-sized bed.

—Awwwww! Rafa, I think this is the nicest bed that I have ever lied down on in my life.

—Let me see! Watch out, I'm jumping on.

While Rafa and I were laying on the bed together, I pulled back the bed sheets and noticed that they were silk.

---Feel these sheets!

---Wow, they are so luxurious! I love it. I wish I could take this bed home with me.

The bed wasn't the only nice feature of the hotel room. The shades on the windows and the lights opened and closed by a computerized panel on the wall next to the bed. The room came with plush towels and bathrobes. We turned on the large-screen television and watched *YouTube* videos for a while before leaving to go say hi to some of Rafa's friends, who were also visiting the city. When we arrived at their hotel room, I noticed that his behavior changed. Rafa was suddenly much more natural, relaxed and gregarious with these two guys than he'd ever been with me. He let his guard down while laughing and joking around with his friends. He and one of his friends chased each other around the beds, then wrestled each other until they both fell onto the floor. It made me happy to see Rafa enjoying himself. Seeing him relaxed also relaxed me. It was fun to see a different side of him. I hoped one day, we would be able to be as fun loving and playful. After a while, I was ready to leave.

—I will be outside when you are ready to go, Rafa.

—We will be leaving shortly. I know I promised to spend my time with you, and I will keep my promise.

After leaving the hotel, we decided to take a Didi to the *Paseo de Santa Lucia*, a tourist attraction, where we took a fun boat ride on the artificial lake in *Parque Fundidora* (Foundry Park), which is a former steel factory turned into a recreational area. Afterwards, we laid down in the park and soaked up the glorious Monterrey afternoon sun while taking in the spectacular view of the large mountainous area in the background.

A few minutes later, we headed over to have a delicious lunch at the *Cafe del Museo* (The Museum Café). After the good food and conversation, we capped it all off by heading to the surrounding park to take a walk around its circular pathway. My first impression was that the park was so clean and well maintained. I felt the light wind cress my face and watched as it rustled the leaves in the nearby trees. A mobile vendor's bells rang out, alerting people nearby that roasted corn on the cob was for sale. Children's laughter echoed around us as they played in the park. Their families sat nearby, enjoying a well-deserved respite from the grind of the workweek. Orange-crowned warblers jumped from bush to bush. The scent of the native wild lilac shrubs filled the air. Yellow trumpetbush flowers littered the lush green grass. While I was busy taking in the splendor of the park, Rafa was mostly ignoring it, staring at his cell phone.

---Rafa, enough with the phone. Enjoy the park!

---Okay. Just a minute.

---Hey Rafa, watch me! Weeee!

Rafa put his phone down, looked up at me and began to laugh, as I playfully chased after a flock of pigeons that scattered and flew away. Next, Rafa put his phone away and joined me in my frolicking, He proceeded to do backflips and leap around while bathed in rays of sunlight filtering through a large canopy of nearby trees. It was a glorious moment of nature-inspired spontaneity.

Newly revitalized, we decided it was time to head back to the hotel. After we arrived, Rafa invited Hector Martinez, one of Rafa's two friends I had met earlier, to come over to visit us. We all enjoyed a nice chat. After Hector left, Rafa was apparently all chatted out, as he went back to watching the television and playing video games on his cell phone. In an attempt to reengage with him, I did what our history demonstrated was most successful---I began texting him. The tactic worked. We were soon texting back and forth while lying next to each other on the bed.

Rafa sent me a link to a music video of Swedish composer and film sound designer Jon Ekstrand's song *Godspeed, Doctor*, from the motion picture *Life*. He asked me to watch it and let him know how it made me feel. I closed my eyes and I listened to it twice on my headset. I texted my response.

—It was so calming at first then the sound began building up until finally something was released. Then there were peaceful sounds again. Next, I heard unusual sounds, like something was hitting me, then it calmed down again. It was like a roller coaster ride of sound. I felt like I was somewhere in space for sure. I enjoyed it. What did you feel, Rafa?

—I felt mystery and calm, like I was discovering something incredible.

—Yes, it was so unusual. How music makes us feel often can't be described adequately in words. I really absorbed the sound, like I was there inside the vibrations. Thanks for sharing it with me. I have a unique song for you to listen to as well, if you don't mind. Have you ever heard the song *Weightless* by Marconi Union? It was a song specifically created by a professional sound practitioner to lower anxiety. The tempo of 60 beats per minute reflects the average adult's resting heartbeat.

---Okay. By the way, what's a professional sound practitioner?

---I'm not entirely sure, but I think it's a person who is an expert in using voice or instrument sounds to stimulate self-healing in their clients.

---That's awesome.

---I just sent you the recording, Rafa.

I waited patiently as Rafa finished listening to the over eight-minute recording.

---I liked it, Socrates. It was very unique and relaxing. It's the type of eerie song style that I enjoy. What do you think of this music from the

Lucy movie soundtrack that I attached? I'm thinking about using it for some choreography I am creating, to be called Beating.

I laid in bed with my headphones on, listening to the song twice.

—It's definitely a great selection for your presentation, Rafa. I felt that the music was very much in rhythm with the beating of my heart. Even more so than *Weightless*. I liked it a lot. I didn't care for some of the background noise, which sounded like someone was shaking some coins or a tambourine.

—It left me speechless.

I loved this aspect of the young man. Rafa was constantly searching for music for his dancing, but it often wasn't the typical music someone might normally select for a performance. His selections were, more often than not, haunting, thought- and sense-provoking music. Except when they weren't. He was back to being silly, showing me short videos of cats and now explosions, in an attempt to spook me. Ever since he discovered that I can be sensitive to disturbing or scary images, he was constantly trying to scare me. Our random text conversations eventually morphed into actual conversations. This time it was the subject of hair styles and fashion.

—Has your hair always been very short, Rafa?

—No. Before, as a teenager, I had long, curly hair. My family and friends often called me Broccoli.

—Wow. Broccoli. I love that nickname! Wait a minute. I think I remember seeing some social media photos of you with long, bushy hair on a boat in Veracruz. Maybe five years from now, your hair style will be long and curly again.

—No, those days are gone forever. I didn't like that style. I do, however, change my short hairstyle quite a bit.

—Yeah, I suppose it is nice to have it short and not have to worry about it. Especially during the hot Monterrey summers.

—I agree. Also, I can get very lazy about combing my hair.

—Speaking of long hair, my dog's hair is super long. Every time I cut it, people on the street ignore him. They loved him for his hair. And he is a diva about me combing it.

—That's funny.

While we were talking, I was checking out some cool clothes on my cell phone that I was considering purchasing.

—What about this one, Rafa? The red and yellow one.

—I don't like to wear happy colors. Only black, gray and white. Sometimes I wear other colors but not often. I'm wearing a light pink shirt today but when I am wearing happy colors, it is because they were gifts from my friends, my mother's friends or my sister.

—The reddish-pink shirt goes well with your lips. Maybe I'll buy you something on this trip, if you are a good little boy.

—What do I have to do, Mr. Chamberlain, to get it as a reward?

—I don't know. Is a sweater worth a suck or a fuck?

—You need more than that.

—Just being with you is all that I need.

—Okay, okay, but wait. This is getting hot. As Katie Perry says in her song *Dark Horse*, once you are mine, there is no going back. I love that song and the video is epic.

—You are funny.

Once I discovered we had shared interests, I put them in storage in my brain for future mutual enjoyment and bonding. Clothes shopping was one of them. As was my custom, I changed the subject, asking more random questions.

—Hey Rafa, have you seen the new *Netflix* series about two high school gay youth? It's a popular series now. The other day, I bought the book version of it in Spanish at Office Max.

—No, I didn't.

—You probably wouldn't be looking for it anyway. I know you don't like romantic movies.

—Well, yeah that, and just because it is popular is reason enough for me not to watch it.

—Hmmm...well, you are fanatical about Lady Gaga, and she is popular.

—She is an exception. I mean come on. Lady Gaga. Need I say more?

—I guess so. Rafa, I have another random question for you. Do you like your body? If you could, what would you change about it or are you happy the way it is?

---I have been wanting to be a little fat since I was younger. I don't like being so skinny. I wish I had a slightly stronger upper body. What about you?

—I generally like my body. I wouldn't want to be fatter but a little bulkier wouldn't be bad. I have a nice chest and back. My forearms and calves are too thin for my liking. It's hard for me to gain weight. I want bigger legs but it's harder for me because I am a bit tall. But I like your legs. They are so beautiful, strong and flexible. You have a nice little butt, too. But yeah, it couldn't hurt you to gain a little upper body strength. And where is your chest? There's nothing there except a couple of bee stings for nipples. No boobs at all. Nothing to grab on to.

Rafa laughed and so did I.

——Shut up, Socrates.

—By the way, I showed your photo to my friend Rhonda. She thinks you look Arabic.

—Really? No.

—I think you do too.

Rafa was quiet for a moment, apparently contemplating why people might think that he looks Arabic.

—You know, you change the subject so quickly sometimes, Socrates, that I can't keep up with you.

—Opps, sorry.

—It's alright.

—You must think fast with me!

—By the way, yesterday I saw an ad with the French song that you sang to me the other night.

—*Je Ne Regrette Rien*? (I Don't Regret Anything) Yes, I've seen that commercial. Every time it comes on, I stop what I'm doing, and I start singing! Rafie starts barking when I do it. It's like he's saying no more, daddy, please!

—That's funny. You certainly have an unlimited mind. Your poems, funny text messages, writings, singing songs, your graphic design and paintings are all very creative.

—Is my creativity all too much for you? Am I too much for you? I'm a lot to deal with, I know. But this is who I am.

Rafa thought about what I said for a few moments. Just when I thought he was ignoring the question, he answered.

—Yeah, you are a lot to deal with. It would probably be a shock to someone who doesn't know you. For me, you are a nice, special friend, a real friend. I don't even know how to describe you. You are many things to me. You care about me more than anyone ever has, except maybe for my mother. Truthfully, it seems like you came from nowhere. You are one of the few people that has made me feel valuable and I am grateful for that. I respect you a lot. I'd never take advantage of you because of the respect I have for you, Socrates.

—Thanks. I wouldn't be much of a friend if I didn't help you be the best person that you can.

—I would say the same, but I can't.

—Why is that, Rafa?

—I would like to say that I want you to be the best you can, but I can't because you already are.

—Awww.

——I said it to surprise you.

—You did. You are full of surprises. Usually, you don't say corny things like that. It's one more reason it's so much fun to be your friend. Whether you meant it or not, I don't care. It was a nice compliment. And by the way, I also have a hard time describing you. You haven't been easy to get to know, but I also like challenges. Many times, I don't like "easy." You have a thirst for knowledge. You are a talented dancer, a virtuoso. And you are authentic, sometimes too authentic. Your actions are often contradictory. You often underestimate your talent. I like that you are a perfectionist, expecting the best out of yourself. You like to test your limits by being excessive and surprising people. Despite all the times you've told me that you are tired, you always seem to have tons of energy to do all your projects. I feed off your energy. You are unique and I'm grateful to be a part of your life.

—*Muchas gracias*, (Thanks) Socrates. Your words are very beneficial to me.

Since I was here in Monterrey on vacation, I wanted to get out of the hotel for a while. Rafa agreed to go with me to *Galerias Monterrey*, one of the nicer shopping centers in the city. After a little bit of shopping and people watching, we returned to the hotel and enjoyed some food at a taco stand across the street. Later, we kicked back on the bed while drinking two miniature wine bottles that I brought with me from San Diego. As we were starting to get sleepy, I went to the bathroom to brush my teeth. I pulled out a condom from my toiletry bag and brought it back to the bed with me. I wasn't expecting anything to happen, but I wanted to be prepared, just in case. When I got back into the room, I turned off the lights. After about ten minutes, Rafa had started to fall asleep, but I was having problems doing so, most likely due to sleeping in a different bed.

—Rafa, would you mind if I held you in bed for a few minutes to help me fall asleep?

—Okay sure, go ahead.

When he said 'Okay, sure,' he was already half asleep. I lay behind Rafa, spooning him, with my arm around his waist. Both of us were shirtless, wearing only our warmup pants. I could hear his heart beating as my bare skin touched his slender, delicate body. After about 10 minutes passed, Rafa startled me as he suddenly gasped and yelled, jumping halfway up out of bed before laying down again. The next thing I knew, he grabbed my hand and moved it, so it was touching his penis, which was beginning to get hard under his warmup pants. He started moving my hand up and down, as if to help him jack off. I could hardly believe it. For a moment, I paused, wondering what I should do.

I then decided to play along and see what happened.

He started to groan a little as I was touching him. I assumed he was awake, although he never said a word. He lowered his underwear himself and his erect, long penis popped up. It was very nice looking, more beautiful than most I'd seen, with a pinkish red, smooth, rounded head. I got a little more daring, positioning myself over the top of his legs. I began to slowly and tenderly kiss and suck the head of his dick. His other head turned to the side as he let out louder groans. I went down further and further, until I had his whole cock in my mouth. I then slid up and down his long shaft, stopping only to suck and lick the side of it. He let out a little yell as he twisted and squirmed away. He seemed to be enjoying me sucking him on the side of his cock, but at the same time, it was obvious that it was a very sensitive pleasure spot for him. I pulled away time and time again to allow him to recover.

Next, I sucked and licked his large, tight balls for a while before putting my entire mouth on his cock again. Sweat glistened off my leg and chest muscles as I sat perched over him, my cock as hard as a rock while he moaned in ecstasy. I pulled up for air, but only for a moment or two before diving back down on him again, sucking the side of his dick. When he twisted his body and groaned loudly yet again due to his sensitivity, I decided to move on, in search of other erogenous zones. I kissed and tasted the sweat on his stomach and navel with my tongue, The musty smell of his smooth-skinned body was a turn on for me. I then proceeded to taste other parts of his body, including his chest nipples and neck, periodically checking to see his facial expressions. I decided to kiss him lightly on the cheek and lips, then went back to work on his cock.

After about half an hour had passed, he turned to his side completely, bending his smooth butt up towards my face. I did not waste this fortuitous twist of body and fate as I licked and lightly bit his butt. It was so soft to the touch, yet perky and strong, due to years of dancing. I pulled back from his sweaty rear end before I dove into his butt hole with my face, rimming around it with my tongue. I took a deep breath, then began to stick one finger, then two, inside of him. In response, Rafa groaned in delight. His plush hole felt so good, better than I imagined it in my dreams. I suddenly felt my manhood rising to a feverish pitch. The excitement of it all was building up inside of me, flowing large quantities of blood down to my throbbing erect penis, causing it to wildly bounce up and down. I was able to steady it long enough to put on a condom. As he lifted his butt towards me, I began to rim his hole with my large, mushroom head cock. I teased Rafa by slowly sliding the head of my cock inside and out of his sweaty hole. I continued doing this until I acquiesced to his moans, which were pleading with me to stick my entire meaty appendage inside of him. I couldn't resist the urge any longer. My mushroom head and cock slowly penetrated his opening, until I was as deep inside of him as I could go. It felt incredible. I partially pulled out, with only my head inside Rafa. Then I began to pound away at his tight hole repeatedly, fast and hard.

Soon, I felt my cock vibrate like a jackhammer, ever so close to squirting my load. That's when I pulled out and ripped off the condom. I went back to sucking Rafa's still erect cock, then pulled back, sensing from his increased 'ohhhh' sounds that he was close to exploding as well. I could no longer contain myself, as my balls swelled up. I moaned in relief, suddenly shooting a large load of cum that flew in the air, landing on Rafa's chest and face, dripping off his lips. I immediately went down on Rafa's cock once more, violently sucking him off. With one last strong suction, I backed off a bit to watch as he finally exploded into my mouth, with some of his semen dribbling out of it onto his stomach. I lifted my head back as I savored the taste of the cum he had shot into me. I immediately sucked his wet cock once more, causing Rafa to tremble. The final touch was kissing Rafa on his cum-covered lips.

Sweating and breathing profusely, I fell onto Rafa's body, exhausted but happy. As I got up, I lifted his tender butt up to kiss it once more, before I grabbed a towel to clean Rafa and myself up. When I got back from the bathroom, Rafa was quiet once again, sleeping, seemingly oblivious to what had just transpired.

About an hour later, I was awakened by a loud thud. While sleeping, Rafa had drifted towards the edge of the bed and had fallen on to the floor. I pretended to be asleep. As he got up and headed to the bathroom, he spoke out loud to himself.

—Why am I naked?

After using the bathroom, Rafa crawled back into bed and fell asleep. When we both awoke later that morning, I wondered whether he would say anything about our night in bed together, but he said nothing. He did not even seem to realize what had happened only a few hours before. I was nervous about saying anything. We got dressed and went to breakfast at a restaurant a few miles away, then came back to the hotel room. I finally decided to bring up the topic.

—Did you sleep well last night, Rafa?

—Yes, I did, thanks.

Rafa was busy, distracted as usual, on his cell phone.

—Come here. I have something important to tell you.

Rafa jumped on the bed, with his arms supporting his head, right next to me. He was smiling.

---What it is?

—This is going to be difficult for me to say. Do you remember anything from last night?

—Yeah, we watched some videos on the television, had some wine and went to sleep.

—Nothing else?

—No.

—Nothing? Really?

He shook his head sideways. I briefly went on to explain what had taken place between us. He was expressionless at first, but then a perplexed look appeared on his face. He said nothing, so I continued.

—So Rafa, when you fell off the bed and were naked, you didn't wonder why?

—Well, yes, I did, but sometimes when I get hot, I take my clothes off.

---Do you remember taking your clothes off?

---No.

—I feel sorry now that I had sex with you. Honestly, I thought that you were awake. So really, you had no idea that we had sex and that you were asleep despite encouraging me to do so? You were really enjoying the experience.

Rafa rolled his eyes up in his head, pausing to try to remember anything.

—Maybe it was the wine that caused it.

—Really? Rafa, we didn't have that much.

—Well, sometimes I don't need to drink much for it to affect me.

—I'm the same.

While we were still lying in bed, I googled whether having sex while asleep is even possible and as it turns out, yes, it is. It is called sexsomnia. It is the result of the brain being caught between sleep stages, which makes a person act like he or she is awake while still asleep. The medical information I read stated that the person with the condition may not know it's occurring until someone else brings it to their attention. I put my phone down and tried to assuage any anger Rafa might be feeling.

—Don't worry, Rafa. We don't have to discuss this ever again. I have had sex with some of my friends. Those were also one-time encounters. When we remember them, it's a good laugh and that is it.

—It's okay.

I was worried how this act would affect our relationship going forward. I assured him that one sex act isn't going to affect how I see him. We stayed another night. This time, we slept far apart on the large bed. But in the middle of the night, he moved next to me in the bed and put his arm around me. I wondered what to do. Eventually he moved again back to where his spot on the bed was. I imagined what it would be like to sleep with him every night. It seemed like he would be a fun person to sleep with. He was a creative sleeper, for sure. When we woke up, I reminded Rafa that he promised to teach me some stretching exercises.

—Oh yeah. Let me demonstrate a few that will help you eventually do the splits. You might want to buy some yoga blocks later.

I was trying to not get turned on as he performed various stretching exercises. I repeated each exercise with him.

—Rafa, I am so envious of you, how your body so easily falls into the splits. I am flexible, but I just seem to have limits to how far I stretch. I start to get sore or feel I might tear something, so I stop.

—Believe me, it looks natural, but it took a lot of work and dealing with some light pain to get where I am now. I am naturally supple, so that helped me. And it's true, each body is different.

—Yeah, and you don't seem as boney as I am. My hamstring muscles always feel so tight when I stretch. I tremble too.

—Trembling is natural and happens to everyone. Just do it little by little. Here, let's get on the floor together now. Okay, now grab my arms and spread your legs so your feet are pressing against mine. Now stretch as far as you can.

He kept imploring me to stretch further and further, but I knew my limits and told him I had to stop. Maybe he didn't think much of the exercise since it probably came second nature to him. For me, though, it was more than a stretching exercise. Holding and touching each other was a unique way to bond with him. To become closer. After it was over, I was spent.

—Thank you so much, Rafa. This has been very helpful.

—You are welcome. Now you know about some of the basic stretches. Keep at it.

—I will. I promise.

We went downstairs, enjoyed our complimentary breakfast in the hotel's restaurant, mostly in silence, and then checked out.

—You know what Rafa?

—What?

—Remember those incredible blue eyes of the hotel attendant? I have a better look at them now. They are colored contact lenses. It's a cool effect, anyway. But things aren't always as they seem. But for me, what is real and what is an illusion isn't always clear.

We went back up to our room, packed up and checked out. Rafa then accompanied me to the airport. Once we arrived, there was a little time to kill before I got in the security line, so we sat down and chatted for a few minutes.

—Have a safe trip back to San Diego, Socrates.

—Thanks.

—I know long trips are painful for your ass. On my last bus trip, I didn't even feel my ass on the trip until after it was over.

—Just so you know, the word "ass" is a little stronger than "butt" or rear end."

—Okay thanks. As I told you before, I say cuss words all the time. I usually don't feel comfortable using them with you because you don't speak that way. With people who don't use foul language, I don't either.

—I understand. I do that too, although probably not to the extent that you do. People who use foul language a lot are often younger or uneducated, with limited vocabularies.

—Mexicans use foul language all the time, even the highly educated. It is part of our culture. I say foul language in Spanish very naturally and that is very strong.

—I wasn't saying educated people didn't, just that they probably use them less. Like you said, people change their behavior according to who they are with and the setting. Another thing is when you become older and wiser, you will learn that words vary in their power, according to their usage. I will say cuss words but use them sparingly. They lose some of their power by saying them repeatedly. That is why I choose specific moments to say a cuss word to have maximum impact, for fun or to be nasty.

—True. I didn't think about that. When I am at home, I say them all day. I also call people disparaging words for fun. For example, I often call my friend Susana a *pendeja* (stupid girl). But that is how we talk to each other. My nephews use bad language more than I do.

—Do you ever say *hijo de tu pinchi madre* (a loose translation is son of a bitch) to anyone?

—Ask my mother!

I laughed.

—You know, Socrates, I realize that I am starting to say more foul language with you. That is a good sign. When a Mexican says foul language to you, it is because he or she trusts you.

—Nice. Well, don't overdo it with me. Don't trust me too much.

We both smiled and laughed. It was finally time to get in line. We hugged each other and I kissed his cheek while saying goodbye. Rafa left to catch a bus back to his house. It was an unforgettable weekend, for sure.

18 A SUGAR DADDY AND
TRIP TO ROSARITO

During my text messages in the last couple of days, I asked Rafa twice how he was surviving without a job. If was one of the few times he didn't answer one of my questions. I started to wonder why he was so furtive. I finally got an answer.

—I have a friend helping me with money.

—A friend? He must be an awfully good friend.

—Well, I didn't want to tell you this, but I have a sugar daddy now who comes across the border from Yuma, Arizona to visit me. I'm not proud of it. He is married, so he comes when he can. He is older than me, but not by much. He already has helped me buy my mother a new stove, remodel my room, and buy a television he got me from a *casa de empeño* (pawn shop). He also bought me a new bed. Before that, I was sleeping on the floor. And because of him, my mother is not hungry anymore. He knows that this is temporary.

—Wow. A sugar daddy not much older than 24 living in a poor city like Yuma? Hmmm. Do you have sex with him frequently?

—Not really. Maybe a couple of times a month.

---Do you talk every day?

—No. Just occasionally. He told me to leave the club job because I was working too much, and I wasn't doing enough dance training. I had a problem in the club, and I started to cry when I told him, so he told me to leave the job. He said he would pay my school bills. He told me that he knows I work really hard for school, and that I deserve more. He said keep studying, he'll be in charge.

—Look, if you change your mind, I can help you with your school money. You don't have to do this.

—I don't want to bother you. Oh my gosh, you are going to make me cry. I'm feeling bad now because there is another negative thing you know about me. You aren't going to be proud of me anymore. My sugar daddy is a nice guy, but he isn't even in the same league as you, Socrates. I must confess that I was worried you would know about this. That is why I never told you anything after I quit my job at the club.

—Well, life is about making sacrifices. I suppose having sex for money with one person is safer than being a prostitute.

—I think I'm literally a prostitute.

—Maybe you need to stop whoring so much. Just a little only.

—For me, that would be like asking me to stop breathing. Hahahaha.

—Oh gawd.

A few weeks later, he told me he was planning on breaking up with him. The more he described what was happening, the more I suspected that this sugar daddy never existed. I mean, there aren't many sugar daddies, if any, who are a little older than 24 years old and living in a city where the medium income is $27,000 a year. And the way he described himself as a prostitute convinced me even more that he made all this up. But I played along with it. A few weeks later, Rafa said he wanted a change.

—*Hola* (Hi) Socrates.

—*¿Qué onda?* (What's up?)

—I have news for you. I am breaking up with my sugar daddy. I want someone new. I want to be single now. You'll be my new sugar daddy, Socrates! Hahahaha!

—Hahahaha. You know I am willing to help you out, without the "sugar."

Two months and hundreds of texts later, we decided to go take a vacation together. With Rafa not working and not having to apply for the University of Monterrey until later, he had some time to refresh and think about his future. I was on vacation for a week, so we were both ready for some down time. We decided to go to Rosarito Beach, which is about a 20-minute drive down the coast from Tijuana, for a five-day vacation. I reserved a top-floor condominium right on the beach at the Rosarito Inn. It had a breath-taking view of the Pacific Ocean. I sent Rafa money to cover the cost of the bus trip to Tijuana. I met the young man, exhausted from his long trip, at the bus station in Tijuana and together, we took a taxi to Rosarito. When we got to our room, we both were shocked at what we saw.

—Oh my God, oh my God Socrates, how much did you pay for this?

This is awesome!!!

—Yes!!! I can't believe it either! The sound of the ocean waves makes it seem like they are only a few feet away.

—That's because they are only a few feet away. I love it!

After getting settled in, we walked out onto the balcony and collapsed our bodies onto the two chairs. We both looked at each other and let out sighs, as life's stresses drained out from our bodies. We turned our heads towards the sights, smells and sounds of the beach below us. The salt water in the air filled our lungs as the soothing sounds of the ocean waves reverberated around us and inside of the condo. We soaked in the Rosarito afternoon sun as a group of seagulls flew high above us in the deep blue sky. One of their solitary compatriots lurched towards us, squawking as if to say welcome to Rosarito. Off in the distance, a pair of pelicans skimmed the surface of the coastline water, looking for prey.

After eating a few snacks, Rafa and I decided to hang out by the pool for a while. When we arrived, we had it all to ourselves. We laid in the sun in our lounge chairs for a while after applying sunblock to each other. I finally decided I was too hot and got up to go in the pool.

—You want to get in the water with me?

—No thank you. I can't swim, so I'm just going to lay here. Well, I can float and move, but not very well.

—You could swim or float in the shallow end, if you want.

—No.

I walked over to the pool's edge in my short blue gym shorts and sat down, while dangling my legs in the pool. I grimaced a little as I slowly dipped my pale, muscular body in the cold water. After wading around a little to acclimate my body to the water temperature, I began swimming laps. using different swim strokes. As I tired, I then flipped over onto my back, laying peacefully in the middle of the pool, as water glistened off my body in the afternoon sun.

I glanced over at Rafa laying on the lounge chair to see what he was up to. Eventually he got curious and slowly ventured into the shallow end of the pool. His first movements in the water were deliberate and gentle, paddling around with his head above the water. After a while, he became more confident, meandering towards the deep end. Next, he began to float on his back, his slender mestizo body laying spread eagle in the water.

I noticed Rafa was now more comfortable in the pool, so I decided to have some fun with him. I snuck up from behind and dunked his head under the water. Instead of laughing it off and maybe trying to dunk me, he came up from under the water panicked, splashing around, gasping for air. He frantically swam over to the edge of the pool to compose himself. He wasn't happy.

---Are you okay, Rafa?

—Why did you do that?!! Leave me alone! Don't ever do that again.

—Jeez, I'm sorry. That's what friends do in the pool. They play around with each other. I wasn't trying to hurt you.

He didn't say anything to me for a few minutes, as he caught his breath while clinging to the side of the pool. Finally, he spoke.

—I've had some bad experiences being in the water. It's been a long time for me. The last time I was in the water was years ago in Sinaloa with my family. Some of them were jumping in a river and they urged me to jump in with them. After I jumped in, I didn't realize how deep it was and I couldn't breathe. I nearly drowned.

—Oh wow. Well, you can't blame me for not knowing that. Maybe you should have told me that before we got into the pool.

He quietly floated in the water, far away from me, for several minutes. I got out of the pool and relaxed in my lounge chair, as a gentle breeze and the sun dried me off. As I watched my young friend slowly wade around the pool, I thought for a minute about why he criticized me in the past for being sensitive, since he obviously was too. After a half hour of silence between us passed, he finally got out and dried himself off. He seemed to have recovered from the dunking. We took the elevator back up to our rented condo, got dressed and went walking on the beach.

---Rafa, check out the pier. Its supported beams are in the shape of V's, X's and fan shapes. How creative. Did you notice that?

---No, I didn't. Interesting.

I continued to notice random aspects around us.

---Look at our toes. The last two toes on each of our feet are different. Yours are curved in and much shorter than mine.

---That's due to my dancing.

--- Yeah, that's what I was thinking. Hey, check out these seashells, Rafa. This one with the orange, yellow and brown squiggly stripes is beautiful. And did you see that guy on the horse? That would be fun riding on the beach.

---I'm really enjoying this, Socrates. Thanks for inviting me to come with you.

---Me too. And you are welcome.

After we got back to the hotel, I asked Rafa if he wouldn't mind sitting down for a minute or two on the balcony with me to watch the sunset. He obliged.

---Rafa, look at the glorious tapestry stretching out before our own eyes! As a painter and artist, I sit here in awe of nature's seemingly unlimited creativity.

---Hahahaha. You get carried away with your descriptions, Socrates. All I see are some clouds and the sun setting.

---Listen closely. Can you hear it?

---Hear what?

---The day, in a faint voice, is casually saying farewell to us by subtly mixing its colorful palette of light. Just like you express yourself without words by your dancing, nature is talking to us through its artistry in the sky, casting its splendor upon us.

Rafa looked at me, incredulously.

---Seriously Socrates? Stop bullshitting me.

---I am serious! Here, relax for a moment and hold my hand.

Rafa reluctantly took my hand.

---If you sit still and give yourself up to nature, you can also feel it, too. Now, take a deep breath with me. Check out the soft, wispy clouds that are lazily drifting above us, as they change patterns, texture and colors. Let the entire beach experience, including its sounds and smells, fill up your senses, bringing increased energy and joy.

We sat quietly for a few minutes, holding hands, taking it all in. Rafa then broke the silence.

---Socrates?

---Yeah?

---Are we done absorbing the beach experience?

---I think so.

---You know, I think I did feel some of what you are describing. *La parte de mí que es escéptico y lógico a menudo descarta inmediatamente tu obsesión como una tontería.* (My skeptical, logical self often immediately dismisses your obsessiveness as nonsense.) But there often is, how do you say it in English, a method to your madness. I should recognize that and open up more to what you say.

We looked at each other and shared a smile as the sun disappeared below the horizon.

---Maybe one day you could paint all that you are describing, Socrates. Could you?

---I'm not really into painting land or seascapes, but I'd do it for you.

Our evening was spent eating take out Chinese food, watching a little television and listening to music while sitting on the balcony. Rafa eventually drifted off to sleep on the living room couch. I put one of the bed blankets over him and then went to snuggle under the covers in the bedroom bed.

The next day, the sun was out again in its full splendor, and we took full advantage of it. We repeated what we did the first day. This time, Rafa swam in the pool all by himself. When I eventually got in, I made sure I didn't get close to him. I didn't want to spook him again. I wanted to talk more, but I respected his space and privacy. I started taking photos and videos of him with my cell phone while he was in the water. After a while, he became irritated.

—Stop taking photos of me.

—Don't be absurd. We are on vacation. That's what people do. They take photos to remember the experience.

—Well, yes but you are getting carried away with it.

—Maybe. But what I do is take a lot and then select the best ones and delete the rest.

—Well, I don't like it, Socrates. You even take photos of me when I am sleeping. Don't think I didn't notice you taking photos of me yesterday napping on the couch.

—So what? You looked so serene. I couldn't resist.

—People don't do that. That isn't normal.

---Oh, come on. Lighten up. I've seen photos of you on your Facebook page where others took photos of your sleeping. But okay, to make you happy, from now on, I'll ask you first before I take photos of you. In my defense, I feel like I must take advantage of moments when you aren't on your cell phone. Because if I didn't, 90 percent of the photos on this trip would be of you staring at it. Who wants to see that?

Rafa didn't respond to my comment. The next day during the afternoon, we left the hotel to take a long walk together along the shoreline. Soon, we saw several dolphins majestically leap in unison out of the ocean. Rafa and I absolutely loved it. It was one of the first times on the trip where Rafa became animated. That evening, we had dinner at a restaurant that resembled a cave, with plants and rock embedded in the walls and running water all around them. It was a lot of fun. The next morning, we had more fun shopping at a *tianguis* (swap meet), where I bought Rafa a wallet and myself a Rosarito Beach refrigerator magnet.

—Thanks for the wallet, Socrates. I really needed a new one. Hey, would you like to play a game I sometimes play with my friends?

—Okay, sure.

—It involves rating each guy that passes us by, according to how handsome we think he is, on a scale of 1 to 10, with 10 being the most

handsome.
—What do you call it? The superficial game?
—Come on. It's just for fun. I'll start. What do you think about that guy over there? I'd give him a six.
---Why a six?
---For me, he is sort of handsome but doesn't really care for himself. And his face just isn't my type. And his butt is as flat as a pancake.
—Yeah, I guess I'd give him a six too. Rafa, what about that effeminate guy over there wearing flashy clothes?
—He's a zero.
—A zero? Really?
—If I could give him less than a zero, I would.
—What if he was wearing jeans and a black shirt, added a tattoo and a beard? You know, kind of like you do to make yourself look more manly.
—Yeah, maybe if he did that, I'd give him a few points.
—Wow, so Rafa, you judge guys in other ways too, besides their face and body?
—I suppose.
---Would you go out with a four or five?
---Maybe. But Socrates, there must be some attraction.
---There are so many intangibles related to human attraction. But if I feel a super handsome guy is empty inside, he's immediately disqualified.
---You are getting away from the game, Socrates.
Rafa pointed at another guy.
---What about him?
—He's a five to me, Rafa. I don't really find that many guys attractive.
—I give him a six. What about him?
—He's attractive. I give him an eight.
—He's a nine to me.
—Really? a nine? Rafa, he looks just like you, except that maybe he's a little chunkier. What about that robust-looking guy over there?
—A seven.
—Seven? You must like chubby, robust guys. He's a three for me.
—He's not that overweight, Socrates.
—Okay Rafa, so tell me. What rating do you give me?
—Hmmm. Maybe a four.
We both laughed.
—A four?! You bitch. Rafa, I give you a fucking two. You have a nice nose and lips. The rest is a zero. Wait, I forgot that you have a nice dick

too. I raise you up to a three.

We laughed harder.

—You are funny.

---Okay, I can't lie. You're a nine for me. One point off for no chest or definition in the upper body.

Rafa smiled at me as we continued to walk. We spent the rest of the day repeating what we did before---relaxing by the pool, walking on the beach and around town and eating out at restaurants. We had no intention of being like people who go on a vacation and plan so many activities that they come back home more exhausted than when they left. After relaxing on the balcony, we took a long evening walk to pick up a pizza and salad we had ordered. We talked about our lives, our future, and silly things. Once again, Rafa seemed to relax more when walking outside with me. Maybe it was due to the exercise increasing his endorphins, the brain's feel-good neurotransmitters. That's also probably why I always love spending time with my tennis friends as well. After several sets of tennis, everyone is a little tired, and more relaxed, more apt to let our guards down.

The next evening had all the makings of a special moment during our trip. We spent it conversing while sitting out on the balcony while staring out at the empty beach and the dark ocean. A light fog had rolled in, filtering the moonlight shimmering off the waves, as they rhythmically crashed onto the shoreline. A few boat lights were visible in the distance. It was generally quiet, except for some music playing from a distant bar. We both sat leaning back in our chairs as we stretched our legs out on the railing of the balcony. Rafa lifted one of his legs from the railing to his head as he smoked a cigarette, while I drank a beer. He then pulled out his phone and began scrolling.

—Socrates, check this out. I made some videos of me doing handstands and backflips. You will be the first to see them before I post them online.

—Nice.

—Even though I have some time off from dancing, I still like to stay in condition.

—I love that about you. You are constantly stretching, whether waiting for an elevator or watching videos on the couch. If you think about it, there is so much dead time in our lives, waiting for something. Why not use it to improve our bodies? After all, it's the only body we will ever have.

—Very true and thanks for noticing. I often stretch without even giving it much thought.

—So Rafa, here we are on vacation, with some time alone together. It's a perfect time to have a deep, meaningful conversation. Why don't you start it off by telling me a few things about you that most people don't know.

I waited patiently for Rafa's answer while he was still using his cell phone. A minute passed before without a response. He almost never responded until he was absolutely ready.

—I'm waiting, Rafa. Tick tock, tick tock. The question was can you tell me something about you that people don't know.

—I'm sorry. I got distracted. Hmm...here's something. Lots of people live to make money. And they tell me I should study something that can help me make a lot of money. But I'm different because I would rather be poor and happy doing what I love than being rich and unhappy doing something I hate.

—Why not be rich and happy doing what you like? The best of both worlds. Did that ever occur to you? Or do you think that is impossible for you?

---You are right, Socrates. I guess maybe I can't imagine myself being rich.

---Also, you probably know more than anyone that not having any money or enough of it can result in being unhappy too. Always fighting or worried about money is stressful.

—I know.

---I do agree with the first part of your statement though. The most important thing is to be happy with what you are doing. I think the rest, like money, will fall into place, at least enough of it, if you love what you do.

---Another thing is I want to dance in Germany or Los Angeles one day, but I don't even own a passport.

—Yeah, you will need money for that. Or another sugar daddy.

We both laughed. I rethought what I said and continued.

—I think I already told you that money isn't an obstacle if you really want something. Besides Germany and L.A., it seems to me like Mexico City would be the logical place to move to for a Mexican dancer. Have you thought about that?

—Socrates, the truth is I don't like Mexico City.

—You don't? I like the diversity of the people and ideas, and the variety of foods and restaurants there.

—Yes, true, there is good food there but there are too many people living there. It's very ugly and you can't be alone anywhere.

—It's a very beautiful city in certain parts, but not so much in other parts. But that is what every city is like. I don't know if I told you this, Rafa, but I was robbed twice when I lived there. Once I was kidnapped briefly.

—How horrible. There is no way I could live like that.

—Okay, so not Mexico City. But is staying in Monterrey to dance going to satisfy you? With your talent, it seems like you would be settling for less than you are capable of.

—Well, there is the satisfaction of helping to grow a dance culture in my home city where it is lacking.

---Yes, I love that, even though it might be a constant struggle.

---Back to your question, Socrates. I'm not sure what I'm going to do.

—That's okay. You are still young, still finding your way, trying new projects. But at some point, you will need a plan. At least, I hope so. Imagine a sculptor with a block of stone who keeps changing his or her mind about what to make. In the end, the sculptor would have chiseled the stone down to only shavings, with nothing to show for his or her efforts.

---That makes sense.

---Whatever you decide to do, Rafa, I'm expecting great achievements from you in your career. If you fail, just get up off your feet and try again. Of course, no matter what, even if you are sweeping floors, I will still care about you, no matter what.

—Thank you so much. I really thank you. While I'm still getting to know you, you've become someone I can trust.

—You are welcome. So, tell me something else, Rafa. What is something that worries you?

—I'm worried that time seems to be going by so fast. As I mentioned to you before, I'm panicking about turning 30 in a few years.

---Maybe you forgot how old I am. I believe that getting older has its advantages and you shouldn't be so concerned about it.

—Socrates, I'm not sure I see the positives about my body breaking down.

—Well, among many advantages, you learn better who you really are. When you are older, through trial and error, you learn what to focus on and you hopefully learn not to make the same mistakes. You become more humble and grateful. You become more stable. For me, the knowledge I have accumulated has been invaluable. Like when I first had an anxiety attack, I thought I was dying. Now when it happens, I don't feel good, but I know what is happening and I don't panic as much.

—Oh, okay. That's a perspective I hadn't thought of before.

—When you get older, you begin to realize what is important and what isn't. You learn that friendships and relationships take time. You learn patience. I have learned patience just from watching and living with Rafie. You learn to focus on what you can control. Life is often uncertain and is constantly changing, so you learn to be flexible and adapt to the situation. You learn it is important to say how you really feel when you have the chance. Because that chance may not come again.

—I want to go back in time to tell my younger self not to quit school.

—From what you told me, you didn't have much choice in the matter. Okay, so it's my turn. Let me tell you something about me. One thing you don't know is that I often listen to a song repeatedly so that it seeps into my soul.

—Interesting. What type of songs do you listen to most? For me, it depends on my mood.

—I listen to many different styles. And by the way, you definitely are moody. It's obvious. Now that I know you, I've learned to be more patient with you. I need to wait for you to be a little more receptive to talking. Of course, sometimes that wait is a day or two.

—Yeah, I know.

—Socrates, I've gotten good at reading your silence and when needed, letting it be.

—I thank you for that. Maybe that's why I feel comfortable around you. You let me have my silent time. As you well know, I often don't say a lot. I'm not always the best at keeping a conversation going. Not everyone understands that about me. I'm not always open to small talk. I enjoy being in my own little world.

---Yeah, I notice you often don't focus on others. You don't see that as a defect of yours?

---No. I prefer to focus on me first.

---And second. And third. And fourth. I mean, for example, you rarely ask me questions. I've figured out that the only way to hold a conversation with you is to ask you questions about yourself. That would be a complete turn-off to most people.

---Well, that's who I am. I'm not perfect.

---None of us are, but that doesn't mean you can't try to improve yourself. Don't you think part of the reason you sometimes feel unhappy is due to your selfish way of thinking? Asking questions and caring about others' needs besides your own is a way to feel connected to others and to the world. It can ultimately help improve your wellbeing.

Rafa took a long puff from his cigarette, stared at me and then back at the ocean below. He didn't answer. I continued talking.
—I'm not saying you don't have good qualities as well. For example, you can be fun and silly when you are in the mood.
——-True.
——-I love to try to make you laugh.
——-You do, Socrates. And believe me, it sometimes doesn't take much.
—Okay, what else? More, more, more.
—Well, let's see. A simple cold often knocks me out horribly, makes me cry and feel like I am going to die.
—Yeah, I remember you saying that before. Me too. I panic sometimes, thinking the worst, which only makes my cold last longer.

After there was a lull in the conversation, I went to the refrigerator to get us more beer. I sat next to him on the balcony, pulled out my cell phone and decided to show Rafa some old family photos of me and my dad.
—Wow, your father was really handsome. I think I would be attracted to him, but not to mine. My dad was not my type at all.

Next, I showed Rafa a childhood photo of me and my brother together.
—You don't have to tell me which one you are. Your face hasn't changed.
—True. I still have kept my same smile.

One poignant moment in the conversation occurred when it veered towards his career. I asked if being a professional dancer didn't work out for him, would he accept a job as a dance instructor or do something else with his life. Rafa's demeanor suddenly changed. He sternly looked at me directly in my eyes as he responded.
—Socrates, do you really think after all my sweat and tears, that I would give up now?!
—It was just a question. Now that I know you better, I can see that you are a very determined guy.

I sat quietly for a few seconds to allow Rafa to calm down a bit. His words were loud and clear. The mire thought of giving up on his dream was unimaginable to him. In this moment, I could see, etched in his face, his battered soul and all of his past struggles.
—So, tell me Rafa about some of your aspirations in life.
—Well, as I mentioned to you before, besides dancing, I want to be an actor. I also want to direct my own play.
—Very cool.

As we drank some more, the subject changed to his upbringing. He talked in more detail about his dropping out of school at the age of 13. Rafa seemed forever fixated on this particular trauma.

—You know, when I was 14 years old, I even lived by myself for a while at my cousin's house in Mexicali.

—What? How did that happen?

—My cousin got a job in Sinaloa, so he let me use his apartment and my parents let me go since I wasn't in school.

---Holy cow. That's not very responsible of your parents.

---Well, I wanted to do it and they let me.

---But at 14, you weren't old enough to be alone without parents or a guardian.

Rafa didn't say anything, so I continued.

---So, tell me more about growing up in Monterrey.

---Okay, well, as you know, my family was very poor, and I would go to bed hungry many times. But generally, we had enough food. But there were times when I didn't even have enough money to buy candy. There were others in my neighborhood poorer than us, so I didn't feel sorry for myself. I often would travel with my dad and my cousin Jorge, taking trips around Mexico in a big rig truck. Sometimes our whole family went together. My family is a truck-driving family.

I took a sip of my beer and imagined what living like that was like. I paused for a moment to stand up to stretch.

—Sounds like it was a different type of education for you, Rafa. Driving around the country. I bet you have lots of stories to tell about those times.

—Yes, it was very much a different kind of education. I helped to load and unload goods. There were lots of stops in small, dusty towns. We ate lots of gas station food. I distinctly remember the smell of oil and gas and sitting for long hours. But there were a lot of fun times. I suppose that was also when I developed a love for nature and a desire to protect the environment.

—So, what changed from then until now?

—I often say that my dad's death didn't have much of an effect on me, but it did.

—I remember you saying you got mad when he died. Not sad?

—Of course, I was sad too. I don't know why I was mad. Mad at life, perhaps, for taking away my father. Mad he wouldn't be around to see my triumphs in life. Yes, he was homophobic, but he was a good-hearted man. He treated us kids with lots of love. For example, he always waited for the rest of the family to be served food before he ate.

---Nice. I suppose you could be mad at him as well for having conceived you at an older age. He must have been like 60 years old or so.

---Yeah true. Thinking about it now, I suppose that I was.

The conversation was getting a little too depressing, so I asked Rafa about when he first got the idea of being a dancer. His face relaxed and his eyes lit up.

—When I was a child, I wanted to be a singer and actor. I always wanted to be some type of artist. I often closed my bedroom door, turned the music up and danced while pretending I was on videos with Lady Gaga. When I was around 19 years old, I started watching dance and stretching videos on my phone. The first time that I saw a contemporary dance video, I had no clue what it was. It was then that I looked for more information and more related videos. My interest had been awakened. I started stretching regularly until I was about to turn 21 years of age, when I entered a beginner's summer class at the Grace Dance School. I began taking yoga and stretching classes soon afterwards. As time passed, I learned more styles of dance at Grace. I had money to live, but dance classes were expensive. That is when I got a job at a chemical plant. At 21, I also began taking the National Education System's adult classes to obtain my high school equivalent certificate. This was to make up for dropping out of school.

—You were a busy guy. What did you do at your job?

—I was mixing chemicals for two years. Later, they moved me to a warehouse where I just threw out trash most of the day. That is when my employer kept changing my work location. Later, I worked as a waiter and on an assembly line. None of this work paid very much. Maybe at the most, I would earn 100 pesos a day. What was most tiring was the physical labor during very late work nights.

—Wow. It's unbelievable that you survived all that.

—Yeah, the pay was so low that I would quickly run out of money. When that happened, I couldn't take the bus to go to dance school, so I walked to school for two hours, sometimes in the heat of the summer.

—That's crazy! I wish I knew you back then, Rafa, so I could give you some money for your transportation.

—Those times were some of the toughest for me. After work, I took dance classes, which were hard and very exhausting. I was averaging about four hours of sleep every day. I would often cry due to the toll this was taking on me. I was either working, dancing or studying every day of the week. I got up at 5 a.m. to be at work at 6 a.m., then leave at 4 p.m. to go to dance class at 5 or 6 p.m. After that, it was off to school classes, which would end at 10 p.m.

—Wow, that's a very full schedule of activities. I'm not sure I could do that. It sounds like you prided yourself on doing it all yourself. Why not ask for more help from family or friends? Pride isn't going to put food on your table or help you when you are heat exhausted.

—I know. I just didn't and still don't want people to know when I feel vulnerable. As you know, people telling me what to do is what I hate the most, Socrates.

—I understand that. But risking your life, taking long walks in deadly heat just because you refused to ask for help? That's insane. And if you don't mind me saying, very stupid. Asking for help doesn't mean you are weak or incompetent. You need to acknowledge your limitations. Most of us do not have all the skills, expertise and even money necessary to navigate life. Well, anyway, kudos to you for surviving that period. It really showed how dedicated and determined you were.

—Thanks for the advice. I'm not sure how I survived it. The first year at Grace was only training. I learned a lot. The instructors noticed right away that I was much more advanced than other dancers. One teacher told me that I have a dancer's body. And she's right. I can do many movements with my body that aren't as easy for others. Dance has helped me in so many ways.

—Tell me more dance stuff. What are some of the limitations you face as a dancer?

—Hmmm…well…one issue us dancers deal with is our legs. Often, a dancer can lift one leg higher than the other. For me, I can lift my right leg higher than my left.

—I didn't know that.

—Another issue is the constant care of one's body and the need to stretch so much. I want to be even more flexible than I am right now, as if I didn't have bones.

—Very cool. That's going to be my nickname for you, Rafa. No Bones. We both laughed.

—What would you say is the most important part of the body to stretch?

—The back. By stretching the back, you also end up stretching the shoulders. Two for one.

—Okay, I'll try to focus on back stretching more. I know we got off track. Feel free to continue talking about your dance history.

—Let's see. The second year, I was moved to the competition team. This was the most difficult year for me because I was doing a job that involved hard physical labor and I was also dancing. The good news was that I received a one-year dance class scholarship. I moved in with

my sister at the time, assisting her with paying her apartment bills.
—Hopefully you saved some money for yourself during that time with the scholarship.
—Yes, I did. For the third year, my dance classes were all paid for. The money I wasn't paying for classes was used to pay for participation in regional and national competitions in Tijuana and Mazatlán. I received instruction from local, national and international teachers. After the third year, the instructors at Grace promoted me to be in the group with the best students. But after I lost my plant job, I couldn't dance as much because I had to work at my new job as a waiter. I was also preparing myself for an audition for entering the music and dance school at the University of Monterrey.
---Nice, nice. So, at this point, you are really growing fast as a dancer. Love it.
---Yes, I was. Hold on a minute. I have to go to the bathroom.

As I sat on the balcony waiting for Rafa to return, I pondered what Rafa had just described to me, as well as past comments. The path he had taken to get to this point in his life and dancing career seemed so daunting, yet he somehow had survived it all. I admired his fighting spirit. It was like he was wearing an invisible, multi-layered coat of constant struggles, which reeked of depression and desperation. He often faked smiles or happiness to distract himself from its burden. Its fabric was years in the making and the layers were too numerous and entangled to easily remove at once. A psychologist might be able to help Rafa remove some of the layers to free him up some. The problem was that Rafa had little time for self-examination, which is often required to change thought patterns that don't allow one to move forward in a more positive way. He also didn't have the money to seek help.

What was a little perplexing for me to understand was that Rafa often took a perverse pleasure and pride in wearing this heavy coat. It was almost like he intentionally was creating drama and obstacles in his life so that when he achieved his life goals, they would mean more to him. This paradoxical way of thinking appeared in other aspects of his life as well, such as with his smoking habit. He seemed to be playing with fire. Being an enemy to himself could easily sabotage his best efforts. Seeing him behave this way made me reflect on actions I may have taken to hinder myself in this way in my life.

Our in-depth conversation on the balcony that night drifted into the morning, finally ending as the sun was rising. Rafa eventually fell asleep, but try as I might, I couldn't sleep at all. After a few hours of lying in bed, I decided to take an early morning walk on the beach by myself. Later when I came back, I discovered Rafa hadn't slept much either. He pulled out his phone and showed me a video he had taken of me from the balcony as I walked on the beach.

We were having so much fun that I decided to extend our trip for another night. I also felt like a zombie for not having slept at all. We took advantage of the extra night by going out to a nearby bar for a drink and then came back early. The next morning, we packed up, leaving Rosarito with great memories of a fun trip. The trip served its purpose; we were very relaxed, happy and ready to continue with our lives. Our friendship was growing stronger. But despite this growth, being Rafa's friend while being physically attracted to him was, at times, wearing on me. I suspected it was wearing on him as well.

As we sat in the back seats of our taxi ride on the long drive to the San Ysidro border, I intensely stared at Rafa for a few minutes while he looked at his phone. Just at that very moment, a favorite Spanish love song of mine started playing on the radio. I tapped the taxi driver on the shoulder and spoke to him.

—*Disculpe, ¿Usted puede subir un poco el volumen de la radio, por favor? Me gusta esta canción.* (Excuse me. Could you please turn up the volume on the radio a little? I like this song.)

—*Claro que sí.* (Of course)

—*Muchas gracias.* (Thank you.)

The song's lyrics reminded me how I was delving deeper and deeper into Rafa's soul. Sometimes I realized that I'd gone down too far and needed to come up to the surface for air. But I loved going for the gusto, letting my unappeasable passion rush through me, unchecked. I absorbed the lyrics and music of the song and attempted to send their vibrations out towards Rafa, but today it was to no avail. He remained hypnotized by what he was looking at on his cell phone. I wanted to kiss him right there in the taxi, but I could never do something like that. I always left those sorts of desires to my imagination and my dreams, to not scare him away. If I did kiss him, it might end our friendship and his confidence in me as well. If I couldn't kiss and hold him, the next best thing was being his close friend, and I didn't want to ruin that.

19 UNIVERSITY DRAMA

A few weeks later, Rafa began studying for the University of Monterrey entrance exam.

—Sorry I haven't texted you in a while, Socrates. I'm taking an online class to prepare for my exam. It's eight hours long. I am six hours into it, and I think that my head is going to explode!

—I can only imagine. Plus, focusing on anything for a long time can't be easy for you.

—Yeap, but I must do it.

A couple of days later, I got a text from him.

—*Hola* (Hi) Socrates. Guess what? Lots of people found a sheet of answers to the entrance exam and passed it to each other. It is a big scandal over here.

—Oh wow.

—I'm getting nervous since tomorrow is the exam date for me. I'm going to stay tonight at my sister's house, since she lives closer to the university. I'm going to study all night and then I will get up early in the morning to study some more.

—Good idea. How long is the test?

—The exam has 122 questions. It is multiple choice. I've got two hours to finish it. I've been studying 12 hours a day. I'm super nervous. I'm probably not going to sleep the whole night.

—Well, try to sleep a few hours.

The next afternoon, I asked him how it went.

—I just smoked a cigarette. I don't think it went well. I really thought I would cry but I am calm. I had to guess on the last 30 questions because I ran out of time. The exam wasn't that difficult, but I just ran out of time. There were some parts where I got confused. Next week, they will provide the results. I will be a nervous wreck for a week.

—Well, Rafa, you tried your best. There is no shame in that.

The entrance exam wasn't the only criteria for acceptance at the music and dance school he was applying for at the university. Also required was a submission of a video of basic dance skills. His video almost didn't get submitted before the midnight deadline due to a slow internet connection and Rafa waiting until the last minute. The wait for the exam results was excruciatingly long. A few days later, I received an unexpected call via video chat call from Rafa. When I saw the screen of my phone, Rafa had his hand over his mouth and seemed to be in distress. Tears were falling down his face.

—What's wrong? Are you okay?

—I got my exam results back.

—Oh my gosh, you didn't get accepted. I'm so sorry. Really, I am.

He then showed me his computer screen, showing an acceptance email from the university. I soon realized he was crying tears of joy.

—I was accepted.

—Oh my gosh!!!!!!!! Congratulations! I am so happy for you. You see, all your hard work is paying off. This is just the beginning for you.

—You are the first person I've told. I wanted you to know first. Well, I did tell my sister too. You've been so supportive. Thanks so much. Really.

—Of course! I support you 100 percent. You see now? All the hard work you did to get to this point was all worth it.

—You know what I've gone through. Thanks for being there for me. You are the best!

Rafa doesn't get excited very often, if at all. But this time he couldn't hide how he felt about this special moment.

—Rafa, it's your time to fly!

Even though Rafa passed the university entrance exam, he still had not completed his general education degree, but he had hoped the university would give him a few months to finish his exams and provide proof of the degree required for enrollment before the first semester started.

—I just sent an email to the university coordinator to let him know that there will be a delay in getting my high school equivalence certificate delivered to him. Thanks again for your support. I really haven't believed in myself. I continue to wait for a response from the university regarding how long they will give me to provide my certificate.

The next day, Rafa texted me to say his dreams of attending the university were in jeopardy of not coming true.

—Hey, I am not ignoring you. I am having family problems. I'll text you later, okay?

—Okay.

A few hours later, I got another text.

—My drug addict brother stole all my savings and left me without money. I work hard to save money and it is gone. I'm angry. I cried. I broke a fan. I'm standing against a wall right now in my room. I can't deal with this damn life. I've had enough.

—Rafa, I don't know what to say.

—I can't save money to go to the university because I keep getting robbed. Everything is against me. I have no money. I can't eat without money. You know what? It's best to talk to me later if you want. I am very upset. If I don't answer your texts, it is because they cut off the internet because Eduardo stole the money to pay it. Oh, and the university said no, they require the high school equivalent certificate now. I guess that I will try next year.

—What???!!! Oh no. I'm so sorry. How frustrating.

—I always had a dream of being a student at the university. Misfortune continues to chase me. You have no idea of how I feel. After I finish my high school equivalence certificate exams, I'm going to Mexicali to live with my cousin. I already sent him a message. I am so depressed. I only want to cry myself to sleep in my bed. It doesn't matter how hard I try. It isn't worth it.

—Please don't say that. That's not true.

—It's the truth. My savings were stolen, I don't have food, they rejected me in the university, and they are going to cut off the basic services in my house. It doesn't get any worse. There is no doubt that God hates me.

—Wait a minute. You don't even believe in God. The money can easily be replaced, and I can give you money for food and to pay for your phone and utility services. And they didn't reject you. You just didn't have the paperwork they required. Try focusing on what you do have. You are young. I would love to be 24 again. You have your health. You have family and friends who love you a lot. You are intelligent, funny and handsome. And while I am still your friend, you will never lack anything you need. Understand?

—Thank you, but this doesn't help me get into the university.

—It's a momentary setback. Take it from an older, wiser person, sometimes failure is just part of the process. The majority of successful people have dealt with significant setbacks. You might even say failure is a steppingstone to growth and success. It teaches us resilience, how to be flexible and adapt to life's challenges. The sooner you realize this, the better. If you need to, cry tonight and call me in the morning. You will be fine. You have a big heart.

—What I have is rage.

—Well, if it makes you feel better, break something else.

—It's not worth it. My life is broken. I can't do it anymore.

—Don't exaggerate. Tomorrow is another day.

—You don't know how it feels when they ruin your dreams. I fought so hard for nothing.

—How exactly did the university ruin your dreams? By following their own rules for entrance into the university? Rules that you didn't verify before you took the exam. Maybe just think about how sweet it will be when you achieve your dreams despite all of this?

—I don't believe you. It is all over for me. I am old for a dancer. Maybe I just wasn't born to dance.

—I have no doubt that you were born to dance.

—I believe that I need to do something else now. Maybe my destiny is not to study, and I must live this way, poor and unfulfilled.

—I don't believe that. You also don't believe in destiny. You are saying foolish things. You can dance at any age. Step by step. Finish your exams for completion of high school and plan what is next. Have a good cry and then you'll feel better. I'm not going to let you give up on yourself. You still have lots of options.

—This makes four universities that have rejected me now. Four. I was accepted at a university in Puebla, but it costs $7,000 pesos a month. You know, I don't like to dream because if my dreams don't come true, the disappointment is bigger than if I never had a dream in the first place. This hurts so bad.

—I know it does. Again, I'm so sorry. Don't worry about the number of universities that have rejected you. It doesn't matter. Universities I have applied to have rejected me as well. I didn't let that stop me and you shouldn't either. Besides, there isn't just one way to achieve your goals.

—I can't. I just can't. I'm too old. This isn't for me. The university doesn't want old people like me.

—That's nonsense. Just keep dancing. If you really love dancing, you'll dance anywhere, at any age.

—I've been rejected. There is no place for me. I don't care now. I'm not as good a dancer as you think I am. I'm not good at anything. This part of my happy life has died.

—Stop saying that. Maybe let's get you enrolled in a U.S. university.

—They are too expensive. I don't even have money for the bus.

—Well, at least meet with the director in person. It's worth a shot.

—Maybe you are right. Tomorrow I will go to the director's office to explain my case.

—I can send you money. I just now sent you $50 dollars. You can go to pick it up at Oxxo.

—What???!!!! You always come to the rescue, Socrates. Thanks so much.

—You are welcome. It is a pleasure. Maybe use some of it to pay for your internet. Tomorrow, I will send you $200, in case the director gives you more time.

The next day, Rafa audio messaged me the bad news.

—The director's office said no. I feel resigned now. I cried yesterday. Today, I could have gotten mad, but I didn't. I can wait another year.

—Keep the enrollment money I just sent you. It is a gift. Use it to pay your bills.

—I will save it. This will be a nice break for me. I can take trips and visit family.

---I'm not giving it to you to take trips. I'm giving it to you to pay for food and bills, understand?

---Okay. Hey, you know what? Lots of people say don't cry but it's the best medicine. Yesterday I cried and I feel cured. When I get mad and sad, I can get very dramatic.

---No kidding.

I left Rafa alone for a few days to cool off some more and reevaluate his situation. When I texted him again, he'd calmed down and was more rational.

—How are you this evening, Rafa?

—I'm good, thanks.

—I'm glad you are feeling better. Now it's my turn to not feel good. I've been suffering from a bad case of acid reflux for days now. I feel like I want to cry. The pain is so bad.

—Oh no. I wish I could do something to make you feel better, Socrates.

—Before I die, I will send you instructions on how to manage your webpage.

—Hahahahaha. Shut the fuck up. Don't say that. Okay, well, go ahead and die. I promise to cry. Hahahaha. Just kidding. I'm going to sleep.

—I will suffer alone then. Well, I have Rafie, but he is sleeping.

20 GOODBYE, HELLO AGAIN
AND THE ESCORT

A month later, I did something stupid. Love makes you do stupid things, but this was beyond stupid. It was an overreach on my part. I pretended I was someone else while texting Rafa via the gay men's hookup app *Grindr*. I knew he used the site. I had not used it for a few years, but I logged on to find him and I did. He had mentioned to me his burning desire to go to Germany many times, and we both talked about taking a trip there together one day. He was also attracted to its men, especially if they were white, tall and had nice legs. So, one day I decided to fabricate a profile of a German guy with the characteristics he liked. I posted a stock photo and texted him. He easily fell for it. For a few hours, I texted back and forth with Rafa as this made-up guy. During our texting on *Grindr*, I finally felt what it was like to be the center of his attention. For a few moments, I was very happy. It was all meant to be a joke and I planned to say it was me.

But he figured out it was me before I could say it was a joke, in part, due to me being inept at turning off the distance marker on the app, which showed I was in San Diego. Instead of Rafa shrugging it off, he exploded in anger. A few moments of happiness cost me my friendship with Rafa, for the moment, anyway. I regretted doing it immediately and was ashamed. I couldn't even bear to admit I did it on a video chat with him, which made it even worse. He deleted me off all his social media again. As much as I attempted to resolve this, it was to no avail. He was upset and probably justifiably so. Not that Rafa never lied to others. I recently witnessed him tell his friends that he was in Tijuana at a concert, when he wasn't. I later learned that he used anonymous profiles on various sites as well, pretending to be someone he wasn't. But just because he lies as well doesn't condone my actions.

Months passed by, and a new year began. Every now and then, I sent Rafa a text message but received no response. It was during this period, I discovered that my suspicions were true---he was working as a gay escort. I stumbled upon a profile of his on a Mexican escort webpage. Okay, maybe I didn't exactly stumble upon it. It was a site I infrequently visited, not to use its services, but to check out the hot photos and videos of local Mexican men. As I was scrolling down the list of photos with profiles, there was Rafa with a facemask on. I recognized his photo as one that I'd seen him previously post on his Instagram page. In all of his other photos on the site, his face was hidden, and his tattoos were blurred out in photos. He was careful not to show his face and tattoos in the videos he posted as well, but I knew it was him. In fact, I was so familiar with Rafa by now that I probably could tell it was him just from seeing one of his legs. Also, he was careless and forgot to blur out a few of his tattoos on three photos, which easily identified him.

I was shocked to discover that he also had another webpage as a link on his escort site, where he advertised his services. It was very sexually graphic, including photos and videos of him having sex with his clients. Searching around the internet, I discovered he was also using other different social media apps and websites to reach clients. To let him know that I knew, I sent him a message on one of the sites, saying I was Socrates and joked that I wanted to use his services. There was no response.

On Valentine's Day, which in Mexico is also referred to as the day of love and friendship, I decided to again attempt to communicate with Rafa via text. This time, he answered.

—Hi No Bones. Happy Valentine's Day.

—*Hola* (Hi) Socrates. Happy Valentine's Day.

—Thanks! How is my favorite prostitute doing? Well, you are the only prostitute I know, but that doesn't mean that you aren't my favorite. Hahahaha!

—Hahahahaha. I prefer to be called an escort.

---Okay. Or maybe you'd prefer to be called a genital engineer. Hahahaha.

---Hahahaha. It feels weird that you know my secret. Now you know everything about me. I wanted to tell you about it a long time ago. I almost told you in Rosarito. I just didn't have the courage to do so.

---It has taken me a while, but I finally possess all of your infinity stones. The whore stone was the one I was missing. Hahaha! I already had the space, reality, power, mind, time and soul stones. Now you are all mine!

—Hahahahaha.

---So why didn't you tell me?

—You know me. I don't like to talk about my personal life much with anyone. And it's not something I'm particularly proud of.

—Yeah, I understand, but I'm not just anyone.

—True. I was also afraid of how you might react.

—Well, honestly, I was surprised, but I kind of suspected it. I already knew that you were a sexaholic. While I understand why you might keep being an escort as a secret from me, I do prefer honesty. But I'd be a hypocrite to judge you for that, since I've lied too. Of course, we all keep secrets or don't talk about private matters and that's okay. But it's not like I wasn't going to find out eventually. All that really matters to me is if you are safe and happy with what you are doing. How long have you been an escort?

—I've been doing it for a year now. When I first met you, I hadn't started yet, but by our second meeting at Real Inn, I had been doing it for about month. That's when I said let's just be friends. My friends that I met up with in Tijuana were escorts too. So yeah, I am a prostitute, but a respectable one. Hahahaha. I never had a sugar daddy.

—I'm curious. Why didn't you just tell me that you were an escort, instead of saying that you have a sugar daddy?

—Well, a sugar daddy doesn't sound as bad.

—You judged me for lying to you, when you are just as much a liar as I am.

—I know.

—The difference is, when I lied, you stopped talking to me. When you lie, I'm like, whatever, it's not that big of a deal.

—You know I explode sometimes.

—Obviously. Except I wish the explosions would not last a couple of months.

—I know.

—So how does it feel to earn more money per hour than me?

—Hahahaha. I don't think so, Socrates.

—I don't earn as much as you charge an hour. Now I am going to ask you for money! Hahahaha.

—Hahahaha. Yeah, you rub my back and I rub yours.

—Can you tell me about your life as an escort? If you feel comfortable about talking about it, of course.

—Well, I don't like to talk about it, but I will for you. A friend told me about it as a way to make money without working so much. I created the fake name Rocco on the escort website you found.

—Is that the same friend who told you that you could get a job as a masseur?

—Yes, sorry Socrates, another one of my lies. As you can see, I kept hesitating about telling you the truth.

—Thinking about it logically, it makes sense. It is quick, easy money. You can earn more in an hour than it might take a week to earn at a standard job. And it frees up your time to be able to dance and go to school. The problem is that it is very risky. A high risk, high reward job.

—Yeah, it's great because I can make appointments to fit my busy schedule.

—Sounds like it works for you.

—It does. Some months I get more clients than others. I'm busier during the week than weekends, probably because the men are busy with their families on the weekends. Sometimes weeks pass without clients and then suddenly I get lots of requests for my services.

—Interesting. So how do you promote yourself?

—Besides the main escort website, I advertise on other sites, as you know. I have special social media accounts with only clients, and I belong to escort sites on them as well. I use all the social media and apps I can to get business. I first started with *Grindr*, but they don't like people selling sex on their site, so I stopped.

—I see. Tell me more about "Rocco."

—Well, I refer to my escort name as if he was someone else. Rocco doesn't work in the early morning hours. I have a few repeat clients, even one who comes from the U.S. People are surprised, due to how effeminate I can be, that I prefer to top guys. And that works out, because most but not all my clients are passive. They are of all ages, but most are older. Many are married men.

—Yeah, I assume few younger guys have enough money to pay for sex. I saw that you charge about $60 US. That's a lot of money for a Mexican to pay.

—True.

—So, what do you typically bring with you when you leave to see a client?

—Well, mostly what you'd expect. I bring a pocket purse with flavored condoms, lubricants, body lotion, toothpaste for my breath, a razor to shave, lip balm, butt plugs, cock rings, gloves, my blue dildo and Sildenafil.

—What is Sildenafil?

—It is the name for what I assume you know as Viagra, an erectile dysfunction medication.

—Wow, so even you, Mr. Escort, have problems staying erect?

—Not usually, but sometimes. I must keep my clients happy.

—I guess.

—I assume you shower beforehand.

—Yes, at the hotel or home. I also use an anal wash device.

—Okay, so you are well prepared. But what about the unexpected? Aren't you ever afraid something bad will happen to you as an escort? People are killed, injured and robbed working as prostitutes.

—No, I'm not afraid. I try to lower any risks. For example, I don't accept clients from the outskirts of the city, the more dangerous parts.

—Makes sense. Are there moments when you have felt uncomfortable?

—Not really.

—Do you ever get nervous going to the house of a client? I think I would, thinking a wife or husband might come home and catch you guys in the act.

—Mostly it is at hotels. I'm not really that worried.

—Yeah, I suppose the spouse would shoot the husband and not you, but you never know. Are you registered with the government as a sex worker?

—No.

—And you aren't worried that the police could potentially arrest you at any time?

—Not really. Like I said, we all take risks.

—I read the Mexican law, and it says that you can be a sex worker if you register with them and prove that you get tested regularly for sexually transmitted diseases. What else? Do you fake like you cum sometimes?

—Yeah, I do. Especially if I have more than one client a night.

—I guess when you do that, you better flush the condom down the toilet quickly, so the client doesn't see that you faked it. Otherwise, they might be tempted to ask for their money back.

—I suppose.

—I'm lucky in that regard, Rafa.

—What do you mean?

—Well, I'm usually alone when I'm having sex, so I don't have to fake it when it's over. Hahahahahaha.

—Hahahahaha. Oh Socrates. If you could see me, you'd see I'm really laughing out loud over here. I even startled one of my cats.

—I see you advertise for providing services for more than one hour. A two-hour escort service is a lot of money for you.

—Yeah, but guys usually never pay for two hours.

—Do you get lots of couples?

—No, but occasionally.

—What about problems you've had with clients?

—Well, some clients want a discount for services or even worse, they want it for free. Rocco doesn't do free. Sometimes clients call me and want a free video sex call. I don't do those either. And when some clients look unclean, I ask them to first shower and clean inside themselves. Sometimes the closeted guys tell me they have never had anal sex, so I give them tips about cleaning themselves and what to expect.

—I saw some of your videos on the websites. I can't believe you had sex in your room at your mom's house.

—Most of my work is done at hotels. I've probably been to half the hotels in Monterrey. I could be a good tourist guide. And yeah, I've done it at my mom's house, but only when she is out on a trip.

—Hmmm. I wouldn't want some stranger to come to my house, but that is just me.

—Yes, I understand. It's a risk.

—Can you tell me some stories about your clients?

—Okay, let's see. One guy wanted me to pretend that I was raping him. I did it, but I didn't feel comfortable doing it. Another wanted me to pretend to strangle him. One guy wanted to be tied to the bed. Another client, a young guy maybe 25 years old, just wanted me to hug him. Well, at first, he did. Then he penetrated me. Some guys just want to talk to me about their problems. I feel like a psychologist or therapist for them. It happens more than you would think. Mostly though, it is just sex.

—That's very interesting. Another question. How does the $60 you charge compare with what other escorts charge?

—Some charge over $100 dollars. My body isn't big and muscular, so I can't charge that much. I've lowered what I charge to $50 now. I charge less than others. I used to charge close to $75. I get tips too, as well as gifts like dildos, wine, liquor, cologne, and other items.

—Has anyone said he was going to pay you and then not paid after the sex was over?

—-Yeah.

—Gosh, I don't know how you do it. You must enjoy it, at least sometimes.

—Yeah, I do, but it's mostly a performance. A fantasy.

—I noticed that on your escort and other related social media pages, that you pose in all kinds of positions. Your clients must love your flexibility. I love those photos of you doing the splits. Hahaha.

—Yes, as I've said before, I can do many types of movements with my body.

—There is no doubt about that, Rafa. From what I've seen, you have been very creative in advertising to new clients. You posted several videos of you having sex with others, adding comments about the sex. You solicit clients to do videos with you. In one photo I remember that you posted, it showed cum spots on your underwear, stating that "Someone has their tank full, and the milk is starting to overflow." Other times, you posted questions like "Do you like my body?" "Should I post a video of this (a photo of you cumming)?" Another photo of you being penetrated came with the caption "They stuck it in me, and it felt so good." There were videos and photos of you masturbating and cumming, sitting on a dildo, dancing naked, moving your butt and cock around, and you standing in front of a hot tub, among others.

—Yes, I have been working as many angles as I can to drum up business.

—And speaking of angles, I loved the angles of many of the photos you took. My favorite was the one of you naked, standing on your head, on a hotel bed, using the mirror on the ceiling to take the photo. There were so many creative cum shots and hardon photos, too.

---Socrates, you are amazing. True to who you are, you notice all the details. You see my creativity, even in being an escort. Nobody sees what you see.

---That's me. Hey, I saw the photos you posted of your feet too. Do you have a lot of feet fetish clients?

—More than you'd think.

—I noticed your escort ad said you are 21 years old, provide services to young, old, married, single, curious and threesomes, that you are serious, discreet, clean, and versatile regarding sex. And you weren't lying completely about being a masseur. You do offered massages!

—Yes, I offer massages, but very few clients request one.

—Rafa, you also claim none of your photos were edited, but they all were. You edited out or hid your face and tattoos.

—Well, yes, you are right, but my body parts weren't edited.

—I was wondering whether you obtained a lot of escort business using the sex groups on social media sites. Also, do you get business using your personal sites where you are posting porn videos?

---No, I don't get much business from them. They are more for my enjoyment. You know I love porn.

---Yeah, I knew that, but you seem to be beyond loving it and closer to being obsessed with it.

—Surprise. What can I say?

—Rafa Galarín, the serious sex addict. Well, I have to say, learning all this just adds to what makes you so intriguing and mysterious. You even said it yourself, that your head isn't just a world, it is a universe.

—Yeah. I suppose to the outside world, I seem normal, but I'm really crazy.

—I wasn't completely fooled by what you are telling me now, but maybe I was sort of stupid to not pick up on it right away.

—You aren't stupid. Guess what? One of the benefits is I finally have enough money saved now to fix my teeth!

—That's great. It was nice that you were able to help your mom too. And all those things you bought for your mom's house.

—How did you know about all that? Oh yeah, I told you my sugar daddy bought those items.

—Yeah, you did. Oh, and please let me formally apologize for the *Grindr* thing. I feel horrible. I really do. It wasn't worth losing your friendship for.

—Don't worry. It's okay. Everyone makes mistakes. Forgive me again for all the bad things I said about you. I was really mad. Later, I will give you a class on how to spy on someone without them knowing it.

—Hahahaha. Okay, thanks. I do need that class!

—Totally, you really do.

—So how is your dance career going?

—Well, I am taking another dance class. And I was accepted to be part of a small contemporary dance company called *La Terraza*. In fact, I'm going to dance at a presentation next week. And I have added more two tattoos, one on my arm and another on my back. Now I have six.

—Oh nice. That's great that you are with a dance company now. I am so excited for you.

—Yes, me too. We have great camaraderie among us all. Did I use that word correctly? Camaraderie?

—Nice and yes, you did. Professor Chamberlain is proud of you. Hey, I heard a noise. What was that?

—That was my knees and joints cracking. It happens all the time. A dancer's life. You know, I often do my leg stretches while sitting in a chair or lying on a couch. So, tell me Socrates, how are you? What have you done lately?

—I'm fine. I finally got my SENTRI border crossing card, but I haven't used it yet. No more waiting in line at the border for three hours.

—Wow! That is great.

—I continue to write my book and I have been painting.

—Cool. Besides wanting to be the first person to buy your book, I also want to be the first to buy one of your paintings.

--- I've painted five of them since we last chatted. Here, I'll send photos of them to you now.

---Wow! I just received them. I never realized you were so talented. They are all so different. Do you have a favorite style of painting?

---No, not really. My style is anything. I like what Vincent Van Gogh said---"I paint what I feel and I feel what I paint."

---Nice.

—I was going to do a painting of you, but then I thought that I didn't want a painting of you in my room reminding me that you hate me.

—I never hated you. I was mad. But that feeling goes away easily for me.

—Well, it lasted a couple of months. That's not going away easily.

—True. I need to work on that.

—Yeah, you do. You know, I think my self-punishment for what I did was greater than you not talking to me.

—How so?

—I kept thinking how deceitful I was and that made me lose confidence in myself. I had months to think about that.

—I understand. I still love you the same as always. Just don't be as obsessed with me.

—I will try. I know that I am a lot to put up with. Just don't be afraid to tell me when I get carried away.

—Hahahaha! Sounds good. I will let you know.

—Thanks. Maybe it would help if you changed your perspective of me as obsessed, so you wouldn't get so upset. Try saying to yourself 'When people I know love me, they touch my skin. But when Socrates loves me, he touches my soul.' Hahahaha.

—Oh Socrates, I missed you and your corny comments. There is nobody like you. And you've been so supportive of me. And I admire you as a person in many ways. You got all you have on your own and you became the person you are without help. I want to do that for myself.

—Well, thanks. And that is true to a certain extent. But without the help of others along the way, I never would have achieved half of what I have. I always give credit to others. That is an important life lesson you need to know. We all need a Rafa or Socrates in our lives. It's okay to let others help you. It doesn't mean you are less of a person to do so. Stop worrying about whether others are going to throw their help in your face. Who cares?

—I know. I'm still learning to accept help from others.

—It's a process. Open up your heart a little to not only receive, but to give too.

---Yeah, as you not so subtly mentioned to me before, I'm too selfish. I need to be a better friend.

---Well, at least you recognize it. That's the first step to changing.

---Thanks for your patience with me.

21 FOCUSING ON THE DREAM

Today while we were texting, Rafa and I sent each other the usual exchange of texts, emojis, GIFs and graphics. For fun, mystery and to see if he was paying attention, I included an emoji of an orange.

—Why did you send an orange?

—Wow, you noticed! I like to surprise you every now and then. I live to make you laugh, Mr. Serious.

—You do it very well. I thought you were sending me a hidden message. Hahahaha. You are now Socrates Orange. I am going to think of you every time I buy an orange, from now on. I love oranges.

—*¡Que viva la naranja!* (Long live the orange!)

—Hey Socrates, I have something important to tell you. I have had a boyfriend since December. His name is Enrique. He's 35 years old. Of course, you know I like older guys. He is married to another man though. He lives kind of far from the center of Monterrey, in a ranch house in the direction of Reynosa, but still in the municipality of Monterrey. I go see him and his husband each weekend.

—Hmmm. I'd normally say congratulations, but this is out of the ordinary. But I've also come to expect the unexpected from you.

—Hahahaha. True.

—Do they know you are an escort?

—No, neither of them knows. I know it's kind of weird. I use a second phone only for my escort services, so they don't suspect what I am doing.

—You know, of course, that it is very irresponsible and dishonest of you not to tell him, but it's your life.

Rafa didn't text a response to my comment, so I continued.

---Also, you could easily and unknowingly expose him to HIV or a sexually transmitted disease.

—I haven't gotten any diseases.

—Do you know that for sure? Sexually transmitted diseases can be insidious, passed on without having symptoms. If you truly don't, that's fortunate for you, but obviously you could get one with your next client. I know you advertise condom use and ask your clients to use protection, but that only goes so far. You also can get diseases in many ways, with or without a condom. I'm sure you never use a condom for giving and receiving a blow job, which is a common way to get a disease. Do you offer to rim clients?

—No, I don't.

—Okay. That's one less potential problem to deal with. It's hard to believe that you haven't discreetly gone to a clinic to get a disease taken care of, given all the men you've had sex with. But I'm not even sure you'd admit it to me anyway, which is fine.

—No diseases. I guess I've been lucky so far. We all take risks.

—When I was looking at your online videos, in most I saw condom use, but in others I didn't.

—I always use condoms.

—Hmmm. A few of your videos show otherwise, but I am not going to argue with you. I just hope you stay safe. Even if you haven't been abused or attacked, that risk is always there, so please be careful.

—I always am. At least I try to be. Hey, you know what I was thinking?

—About what?

—About us. You want to know why I didn't want to have a relationship with you? Because you found out who I really was.

—Now, you know that's not true at all. I didn't know you were an escort a year ago when you said let's just be friends.

—True. Well, I was just starting my escorting then and I couldn't do that to you. You are an amazing person. You don't deserve it.

—Yet your current boyfriend or boyfriends do deserve it? Come on. Really? Give me a break. That makes no sense at all. You were lying to protect my feelings. I'd prefer you tell me the truth. You are amazing too, but if you had just said that you aren't attracted to me, it would have saved me from a lot of pain.

---It's wasn't that at all. I just wasn't ready, emotionally, for a boyfriend at that moment. I still wanted you in my life because I did and continue now to feel something special, being around you. And my relationships don't last very long. If ours had ended, I'd never be able to see you again.

---I understand. Well, I'm off to bed. Sweet dreams, handsome.

---Sweet dreams, Mr. Orange.

It was good to be back to normal once more, or what was normal for us. The next day, Rafa texted me with another surprise.

---Good morning. Hey, guess what? I have a surprise for you.

---Good morning. Another one? I don't know if I can take another.

---I want to move to the U.S.

—You are just going to desert what's his name, Enrique, like that?

—I'm not going to stop dreaming about my career just so I can be with a guy.

—Well, you don't have to. You sit and discuss the dreams you both have and work together to support each other.

—Yeah, I know, but Enrique isn't going to leave his husband to move with me or support me traveling. And he isn't into the arts scene.

—Okay. So, he's just a temporary someone to have fun with for the moment?

—I don't know. What I do know is that I want to dance and study acting in the U.S. As I mentioned before, one of my biggest dreams is acting in Hollywood. I don't know when, but I really want to do this. And you'll be my manager. I really want you to be there supporting me. As you know, I want to do many things. I don't say it very often because people laugh at me, but one of my biggest dreams is to be nominated for an Oscar or a Golden Globe award. I don't care if I win. I know it may sound ridiculous. At least I want to try.

—Dream big! You are going to have to work on improving your spoken English. Of course, now lots of non-English films are winning awards.

Right after he told me that, I texted him a recording I made of Rafa winning the Oscars best actor award with crowd noise from a previous Academy Awards show and me announcing him as the winner.

—Wow! Socrates, there is no doubt that you have quite an imagination. Really big. You would be a good master of ceremonies for the Oscars.

—I love to make recordings for positive reinforcement. I find that by listening to recordings repeatedly of anything I'd like to accomplish helps give me the confidence to make it a reality. Thoughts are things. I methodically pound what thoughts I want into my brain.

—You are right. You know what I do sometimes? I read scripts of movies or series as if I was acting. It also helps me with reading English.

—Very cool.

—I want to study hard so I can sound like a native English speaker. I also want to be only a massage therapist, not an escort in the U.S., because the paparazzi will figure out what I do for a living. Hahahaha! The surprises continued as Rafa texted me first the next day. It was the second day in a row he had done so.

—Good morning, Socrates.

—Good morning, Rafa. Another day, another chance to excel. Excel means *sobresalir* in Spanish.

—I was going to ask you.

—I knew you were! I already know what you are thinking sometimes.

—I knew the meaning before, but I forgot.

—My boss says it to me almost every day to motivate me. Sometimes when she says it, it makes me laugh. Sometimes she says it sarcastically. But I've ended up taking it to heart.

—Nice. What are you doing, Socrates?

—I'm eating breakfast before going to the supermarket. I plan to go run and workout. And you?

—I'm heading to a calisthenics gym. I've been going to a regular gym too. At the regular gym, I feel like the guys are looking at me like I'm a weirdo.

—Well, you are a weirdo! Hahahaha. Embrace who you are.

—I know. I don't like to go alone, so I go with a girlfriend. I am a little ashamed of my body. Everyone in the gym is very strong and I am skinny.

—I understand you feel self-conscious. But people at the gym are usually focused on their routines, so try not to worry, okay? Besides, I'm guessing few of them could do the splits, jump as high as you, are as flexible as you or as talented a dancer as you. Be nice to yourself and focus on what you bring to the table.

—Okay, I'll try. And you are right.

—Did you have breakfast, No Bones?

—Yes, I did, Socrates Orange. I had two beef tacos.

—Awesome. The breakfast of champions. Hahahaha.

---Speaking of breakfasts of champions, near the regular gym I go to, there is a bakery behind a shopping center where for 50 pesos, I buy these large *conchas* (sweet bread) that are super delicious. I have them with a cup of coffee. It's my reward for finishing my workout.

---Nice.

---What did you have for breakfast, Socrates?

—I ate oatmeal, blueberries, some nuts, and a banana.

—Very healthy.

—Yeah. You are going to think that I am strange Rafa, but eating the banana made me think of your escort service. Hahahaha.

—Hahahaha.

—I was thinking about how amazing it is that you can get an erection with people you aren't attracted to. I mean, when you aren't using your blue pills.

—Yeah, I guess it's a talent I have. I always say, if you touch it, it will grow. As you well know, it even happens when I am sleeping. Hahahaha.

—Hahaha. I'd love to see it grow again.

—Well, as I said before, Socrates, now that you know my secret, I wouldn't mind letting you do it again.

—Okay, you don't have to say it a third time. Hahahaha. I'll keep it in mind.

—Hey, I decided not to go to the gym after all because it is really windy, with sand blowing all around. I'd have to walk 20 minutes to make it to the bus stop, dealing with all that.

—Really? Just because of a little wind? So, put a jacket and glasses on.

—I do, but it's more than just a little wind. The sand really hurts when it hits you. OMG, it is starting to rain super hard right now. I'm glad I didn't go now.

—Jeez, I forgot about that. Before I visited you, Rafa, I thought okay, the wind is blowing, big deal. But now I remember. On some days, I could feel it in my lungs and there was dust in my nose. You need a spacesuit for protection from the blowing dust and sand. I wish the governor of Nuevo Leon would start a tree planting program to help mitigate that issue. Stay safe.

—True, we need more trees. I'll text you later.

22 MAJOR LIFE CHANGES

Rafa was continuing to move forward with his efforts to achieve his life goals while I was preparing to leave my graphic designer job. I got up out of bed today, figuring it would be another ordinary Friday, my day off from work. But it wasn't going to be an ordinary day. Not by a long shot. After finishing my usual bathroom routine, I changed my clothes, and grabbed my dog Rafie's leash to put it on him to go on our usual morning walk.

---Come on, *mi bebe hermoso* (my beautiful baby), time to go out.

As I walked over to him, I noticed he was panting heavily as he looked up at me.

---Hey Raf, you okay buddy?

After putting the leash on him, Rafie didn't move. Eventually, out of force of habit, and a tug of the leash, he was persuaded to stand up and walk with me out the door and down the elevator to go outside to do his business. He managed to finish the walk, but it was obvious that he was not his normal self. I made an appointment with the pet hospital for the next day, and called my mom and friends, asking them for their advice. Rafie was now over 15 years old, past the estimated limit of life expectancy for the Tibetan Terrier breed. He had slowed down the past several months, so I figured the end could be coming soon. But still, even if you realize the end is near, it's still a shock when it happens. During the rest of the day, Rafie refused to eat his food. It was now dawning on me that this might be one of my last days with him. I spent the evening holding Rafie in my lap and lying next to him on the floor.

The next morning, I bent down to greet and check in on Rafi, but he wouldn't even look me in the eye. Besides the panting, he was now glassy-eyed and disoriented, staring out in the distance. After making several attempts to persuade him to stand up, I decided to carry him outside to see if the fresh air would get him moving. When we were outside, I let him down next to a tree and watched as his feet collapsed out from under him. After sitting there for about five minutes, I realized it was time to take him to see his veterinarian.

After Rafa's vet did some blood work and finished her examination, we talked about what to do next. The tests were normal, but Rafie was not. I described to her the many previous signs that my best friend was slowing down. After a moment of silence, the veterinarian tried to offer some hope.
---We can do more tests if you'd like, Mr. Chamberlain.
---Will the tests lead to taking any actions to help Rafie get better?
---I'm afraid not.

Even though I told myself I would never agree to putting my dog to sleep, I could no longer bear to see Rafie struggling anymore. I took him home to spend one last night with him and say my goodbyes. The following day, we were back at the veterinarian's office. I gave Rafie's vet the okay to prepare the medications for his departure from this world. She said she had another dog to attend to, but if I didn't mind, she would leave me in a waiting room alone with Rafie and come back in 20 minutes or so. I agreed and sat down in the room. When the door opened from the exam room, Rafie immediately barked and ran to me. I thought for a moment that maybe Rafie still had life in him. It was, however, all he could muster. For the next 20 minutes, he walked in circles, stood in a corner, bewildered, his mind somewhere else, as he struggled to breathe. The life in him had ebbed to the point where there was no use in continuing.

When the vet returned, I sat in front of Rafie on the couch while she first administered the sedative, then the medication. I watched as Rafie slowly closed his eyes for the last time. My beloved Rafie had passed. She left me alone with him to say my final goodbye. I laid over my precious ball of fur, weeping uncontrollably for several minutes.

Although it pained me to do so, I managed to stand up. In a dazed stupor, I slowly walked away. A huge part of my life was now gone forever. A hole was in my heart. It seems strange to admit it, but my love for Rafie was stronger than it was for any human. It was the worst day of my life.

When I got home, I collapsed on my bed and cried some more. After wiping away the tears, I began to reminisce about my Rafie. I remembered when I first learned that a lost, scraggly one-year old dog was found on the San Diego Trolley tracks, with gum and urine in his long hair. When our first meeting had been arranged at a dog shelter, I remember Rafie rushing past me to the front yard, rolling happily in the tall grass. It was the beginning of a beautiful relationship.

Over the years, I would observe and enjoy the minute details of him, which included his facial expressions, his galloping-style run to the door to greet me, and the smiles he brought to the faces of people passing by when we went on our daily walks.

I will always remember Rafie relaxing with me at my favorite coffee houses, our trips to the beach, watching me play tennis at the tennis club I belonged to, playing with me and his toys, his excited bark for food, and him jumping on my bed every night for treats. He was often grumpy and growled at me when I was too sweet with him, but then he'd appease me with a lick. His baths and the afterbath combing and unsnarling of his long hair were arduous workouts. Petting and caring for him when he wasn't feeling well brought the nurturing parent out in me. Laying on the floor with him at night when I couldn't sleep brought me peace and relief. Some of my simplest yet most joyful pleasures involved holding him in my lap and him falling asleep with me on my bed.

Later that day, I texted Rafa about Rafie's demise. He sent his condolences via text, saying without even meeting my dog, that he strongly felt my pain. This devastating blow left me numb for a long time afterwards. My life involves intensely living, which often means the lows can be very hard to recover from. For a few weeks, I had no energy to give to anyone, including Rafa. We continued texting, but he could tell I wasn't the same. He tried to keep my spirits up, but no words were going to soothe my pain. I was just doing the bare minimum to keep functioning. Slowly but surely, after a few months had passed, I was more fully back in the game of life. Even though I was still a bit shaken up, I was ready to move on.

Rafa continued to tell me about his dreams in life, but I also wondered whether he would have the time to achieve all the goals he talked about. We were getting along fine, texting away, updating each other on what was happening in each of our lives. Six months after he had failed to qualify to be accepted at the University of Monterrey, he took the university's entrance exam again after studying hard for it. He passed it again. His dream of being accepted to the university finally came true.

—I'm so proud of you, Rafa! You did it again.

—I'll send you a photo of the acceptance letter. Here it is.

—Let's see. It says Rafael Coria Galarín, accepted for the University of Monterrey School of Music and Dance. Wow! Congratulations!

—Thanks.

This time around, Rafa was happy but not as happy as I expected him to be. I wondered why. With him seemingly locked in for at least five years in Monterrey to finish his degree, I envisioned that his dream of dancing in Hollywood would be delayed. Maybe he'll end up living in Monterrey all his life and that's okay too. But whether dancing in Monterrey or Hollywood is the long-range goal, it helps to plan a roadmap to get there. At least I thought so. But long-term planning stressed Rafa out. It didn't, however, stress me out. My slow but steady efforts to prepare myself for the next chapter in my life had given me the courage to finally take action. I decided that working at the same job for many years was over. I texted Rafa the next day to tell him the news.

—I am leaving my job in March. I notified my boss today.

—You're going to leave your job? OMG. Can you do that at your age?

—-Well, I'm deferring my pension until later, but I've done a good enough job at saving money and investing it so that I can quit working now. Well, I want to keep working per se but do my own thing. I want to paint and to write.

—Wow, that's great. I wouldn't know what to do with a lot of free time. How lucky you are.

—Well, it wasn't luck. It was years of hard work and investing my money.

—That's true, Socrates. How exciting.

—I really can't believe it. What would you think if I came to Monterrey and helped you with your dance career?

—No, don't come just for me.

—Well, it wouldn't just be for you. It would also be a chance for me to improve my Spanish, paint and finally finish my book. But perhaps most importantly, moving to Monterrey by myself would remove me from the constant distractions I have in San Diego. I'd like to use my time to transform myself. I want to take the time to study how to be a better person.

—Well, it would be nice to see you more often.

—I was thinking of getting my Mexican permanent residency card and then living half the time in Monterrey and half in San Diego. Maybe you could take care of my apartment when I am in San Diego.

—Sounds good to me.

—Then it's settled. I'll let you know when I begin looking for a place.

A few weeks later, as my last workday came closer, I began to receive more emails from my fellow employees. I texted Rafa to let him know.

—Rafa, I received an email from an employee who said she was lucky to have known me. Wow.

—Very nice.

—You know, often we get so caught up in our work that we don't realize the impact that we've had on others.

---That's so true.

---Another employee said "You're intelligent, talented, witty and your deep compassion for others has touched me. I've become a better person because of you."

—I'm guessing that many people would say the same thing. I'm one of them. Truthfully, I'm glad to have met you. You are a blessing to me. You deserve all the good things. You are my guardian angel.

—Thanks so very much, Rafa. You are very kind. The guardian angel comment was a little over the top, but nonetheless appreciated. I hope I don't cry at my goodbye party.

—Do it if you feel like it.

My last workday and goodbye party finally arrived. It included a nice PowerPoint presentation with many beautiful, loving messages. Afterwards, while still at the party, I texted Rafa.

—After the presentation was over, I said to everyone, okay, this was very nice, but maybe too nice. You should have found a few employees who hated me, to write some comments. You know, to balance it all out. Hahahaha!

—It's gonna be hard to find someone who hates you. I'm happy for you. Truthfully. You deserve it. I'd like to see your happy face. I send you a hug and my best wishes. You are my great friend, my Socrates.

—Thanks. I know it's my own party and these are all my work friends, but I still hate being social at parties. I feel like I am being fake.

—I like being social at parties, but I need alcohol to do it.

—It's a work goodbye party, so no alcohol. You seem to be good at socializing without alcohol too. I've seen all your Instagram videos, joking and laughing with the girls at your dance company.

—Well, it took me a long time to get to that point.

—But you are an escort. How can it be that it takes so long for you to feel comfortable with co-workers, yet you have no problem being intimate with strangers? I don't understand that.

—Well, I don't have to feel comfortable with them. I'm just polite. It's acting.

—True, but for me, acting is work I don't like to do. I know you love to act. I guess you can add your escort work to your resume when searching for an acting job. Hahahaha!

—Hahahaha. No.

I said my goodbyes and drove home one last time, with helium balloons bouncing around in my car and cake icing stains on my work pants. I woke up the next day a free man, with nothing to do. I'd dreamed about this moment for many years. I decided to spend my first day of freedom at a nearby coffee house. I picked up my caramel macchiato and sat down outside at a table, next to some older gentleman telling stories and laughing. I soon was absorbed in their conversation, shooting the breeze with them as they discussed their glory days. It was fun, but I thought, wait. Maybe, at my age, I don't belong with this crowd quite yet.

It was joyful to finally be free from having to work. What I didn't realize until later was that even a joyful big change in my life could come with stress that would take my body and mind a while to get used to. Even in my happiness, the shock of sudden change was ever present. For the next couple of weeks, I still woke up early, as if I was still getting up to go to work. And the same nervous feeling I used to get on Sunday afternoons before going to work on Monday continued to occur for a while. After a few weeks, the adjustment seemed complete. The Sunday afternoon stressful feeling finally went away. A well-earned peace was now mine.

My next goal was to obtain my permanent residency card for Mexico. To get the process rolling, I went to the Mexican consulate in San Diego and provided the necessary paperwork and signed documents. Hours later, the first step was complete---my permanent residency card visa was stamped on my passport. It was only valid for six months, so I headed off to Monterrey to get the actual card. It wasn't an easy process. After an almost all-day visit to a Mexican immigration office, waiting outside for hours in extreme heat, it was finally my turn to enter the office to receive instructions for providing the necessary paperwork. After receiving them, I filled out the paperwork at home and went back for another all-day wait in the heat to deliver the documents. This time, I started to feel a bit dizzy and nauseous from the blistering heat. Just when I was about to give up and come back another day, it was my turn to go into the building. After waiting for a few more hours in an air-conditioned room, I was finally approved for permanent residency as the workday was ending.

The simple act of receiving my card, which amazingly had no expiration date, stirred a special feeling in me. I am and always will be a proud born and raised United States citizen, but first and foremost, I am a human being of the world. A human being who now felt a little more accepted and loved in Mexico, my new second home. There might even be a photo of me now on a wall in the Monterrey immigration office. I accepted the request to take a photo standing with Mexican government immigration office employees while holding my card, since I was one of the first applicants to receive their card on the same day it was approved.

My next goal was to rent a house or an apartment in Monterrey. After a couple of failed attempts, I found a newly built, cozy two-bedroom, one bath, furnished apartment, with a patio. The four-unit duplex had a modern design, with colorful floor tiles and flowers blooming outside the kitchen windowsill. The price of the rent was $14,000 pesos ($700 U.S. dollars) a month. It was located a half a block from the University of Monterrey, which was perfect for Rafa to drop by after class to rest before heading off to his rehearsals with his dance company. After I signed the contract, it was all mine. Rafa and I were both very excited. The apartment had most of the modern conveniences that U.S. homes have. I especially loved the big kitchen, since I love to cook.

The morning after moving in, I got up and decided to take a late morning stroll to get to know my new neighborhood. As I walked down a dilapidated and narrow sidewalk, faint sounds of *banda* music could be heard emanating from a nearby house. I dodged a low-hanging telephone pole wire that was in my way. A few yards further down the street, I carefully balanced myself on a curb as I walked around a large hole in the ground with weeds growing around it. Next, I suddenly sidestepped into the street, frightened by the furious barking of three large dogs reaching their heads through bars of a gated home, nearly biting me. Although very different from the heavy-trafficked cement jungle surrounding my former workplace in San Diego, I couldn't help but think that I traded one obstacle course for another.

After finally reaching the main road, I crossed over to a coffee shop, ordered a coffee and sat down at a small outside table. As I looked across the street at the large park in front of the university, I breathed a sigh of contentment. After I finished my beverage, I continued to explore my neighborhood. A little further down the road I discovered a supermarket, an office supply store, a bank, a pizza restaurant, a barber shop, a money exchange house and an automated teller where I could pay my gas bills. I had everything I needed within walking distance. That was important to me, since I was not fond of driving in Monterrey. Stop signs and other transit signs and rules seemed to be suggestions only. I was also aware that getting into an accident as a foreigner could land me in jail.

Slowly but surely, I began to purchase kitchen and home items to make it feel more like home. I went to an art store to buy canvases and supplies. I planned on creating many paintings, including a couple of Rafa. He was very busy, so we initially only saw each other a few times at the apartment. Later, he began to visit more and more to the point where we now had at least a few hours to spend together each day.

When he came over, I was never sure which version of Rafa would show up. There was the happy, energetic, fun guy who would be playful, silly, dancing and stretching. He'd slap the kitchen countertop hard with his hand or on his thigh to try to startle me. Sometimes he'd be flirty, grabbing at my chest or tickling my feet. Sometimes we'd throw rolled up pieces of paper at each other. Once I filmed him with all the rent money in his hand, as he casually threw it all in the air. It was the fun stuff best friends do.

There was also the tired version of him who ignored me, only wanting to eat and nap. And there was a version of him that was distracted, on his cell phone most of the time, serious and quiet. Infrequently, a few of the versions mixed together. I had to be flexible and intuitive to figure out which Rafa showed up so I could adjust my behavior accordingly. Sometimes, I'd stop and wonder why I did this, but I did it anyway.

The daily routine was that he'd get off from school and arrive at the apartment. He'd text me to open the garage door for him, because he was too lazy to unlock and lock the metal door outside. I would have a meal prepared for us both when he arrived, but first he'd go straight to the bathroom and spend at least a half hour there doing who knows what. I figured he was watching videos, reviewing messages for Rocco, posting his porn videos, and chatting with friends, schoolmates and co-workers. When he came out, he'd be ready to eat.

As the months passed, I became more successful at pleasing his discerning palate. I was constantly washing the dishes because he was always hungry. He preferred noise in the apartment, so he'd turn on the television to the *YouTube* app to watch his favorite programs: *The Simpsons*, *Malcolm in the Middle* and *La Familia Peluche* (The Teddy Bear Family). He'd do this, even though he'd seen every one of these shows dozens of times. Sometimes he'd say the actors' lines before they did. He most enjoyed spending time in his room, sleeping and relaxing. The room had an adjacent patio, where he would sit in one of plastic chairs, smoking his cigarettes, while looking at his phone. Later, I would empty his ashtray, sweep the apartment floor, as well as the dust and stray cigarette ashes off of the patio.

When it came time for Rafa to leave the apartment for his dance rehearsals, I would often accompany him to different public bus stops a few blocks away. Several of the bus stops in Monterrey had signs denoting they were designated stops, but many others didn't. They were stand-alone benches or simply common places where people gathered. There was no bus schedule at any official or non-official bus stop, meaning they might come quickly, take an hour to arrive or even not come at all. When the bus arrival was delayed, it provided us with an opportunity to talk, but Rafa mostly stared at his phone. It made me wonder if he could survive life without a cell phone. Each time we saw the bus arriving, we hugged each other goodbye, and in a caring voice, he often would tell me to take care crossing the busy streets. For most of us, that's a normal, habitual departing comment. Take care. Be careful. But with Rafa, it always seemed strangely out of context. He would be the definition of indifference for a half hour and then suddenly seem genuinely concerned about my welfare. More than a few times, we would be arguing about something or not talking, and then, as I was about to leave, he would change character and remind me to protect myself from the cold. At first, this incongruent behavior confused me. After a while though, I stopped attempting to understand why he acted the way he did and just accepted it as his normal, abnormal self.

As the days turned into weeks, and the weeks turned into months, Rafa's habitual routine stayed the same, but his attitude slowly began to change. To my chagrin, his low-level narcissism was now exhibiting signs of growing. He was showing very little appreciation for what I was doing for him. He had begun to take for granted his whole setup— my catering to his needs, the free use of the apartment, the free food, and my washing of his dishes and clothes. While it was normal to see him drifting off into space, he'd usually come back to earth. Now, it was becoming more common to see him spending longer periods willfully entering a black hole that he himself had created. Today, I woke up and wandered into the living room where I found Rafa seated on the largest of the two couches.

---Good morning, Rafa.

Rafa continued to look at his phone without responding. I repeated the good morning greeting. Still nothing.

---Did you hear me?

---Yes. Is it an obligation to respond?

---No, but it is respectful and courteous to do so. I admire that you like to do things unconventionally. But your lack of attention is causing me to feel unimportant and unappreciated.

---All this, just because I didn't say good morning?

---No, it's not just this time. Lately, you have been in the habit of taking for granted that I allow you to share this apartment without paying rent, food or utilities. Is it really too much to ask of you to show common courtesy?

Rafa looked at me without saying anything, and then went back to look at his phone. After this conversation and a few similar ones where he blithely showed disdain, it became clearer that he was not willing to make much of an effort towards demonstrating basic manners. In other words, he was behaving like a spoiled brat. It made me question whether it was worth the effort to continue to do so much for him, just to have him close to me. By now, Rafa wasn't only receiving free rent and food. I was now helping to pay some of his travel expenses on buses and ride shares. I was bringing him back clothes I had purchased in San Diego. And I paid for his university enrollment.

What did I get in exchange for all of this? Not much in the material sense. He did help me with my Spanish, which I very much appreciated. And he did help me get oriented to where places were in the city during breaks in his schedule. It was also important for me to have someone around who I could trust and depend on.

Having Rafa nearby was also especially helpful in dealing with Monterrey's extreme heat. My young friend was able to adjust, no matter how hot it became. It certainly didn't hurt that he was young, in good shape and had skin pigmentation better able to deal with the weather than mine. A recent example of this was when we decided to spend part of Rafa's summer break from school working out at a small, intimate downtown gym. It was equipped with a few fans and one air conditioning unit that wasn't working well. I seemed to be dealing with the conditions okay until one day after a rather strenuous workout. After stepping outside into 117-degree heat, Rafa walked outside with me like it was just another day. I, on the other hand, immediately felt dizzy and nauseated. I was forced to stop walking after two blocks after nearly collapsing. Rafa helped me make it to an air conditioned 7-11 convenience store, where I was able to recover.

Adjusting one's plans to deal with the extreme heat was just part of life here. I would only go buy groceries very early in morning, because even in the evening, it would still often be over 100 degrees. Another time, after purchasing prescription eyeglasses for Rafa and I at the optometrist office, I decided to accompany him walking to his dance company building. When he pointed out that it was 12 blocks away in high heat, I changed my mind and requested a rideshare to take me home.

Despite my suffering from the high temperatures outside, the warmth between Rafa and I inside my dream world was something I was more than happy to put up with. My dreams evolved from us doing random events together to more of a sexual nature. The dreams would often be very abstract. In one dream, Rafa had two mouths. In another, he'd have penises on different parts of his body. Soon, the dreams were of us having frequent sex.

With Rafa's persona so engulfed in my dream state and absorbed into my psyche, I was better able to put up with his lack of attention in the real world, at least for now. It wasn't lost on me how similar this was to our sleep sex at the Hilton Monterrey Hotel. I was the one aware of what was going on, while he was oblivious to it. Still, being intimate with him in my dreams was my only current option. This morning, I woke up from yet another erotic Rafa dream to find he had arrived at the apartment before his school classes, which had just begun again. He was seated at the kitchen counter, finishing up homework on his old, dilapidated computer. I walked down the hallway, in a post-dream, half asleep state, with a strange but happy smile on my face. As he heard my footsteps, he looked up and caught me staring at him. A perplexed expression appeared on his face.

---What? Why are you looking at me like that, Socrates?

---Sorry, I'm sort of in a zombie state from just waking up.

---Did you sleep well? Judging from the bulge in your workout pants, I would say yes.

I glanced down at my pants to see them holding back an erection.

---Opps. How embarrassing.

---It's okay. It's normal. Hey, guess what? My computer is having issues again. It's so frustrating. It froze again. And I must finish this assignment before I go to class.

---Be patient, Rafa.

A few minutes passed as I prepared my coffee. Rafa then excitedly blurted out.

---Finally! Thank goodness, it's running again.

In my non-dream life, I began to assist Rafa with a few aspects of his dance career. While generally unappreciative of help in his personal life, he showed gratitude when it came to assisting him with his work. The help I provided him included publicizing his dance company performances, paying for, designing and writing his dance career webpage, and developing his resume. I continued helping him when I returned to San Diego. Today, I surprised him on his birthday by sending him an article via email that I wrote in English and translated into Spanish about his life journey to become a dancer. I planned to get it published in Monterrey social media and newspapers.

—What do you think of the article, Rafa?

—Oh my gosh, I just read it. Thank you, Socrates Orange. I almost started to cry. You did an amazing job with both the photo and article. You're still surprising me with your memory. I didn't know you remembered all that about me. All that I went through. Truthfully, I'm very happy to have met you. You are a blessing to me.

—You are welcome, but truthfully, I didn't remember it all. I had to review our text and audio messages. I am proud of it. It showcases who you are. I tried with all my heart to put into words who you are as a person. I love writing, as you know. I also wrote it to inspire you.

—You did!

—Happy birthday, No Bones.

I also wrote up a blurb and published it online to help raise money from the public for Rafa's dance career. The process of picking out a photo of him for this effort proved to be challenging, due to him being a perfectionist. We spent over three hours in search of the perfect photo. His comments after seeing the photos I chose included the following: "It's too blurry. My face doesn't look good. I seem a little drunk in that photo. The flag in the background looks weird. I'm too young in that one. I was sick when you took that photo. I'm blond in that photo. People will think I'm from the U.S. That one is ugly. I want a photo of me with my hair combed and where I am clean shaven. You are choosing the worst ones!" We laughed and had fun with it. But it was still frustrating to deal with someone that picky. I wish I could say this was an aberration in his personality, but it turned out I would have to deal with this side of him many times. A week later, I was back in Monterrey, dealing with his diva-like demands.

---Hey Socrates, I'm heading over to the apartment now.

---Okay, our lunch will be ready when you arrive.

A half an hour later, Rafa still had not arrived. When he finally did, he scowled as he looked at the glass of Coke I had poured for him.

—You should wait until I arrive at the apartment before you pour the Coke. I don't like the water melted from the ice cubes above the Coke.

—Really? You've got to be kidding me, right?

—No.

—Wow, you really are a diva. Maybe worse than me. Coke is mostly made of water. Who cares if there is a little melted water on top? Is it too much for you to stir the water into the Coke?

Rafa sometimes accused me of trying to kill him. This happened once after I offered to add hot salsa to his meal when he was still sick after eating some food at a bar on a trip to Ensenada. Another time, he thought I was planning his funeral when I served him container of cream for his chilaquiles that was a few days passed the 'best by used' date. If I was really trying to kill him, why would I be consuming the cream with him? Of course, it's hard for me to be too harsh on him for his sensitivities since I can be diva-like as well. I guess it takes a diva to know one.

When I wasn't dealing with Rafa's diva side, I was doing more than what he expected of me regarding his career. This included me making lists of possible fellow artists who might be interested in attending his performances, as well as a media list to publicize him. Was I getting paid to do this? No. But we were best friends. It was what best friends do for each other. Well, it's what I do for my best friend. Also, I really didn't give much to charities, so I considered Rafa as my charity. Today, we were texting about his next performance.

—Rafa, I can't wait to see you and *La Terraza* on Friday. I've promoted the upcoming presentation to as many media groups as I could.

—Thanks so much. I've got your ticket. My family will be there too.

—Great. Do you really feel like the character you are portraying is part of you now, with so many rehearsals completed?

—Most definitely.

—How have the last rehearsals gone?

—Very good. It's been a lot to coordinate and memorize with 12 or so people. The choreography is going well, but sometimes our timing is off. There are so many wardrobe changes and so little time to do it.

—Well, at least with contemporary dance, no one has any lines to memorize or forget.

—Yes, but dancing bodies have a language of their own to memorize.

—True.

—It should be fun. It's in two parts, two hours in total. Text you later.

---Good luck.

Friday night finally arrived. I got dressed up, requested a *Didi* ride share and 15 minutes later, I arrived at the *Teatro de la Ciudad de Monterrey* (Monterrey City Theatre). The very large and recently renovated building was located in the heart of the city. After I picked up my ticket, I waited in a long line to get in. I learned earlier that the performance was sold out, all 1,315 seats. I texted Rafa from my seat.

—Are you excited?

—Yes, I am.

—Nervous?

—Nope.

---That's hard to believe. There are so many people here. There's a lot of press here too. I see a couple of camera crews.

Shortly after sitting down, Rafa's family arrived and sat next to me. It was an opportunity for me to finally meet Rafa's mother, Lola. If she was excited to meet me as I was to meet her, she didn't show it. She calmed greeted me and we exchanged a few pleasantries. She ended our chat by saying how immensely proud she was that so many people had come to see su hijo (her son) perform with the rest of *La Terraza*. After brief announcements by a representative of the governor's office of Nuevo Leon and the director of *La Terraza*, Salvador Pérez, the curtain opened for act one of *El Ojo de la Tormenta* (The Eye of the Storm).

Dynamic music immediately reverberated from the speakers, capturing the attention of the onlookers. The ensemble darted out onto the stage, timing mid-air splits and tumbles in rhythm with the music. Flowers began to rain down, setting the stage for a beautiful display of pageantry. As horns and trumpets sounded, the dancers stopped in their tracks, as Rafa's character King Fernando took the stage. He made a regal entrance, wearing a light blue velvet outfit, a gold-colored belt, with hair held up in a bun. After gliding across the stage, he showed off his athleticism and agility with a series of twists, backbends, somersaults and acrobatic movements. As the music slowed, so did Rafa's portrayal of his character. His exquisite, deliberate turns and form seemed effortless. No Bones was living up to his nickname, exuding a flexible grace and elegance that seemed to really be resonating with the audience. Next, a young peasant woman appeared on the stage beside him, circling Rafa in an attempt to court him. This continued on as act one ended.

As act two began, dancers flawlessly exchanged props, waving and deftly throwing them in the air and catching them, as flowers and confetti continued to flutter about. What followed ran the gamut of intrigue, contempt, rapture, melancholy and despair. The final scene was an appropriate ending for such a large undertaking. Rafa, wearing a majestic headdress, watched on as his lover pleaded with him not to abandon her. The performance culminated with her suicide. The large audience leapt to their feet as the curtain closed on the Broadway-worthy performance.

It wasn't only the performance and its multiple wardrobe changes that was breathtakingly beautiful. The special effects were as well. They included large waterfalls, lakes of moving water, large skies and wind-blown white and pink leaves drifting from trees. Birds and even large dragons flew around blue, purple and yellow mountain landscapes. It was indeed an overload of sensorial stimulation, leaving the audience mesmerized throughout most of the evening.

Afterwards, the media interviewed the show's director, Rafa and a few of the other dancers. Rafa proudly posed for pictures with his fellow dancers, friends and family. I texted him when I got home.

—Great show. Oh my gosh, there aren't words to describe the grandness of it all. Salvador must be very proud of the result.

—Yeah, he was. Thanks again for coming and for supporting me. I'm so excited.

---You should be! All that hard work in rehearsals paid off. You slayed it. What a stellar performance. You really did a great job displaying your repertoire of dance moves.

—Thanks. There were mistakes, but we all agreed that it exceeded expectations.

—Yeah, I saw a few mistakes but really, they were hardly noticeable.

—There were moments of improvisation as well, forcing us to change the choreography. I'm not sure if you noticed, but during a wardrobe change, one of my fellow dancers took my outfit. I panicked! But for such a large undertaking, there were bound to be a few mishaps.

—True. But regardless, it was a moment of triumph for you all. I think this moment will be key to building your confidence and hopefully removing some of your doubts about your abilities. I know you've been working on being less reserved on stage. Now you are opening up.

—I think so.

---You must feel like you are a prince, with your chest forward and your eyes looking up!

---You are right.

—This performance was most definitely one of your best. It was an honor to be present to see it.

—Wait until next Saturday, if you can attend. I will interpret and choreograph a two-person performance I'm calling it *Hasta la Muerte* (Until Death). It already has a promoter, so there isn't really much for you to do except enjoy the show.

—Great! I love that you will be the choreographer and a lead dancer. Quite a step up for you. Of course, I'll be there, if only to support you and get your autograph.

—Cool. We are out at a restaurant celebrating with the group now. I'm so exhausted and my feet are sore.

—I'm sure. Enjoy your special moment!

—Thanks, I will.

I was excited to be witnessing Rafa's ascent as a professional dancer. It was indeed a glorious time in his life. When Saturday arrived, I was in the front row at Monterrey's *Teatro de las Bellas Artes* (Fine Arts Theater) to witness the Monterrey Dance Festival. As I looked around, I spotted a few of Rafa's family members and friends. He would be performing with Raymundo Garcia, a young and up-and-coming dancer who had previously been a part of the *La Terraza* dance company. They were scheduled as the final dance performance. As the festival started, I texted Rafa, who was stretching backstage.

---How are you feeling?

---Very nervous.

---Really? You are rarely nervous.

---I know. I think it's because we've only had a few rehearsals. Also, because I choreographed this, I feel more pressure for it to turn out well.

---Relax and take a few deep breaths. You'll be fine.

An hour or so later, it was Rafa and Raymundo's turn to present their 10-minute performance. As they stepped onto the stage before a jampacked crowd, both received a warm response from the audience after their names were announced. Rafa's family excitedly began to chant "Rafa! Rafa!" Rafa ignored them, as he stood stone-faced, already in character, waiting for the music to begin. Both young men wore only jeans, showing off their upper bodies and tattoos on both of their arms. As the music started, Rafa and Raymundo sprang into action with a feigned fight, with each attempting to gain leverage over the other. Their movements and facial expressions demonstrated both anger and defiance. They included pushing and shoving, shows of strength with closed fists, and backward kicks as they flipped over each other. At various stages, their two characters crouched down, measuring up the other. At one point, they circled each other as they leaned forward, while balancing their heads on each other's.

Another impressive dance maneuver occurred after Rafa was pushed to the floor. He leapt back to a standing position, impossible for most of us to do. As the performance continued, both executed several highly technical and artistic maneuvers demonstrating false bravado. Finally, they collapsed to the stage floor, writhing in pain after connecting simultaneous, simulated punches. The audience showered the two young men with thunderous applause. This was what I had been waiting to see, a presentation by Rafa, solely focused on him and another dancer. He didn't disappoint, showing off his myriad talents.

After the show ended, I immediately went searching for Rafa in the dressing room. When I arrived, he was sitting alone, hunched over, sweating profusely. As soon as he spotted me standing among other dancers and their loved ones, he ran over to me and leaped into my arms to hug me.

---Socrates! I'm so happy. I did it!

—Yes, you did!

---What did you think? Be honest.

---I thought you both were incredible. Fantastic.

---Thanks. We were a little off regarding our coordination, but overall, not bad.

---Yeah, I noticed, but overall, it was well done.

—Thanks for sharing this important moment with me in my career.

—Of course. You are my muse. I'm enjoying every moment of your nascent career. I videotaped it all, so if you want to and have time, we can review it later tonight when you stop off at the apartment, before you head off to Enrique's place.

---Sounds good. I'm so happy with how it turned out. I can't believe all the praise I am getting. By the way, what does muse and nascent career mean?

—Muse means a source of inspiration and nascent means your career is beginning to show signs of future potential. I added those words to increase your English vocabulary.

—Okay thanks. I'll meet up with you later.

When Rafa finally arrived at the apartment, we sat down on the patio chairs, popped open a bottle of wine, and celebrated his performance. We critiqued the video of his performance, as we drank, laughed and relaxed.

---How do you do it, Rafa? One great performance after another. I am not worthy! Although it was sort of difficult to believe, watching you portray such a masculine role.

We both laughed.

—What a bitchy thing to say, Socrates Orange. What would be more shocking would be to see you behaving in a masculine way.

—Oh, come on. I'm not that effeminate. And I certainly can't roll my hips like you can.

---Yeah, that's true.

Rafa proceeded to wave his hips at me like a belly dancer, as he pursed his lips with a come-hither, come get me look. I laughed.

---Do not tempt me, you vixen! You know, you probably wouldn't recognize me watching sports. I change my voice completely.

—I suppose you are right, Socrates. How we sound often depends on who we are with or what we are doing.

—Yeah, often gay men are much more effeminate around other gays. At least, that has been my experience.

—True.

—What I don't understand Rafa, is why you find overly macho gays so attractive. And why are you so repulsed by effeminate guys like yourself. It's like you accept the heterosexual male's repudiation of effeminate gays. Why don't you instead judge prospective mates more by their character? It might even save you a lot of wasted time and heartache, right? I suppose though that I shouldn't judge you too harshly, since I have my own issues regarding being drawn to narcissists. We all have our tastes and aren't even sure where they come from. Maybe from our youth?

—Yeah, who knows. There could be multiple levels of issues at play that determine why we like a certain type of guy.

—Yeah. All I know is I am the opposite of you regarding tastes in men. A guy who is overly macho for me disqualifies him from being my love interest. If he is incapable of being loving and caring, as well as being comfortable with showing his effeminate side, it's hard for me to overlook those aspects of his personality. Anyway, I got us off the subject. Congratulations again! A toast to another awesome performance.

As we clanked wine glasses, I decided to change the conversation to Rafa's future dance career.

---You must admit that you are really starting to grow as a dancer. After watching you tonight, it made me wonder about you continuing to dance in Monterrey. I mean, it's been great for you up until this point and of course if you want to stay here and live your entire life working and promoting dance in Monterrey, that would be great too. But I also wonder if it's time for you to step up to another level. I know you are committed to your university studies, but I can't help but feel that you should be dancing with a company that's really worthy of your talent and skillset. A place where there is a higher level of competition and instruction.

---Thanks, but I don't like to compete with others.

---I understand that, but there is a benefit to competition. It can push and inspire you towards learning more complex skills and having higher expectations. Maybe think of it as a friendly competition, if that helps. There is also the possibility that you will eventually become bored performing with dancers who have a lower skillset than you. I remember when I was playing tennis in San Diego and was improving, but I soon reached a point where my game began to stagnate. I started hanging out in Los Angeles with the players over there, where the competition was fiercer. I noticed how more was expected of them and how hard the players worked out. They also received more advanced instruction. I began playing more with them and following their routines, instruction and advice. That's when I began to see a big improvement in my confidence and results.

---I understand what you are saying. I'm just trying to take things one day at a time. I haven't closed my mind to alternatives.

---Okay. I just thought I'd throw it out there.

---Thanks.

In the days that followed, Rafa was still glowing, beaming with contentment about his last performances. But that feeling did not last. He was starting to feel the weight of the expectations of others, including his own. In a moment of candor, he texted me his thoughts.

---Socrates, I sometimes feel that I better I perform, the worse it is because then I have more to lose. The dance community is expecting more of me, which makes me more nervous. I worry that I will disappoint them, as well as myself.

---I think it's natural to be a little scared when your life is changing so fast. I'm not a sports psychologist, so maybe I'm not the best person to talk to about this. But I am here to support you, Rafa. I know when I am nervous, I try to change my perspective. Instead of saying to myself that I'm nervous, I say I'm excited about the opportunity. I tell myself I'm doing this because I enjoy it. That makes me smile and relax.

---I like that. Thanks.

It would, however, take more than a suggestion from me to change Rafa's embedded beliefs. The introverted young dancer, who prized his privacy, started to become annoyed at the increasing demands of his peers and even the local media. His discomfort eventually made its way down to me as his manager. At first, he thought it would be nice for me to help him, but now he started to realize how much a manager is involved with their client, especially now that his star was rising. My continued presence in his life, once embraced, now felt more and more like an intrusion. Still, what he texted me next came as a total surprise.

—Socrates, it bothers me now, more than ever, that more and more people know about my life and about our business. When you loaned me money to pay for enrollment in the university, I found out that you told Maria and Salvador about it. Do you know how embarrassed I felt that people knew that I didn't have money?

—I'm sorry. I guess I should have thought about that before telling them. I wasn't intentionally attempting to embarrass you. And it wasn't like I told the whole world. I told your sister and dance director because I know they worry about you. I wanted them to know that I have your back. That you are okay. They both said they were glad I was supporting you.

—Well, I still don't like it.

—I understand that you don't want others to know that I help you, but on the other hand, I feel like you hide me from people. It's like you prefer my support to be anonymous.

—I'm not hiding you. Well anyway, I decided now that I'm going to make my own decisions about my professional life from now on. We can still be friends like always, but you are no longer needed as my manager.

—What? What does any of this have to do with being your manager? And at least you could have had the courage to tell me this in person, instead of by text. I understand you felt embarrassed, but it wasn't like you not having much money was a secret. It's very common for artists of all types to have sponsors or help from friends. It's often a necessity in the arts community. It's nothing to be ashamed of.

—I know, but you must learn that there are things that you just don't say to others.

—Okay, but you tell me so many private things about yourself. I wish you would tell me what to say and not to say. I hang out with and text your family frequently. It's hard not to say anything about you.

—I'm not saying you can't say anything about me to others. You know I'm a private guy. You are overly involved in my life, and I don't like that. Don't live your life living mine. I don't want you to make me happy. I want you to be happy.

—What you don't seem to understand is that making you happy makes me happy too. If you haven't figured it out by now, helping and serving others is something I love to do. And I'm certainly not living your life. I have my own projects. And you know I am very intense with my close friends and with everything that I do. That shouldn't be a surprise. Maybe you don't like it or understand it, but that is just how I am. I'm not going to apologize for who I am, for giving 100 percent effort in everything that I do.

—Well, you are still too much for me. Like every time I send you a text message, you immediately view it, like you are always waiting for me. But then you won't respond for a half hour. What's up with that?

—Yeah, I admit I'm probably on my phone too much. As for me immediately viewing your texts, what can I say? You are important to me. But the reason I take so long to respond is because I prefer to respond to you in Spanish and I'm not always sure how to say something, so I will look it up or translate it first. I also take my time when you say something that requires a longer or more detailed explanation. I want to word it right, so you don't misunderstand me, because you tend to explode if I don't say it right. Other times I see your messages, but I'm at the supermarket or gym or doing something else. My friends do the same thing. To me, it's not a big deal. Sometimes I see you read my messages and don't respond at all as well. It doesn't bother me like it bothers you.

—Okay. I still feel you are all over me. It is not good to text every day. I hope you understand.

—As you wish.

—You are too obsessed with me.

—Passionate is the word I prefer. Call me obsessed if you want, but that sounds overboard. I'm not stalking you or following you around. As far as texting is concerned, you should know that you aren't the only friend I text with every day. Did you know that? Remember all those comments from fellow employees that I received before I left my job? Those comments weren't for nothing. I actively and passionately worked with them. That is how I live my life.

I paused to let Rafa respond. When he didn't, I continued.

—And you aren't the only person I have done a lot for. For example, in the past, I helped two of my friends get their working papers in the U.S. I paid a lawyer over a period of two years to help one of them. When a good friend of mine went to jail, I sent him money for food and called him most days of the week for several years. I sent him crossword puzzle books with inspiring and funny notes for him to keep his spirits up. Every roommate I've had has paid a smaller amount of rent because they didn't earn enough money in their jobs to pay half, so I agreed to pay more. One friend of mine was dumped by his boyfriend and had nowhere to live so he ended up living with me for two years at a reduced rent. Another friend of mine stayed with me for a week after he fought with his boyfriend. What I'm trying to say here is that I give my all to help good friends. If you paid more attention to me and stopped looking at your phone for a few moments to take the time to get to know who I am, you'd already know all this. You'd know that I'm not always focused on you or only care about you. But since you're so self-absorbed, it seems you actually believe that. Well, you are wrong.

—Well, that's all nice what you've done for others, but I still need a break from you, okay?

—Okay. I know I can't force you to do anything you don't want to. I just wish you weren't making such a big deal out of this. Every time I do something you don't like, it's the end of the world. Is "I forgive you" that difficult for you to say?

---Goodbye, Socrates.

23 ALONE IN MONTERREY, WAIT, MAYBE NOT

I was now mostly alone in Monterrey. Well, at least away from Rafa. Today, I received a surprise text from a longtime friend, Marco, who lives down south in Ciudad Victoria. He was in town visiting his sister. Marco was one of my first roommates in San Diego before he decided to move back home with family. We decided to meet up for lunch at *Los Equipales* artisan restaurant in the downtown area. Once we arrived, we sat down at our table and began to catch up with what each of us was doing with our lives. The subject of who we were hanging out with eventually came up.

—You keep talking about this guy Rafa. Can I ask who he is?

—He's a special friend of mine who is a contemporary dancer. I'm trying to help him in whatever way I can, so he can graduate from the university here.

—A special friend? What does that mean? Are you in love with him?

—Honestly, yes, and he knows that. But he isn't in love with me, so it doesn't matter if I'm in love or not. And on top of it all, he is in love with someone else. I've learned how to be a respectful and caring friend without getting carried away.

—I guess that military father of yours was valuable to you after all. All that discipline he taught you. But come on, tell me the truth. There must be times when you are dying to kiss him or touch him and can't. It must be driving you crazy.

—Yes, a wistful feeling hits me sometimes, but I'm mostly fine. Rafa doesn't say it, but I know he feels my occasional looks of adoration and desire. He doesn't like it, but it's not like I can turn it off or unlike him.

When those feelings come up, I just try to refocus on one of the reasons why I'm here—to help him achieve his goals and be his friend.

—No Socrates. You are here to do what you want, not what he wants. I know you get carried aways sometimes when helping out your loved ones. You need to set some boundaries.

—I am here for both reasons---to do my projects and to help Rafa. I'm not lost in this guy. And I haven't given up on my dreams. If our time together ends, it ends. But I'm enjoying the journey into the unknown parts of his personality. Rafa is difficult for sure. Even unpleasant. He shows a recalcitrant attitude at times, which can be hard to deal with. He sometimes thinks I'm trying to control him when I ask him to compromise on our living arrangement in the apartment. But I'm not. I just want to make sure some of my needs are met, too. Is that too much to ask for?

—No, it's not. Not at all. Because he knows you love him, he's probably using that to his advantage. Is he paying rent or for the food or helping you in any way?

---He pays no rent, food, gas, electricity, or internet. I even wash his clothes, clean up after him and help pay for his transportation.

---Wow. He's got a sweet set up with you, for sure. I hope he appreciates it.

—I suppose he is using me, but I am willingly letting him do it, up to a point. Sometimes I do wish he would say he was more grateful or pay attention to me.

—How long have you known him? Can you trust him?

—We've been friends for a while now. Yes, I trust him completely.

—So, no sex at all?

—None. Well, once.

—Wow. Well, as long as you are happy and aren't deceiving yourself into thinking he will come around to being your boyfriend. Or that this will last forever.

—He's certainly a lot to deal with, but at least until now, I am up to the challenge.

Marco and I went our separate ways after lunch, but our conversation lingered in my mind. Later that evening, I went out on my patio to sip some green tea, with candles lit all around. Adrift in my thoughts, I quietly spent some time pondering whether Rafa was doing me more harm than good.

When I woke up the next day, I put aside any thoughts about Rafa and instead focused on my painting and working out at home and at the gym. A week passed without any contact with my favorite dancer.

I completed two paintings—one of a man drinking coffee in his underwear while contemplating what lay ahead for him and another of an abstract painting. This period without Rafa wasn't easy for me. I saw so many things that I wanted to send him, so many thoughts I wanted to share with him, but I resisted the urge. I wasn't expecting Rafa to text me for a couple of weeks, but it was exactly a week later when he did.

—Hello Socrates. How are you?

—Who is this? Hahaha. I'm fine, thanks.

—I want you to know that this distancing is working. It is not to stop talking. But the fact that we didn't talk made me feel like I wanted to connect with you.

—That's fine. I know you needed a rest from me. Maybe the absence of talking helped you, but it was a tough punishment for me.

—Don't take it in a bad way. It is to make our friendship stronger. It helped me not get bored of you. If we stopped talking, truthfully, I would miss you.

—I guess. They do say absence makes the heart grow fonder.

—I almost wrote you an email, Socrates. I was going to say Socre, but it sounds a little weird to me.

—You? Write me an email? The guy who usually responses with a text message of a word or two? I would need to be seated if I received an email from you, because I'd probably faint.

—Hahahahaha.

—And please call me Socre sometimes. I would love that.

I tried my best to see our friendship from his perspective. We all need breaks from each other. After thinking about it a little longer, I grudgingly admitted that Rafa might be right. That the break was beneficial for our friendship. And maybe he was as tolerant as anyone could be regarding my avalanche of texts.

Despite Rafa reconnecting with me, I was still feeling lonely in my Monterrey apartment. And sometimes sad. It's true Rafa never asked me to move to Monterrey, but he did ask me to be his manager and to do that, I felt that I had to be living in the same city as him. Of course, texting someone and hanging out with someone every day is very different. And surprises were bound to have occurred. For example, I wasn't prepared for Rafa changing his mind so frequently. One day we were planning his future in Los Angeles with me assisting him and the next, I was pushed out of his life as he pursued his career on his own in Monterrey. I guess I should have known the uncertainty of dealing with a young artist in his 20s. He now claimed he never needed a manager since he wasn't yet a professional dancer. Fine, but maybe he should have thought of that before he asked me to be his manager. And technically speaking, he was paid at times to dance and that is considered a professional. I know I could have helped him become a big-time professional dancer. But I guess it wasn't meant to be.

Not being his manager wasn't as much of a blow to me as was being pushed aside as his friend. He was a friend I spent so much time and energy on. A friend I connected with in so many ways. We still texted each other but it had become less frequent. I was feeling more lonely than normal one weekend and texted him about why I was feeling this way.

—Hi Rafa. Good morning. Another weekend here by myself. I especially don't like the weekend evenings because my few other friends here in Monterrey all work or are unavailable. I hear the neighbors enjoying themselves on the weekends and I feel left out of the fun. Being an introvert, I'm not really a partier, but I do sometimes like to get together with a friend or a small group of friends.

A few hours passed without a reply from him, so I kept texting.

—I don't even remember the last time we got together to go out or even stayed home for a night. It doesn't seem fair that your boyfriend usurps all your time on the weekends, the only time you have free. I know that is what you like to do. But every single weekend? I feel sad at times not sharing some fun time with you. I mean, we are best friends. I'd even love to spend a weekend day with you and your family.

After an hour passed without a text response, I finally got a message.

—Hi Socrates. To answer your question, I don't like to go out much and with my busy schedule during the week, I just like to relax over here. And my friends that you know, well, I only see one at school and with the other, it has been months since I have seen her. Regarding my family, I don't get along with them very well. I have already spoken about all of this with you. I thought I was clear about what I prefer to do.

—Yes, I know. But there are 52 weekends in a year, and I don't get to spend even one of them with you. I had a boyfriend years ago and we frequently spent time with other friends as well. Why can't we do that?

—I am not that way. Don't expect everyone to be like you want them to be. And you know my boyfriend. He doesn't like you. Honestly, he doesn't really like any of my friends. He is jealous of you, and you wouldn't get along with him anyway.

—I don't expect that everyone is like me, but I think what you are doing is very uncommon and extreme. I just feel left out and sad.

—Socrates, I care about you a lot, but I don't like people demanding my time, like it was an obligation. Nobody does that to me. Nobody.

—Okay, now you are exaggerating what I asked you. I'm not obligating you to do anything. But I know you well and how your mind works. Anyone requesting you to change your routine is met with harsh words. You enjoy being aloof. Of course, I never want you to do anything you don't want to do. I was hoping that you would want to hang out with me, not as an obligation. Anyway, I was only asking you. I can ask you, right?

—Yes, of course.

A day and a half went by sans communication between us. I had nothing to do, so began to read about telepathy, the ability to transmit words, emotions or images to someone else's mind. For fun, I decided to see if I could send Rafa messages while I was away from him. To best do this, I follow the suggestions I read about. I first meditated to calm myself. Next, I visualized Rafa in front of me, using a recent photo of him. I imagined sending messages via a tube connected to each of our heads. I made sure I sent the messages with as much emotional intensity as possible. I can't say for sure if the experiment worked or not, but instead of mostly ignoring me like he usually did on the weekends, Rafa texted me without texting him first. I was always shocked when he did that. He was making a small concession to me.

—Hi Socrates. How is your Sunday going?

—Everything is fine. I was reading and doing an at home workout. By the way, I'm sorry about the other night. I have moments of desperation about being alone. I'm fine now. What are you up to?

—I'm doing homework and preparing for classes this weekend. And yes, I know. Don't worry. I understand how you feel.

---By the way, I noticed that you added a new profile and photos on your escort website. You are now Lu, not Rocco?

---Yeah. I'm testing it out to see if it brings me more clients.

---Good luck with that.

---Thanks.

While Rafie wasn't going to change his routine, at least he knew how I felt. And who knows? Maybe somewhere down the line, he will soften his stance and concede some time for me. But I understood him too. He had a crazy busy schedule. Because of that, friends were a low priority.

Now that I had more free time on my hands, I decided to travel back to San Diego for a few weeks. Before I left, Rafa mentioned that he would be coming over to the apartment in a few days to wash some of his clothes. I asked him if I needed to leave him instructions on how to use the washer and dryer. He acted like it was a stupid question.

—I know how to use a washer and dryer.

—Are you sure? There are a lot of options and instructions about its operation that took me a while to learn.

—I'm fine.

After a few days back at my condominium in San Diego, I woke up one morning to find 25 texts from Rafa. Turns out he got trapped out on the patio. After he went out to smoke a cigarette, the sliding glass door handle unexpectedly fell and locked him out when he closed it. He was calling me all night to get me to call the manager, but I had my phone on vibrate instead of sound. He ended up sitting out on the patio floor the entire night and early morning, until he heard the upstairs neighbor get up. After yelling out for help, the neighbor was able to unlock the door and Rafa was set free. He ended up missing a day of school because of it. Later he texted me again, asking me to call him, so I did.

—*Hola* (Hi) Rafa. How can I help you?

—Promise not to laugh at me, okay? I'm embarrassed to ask you something. How does the washer work?

I laughed anyway.

—I knew it!

—My clothes are locked in the washer.

—You must hold down on the start button for a couple of seconds to manually unlock it.

—Thank you!

—Tonight, I will have my phone next to my bed, with the ringer on, ready for any additional emergencies you might have.

—I will be sleeping at my mom's place tonight, but thanks anyway, Socrates.

—Again, I'm sorry about you getting locked out on the patio. I'll talk to the manager about it later. It was your fault anyway for wanting to smoke a cigarette.

—I slept most of the day with your blanket on the couch.

Rafa texted me a few days later. I asked him how his rehearsals were going.

—They are going well, thanks. My back is sore due to so many contortions.

—Yeah, right, your rehearsals. Maybe stop trying to bend over backwards to please your clients. Hahahaha.

—Hahahaha. No, it was because of the rehearsal. You know what is helping me with the pain? Your bed. Last night, I slept in two beds. At first, I was on my bed, but then I went to your room where less light enters the room. Your bed is also more comfortable and supportive for my back. I love your couch too.

—I'm surprised that you were at the apartment again.

—I had a tough day and I wanted to be alone.

—Well, I'm glad you are using the apartment, Rafa. That's one reason why I got it. It's a place for you to recuperate from work and school.

—I'm beginning to feel more and more like it's my place too.

—Hey, I read that the heat is almost 50 degrees Celsius (122 degrees Fahrenheit) over there right now. Take care. I also read that air conditioning is required to be working on all Monterrey buses or they will be fined.

—Hahahahaha. That is never going to happen. We just sweat.

—That is so sad. And inhumane.

—Each human adapts to his surroundings to survive.

—True, but that isn't to say you should be satisfied with less, especially regarding life-threatening heat. No one adapts to that.

—I'll text you later, okay, Socre?

—Okay, enjoy your evening.

After a few weeks, I made my way back to an extremely hot Monterrey. The apartment was a mess, with empty wine bottles all over the place, dirty dishes, cigarette butts and ashes on the patio, a dirty bathroom and food stains on the floor. I texted Rafa.

—Hey, I'm back in Monterrey. How's it going?

—Great. How was your trip over?

—Well, this time I took the bus from Tijuana to Monterrey to experience it. I thought I would be scared traveling through the *Rumorosa* (mountainous region separating Mexicali from Tecate and Tijuana), but it wasn't that bad at all. One funny thing happened a few kilometers into the trip. The military stopped the bus to check our bags. There were only four of us on the bus. One of the military guys was assigned to write down our names. I told him mine twice and he didn't understand what I said. The bus driver was standing next to me and said just put down Francisco Chavez. So that is what he did! Hahahaha.

---That is funny.

---The bus was luxurious, with curtains, plenty of leg room and a screen and headphones in front of every seat to listen to music or watch videos. Before boarding, a woman gave out water and snacks free of charge.

—Glad you had a nice trip. How was your time in San Diego?

—It was kind of cold for me. When I arrived, a friend told me it's been very hot in San Diego, and I told her I need a sweater. Hahaha.

—Hahahaha. Yes, without a doubt, Monterey will change your perspective of what is hot.

—By the way, you left the apartment a mess, Rafa. That isn't very responsible of you. The apartment should look just like it did when I left it.

—And what if I don't? What are you going to do?

—Just forget it. Among the mess, I found several empty wine bottles. First you started collecting insect repellent cans. And now wine bottles. Your idiosyncrasies never fail to amaze me.

—Hahahahaha. You made me laugh. Really. And it hurts to laugh for me because I've been sick. I'll be going to my rehearsal later, but afterwards, I'll try to come by later to see you. I've been wanting to see you.

—Okay, don't overdo it at the rehearsal.

24 RAFA'S BREAKDOWN

As I spent more time living in Monterrey, I also began to spend time with Rafa's family. They became people I could trust, and I also enjoyed the laughs and comradery. Today was one of those days. It was another hot summer day as I climbed into the Didi ride share. Glancing at my phone, it said 110 degrees Fahrenheit. I texted Rafa.

—Hey, I'm in a Didi now, heading over to your mom's house for a family get together. I'm not happy with this ride. The Didi has no seat belts or air conditioning. I feel like I'm in a sauna. The wind is blowing dust into the vehicle. When I pointed all this out to the driver, he didn't seem to care at all.

—Yes, it should have seat belts. Regarding the air conditioning, you should be fine as long as you keep the car window open. I'm used to it, but I know you aren't.

—Okay, will do. The driver asked me why a gringo like me is going to this poor neighborhood so far away. I told him that I like to suffer. Hahahaha.

—Hahahaha. I'm at the store buying soap.

I texted Rafa when I finally arrived at his mom's house.

—Lola is making some pinto bean and bacon soup while I'm out here in the front yard. I'm still sweating from being in that hot taxi. We almost crashed because the driver was looking at his cellphone. A truck driver attempted to change into the lane we were in and almost hit us. I yelled out and it got the driver's attention. I am not happy about almost crashing without seatbelts. I feel lucky to be alive.

—Wow. How horrible.

—I seem to be calming down now. I was just a little shaken. It was a large semi-truck. Hey, I always get confused about what a semi-truck is called, what a regular truck is called and what a pickup and van are called in Spanish.

—Don't worry, Socrates. No one calls them by their official names. I get confused and just call them all *troques*. A semi-truck is a *trailer*, while a regular truck or pickup truck is called a *troque*. A van is called a *camioneta*, but just to confuse you more, in Mexico City, a *camioneta* is often translated as a pickup truck.

—Okay, thanks.

I put down my phone as Rafa's mom came out with our soups and sat down next to me. We began eating them on a wobbly wooden bench while seated on makeshift wooden chairs. Rafa's dogs were running around the yard, chasing each other, as the cats tried to stay out of the way. Lillie, the largest of Rafa's dogs and my favorite, jumped up and tried to lick me. Lola spoke no English, so our conversation was in Spanish. We began talking about our lives, as well as silly things. At one point, she had me laughing so hard that I almost forgot about the hot wind that was blowing up swirling dust tornados around us.

Lola was a robust, beautiful woman, very calm, not well educated in the traditional sense, but very smart in the street sense. She was a hard, honest worker who had taught Rafa well. Well, okay, maybe she screwed up on a few parts of his character, but my guess is those are all on him. Anway, I felt a special bond with her. She drank too much beer for my taste, and like Rafa, wasn't easy to get to know. But once we became friends, she and I were like brother and sister. The more time I spent with Lola, the more I saw where Rafa got some of his attitude too. I saw lots of similarities between Lola and Rafa. They often used the same phrases and tone of voice. Sometimes we don't like to admit it, but who we are is greatly influenced by our parents. Sometimes it made me cringe when I realized I was talking like my mother. This afternoon, she was attempting to fill me in on some details about her son so I could better understand why Rafa is like he is.

—*Le amo a mi hijo mucho. Sin embargo, es un hijo especial.* (I love my son very much. He is, however, a unique son.)

—*Sí, a veces demasiado especial.* (Sometimes too unique.)

We both laughed at the same time after I said that.

—*Quiero que sepas, Socrates, que cualquier amigo de mi hijo es mi amigo.* (I want you to know, Socrates, any friend of my son is my friend.)

—*Awww...gracias.* (Awww…thanks.)

—*Gracias por todo el apoyo que le has proporcionado. Tal vez, no te lo dice mucho, pero debes saber que lo aprecia.* (Thanks for all the support that you've provided him. He may not say it to you much, but you should know he appreciates it.)

—*De nada. Sabe usted que le quiero mucho.* (You are welcome. You know that I love him a lot.)

Later, Rafa's sister Isabel arrived with her husband Carlos and their two daughters to join in the fun. We all drank, laughed and danced into the evening. After a few drinks, I surprised them all by playfully saying a few of my favorite Spanish cuss words. When they used them in conversation, hardly anyone gave it much attention, but when a gringo like me said the same thing, they'd all bend over in laughter. The fun eventually came to an end, and I took a late-night taxi ride back to my apartment. The next day, Rafa texted me, saying he still wasn't feeling well.

—Hey, I wanted to tell you that I've been depressed lately because Lillie is sick. And my feet hurt from last night's rehearsal. And I have no money.

—Oh no. Sometimes when it rains, it pours. That is an expression in English meaning that sometimes when bad things happen, they all seem to happen at once. And I'm sorry about Lillie. I love her. She didn't look that bad when I was playing with her yesterday.

—Yeah, well, despite her appearance, she isn't well. You know that she's *mi gorda* (my fat one), the one I tell all my problems to. Anyway, I had 8,000 pesos in my piggy bank, but I spent most of that money on Lillie's medicine and veterinary care. I also had to pay for house bills, including for the air conditioning. Now, I have no savings. I always save money, but emergencies and other needs always seem to happen and then I must spend it.

—I told you that I can send you more money, Rafa.

—I know and I thank you, but I don't want you to pay for all my issues.

—*A veces te gusta la mala vida, ¿no?* (You like a life of suffering sometimes, right?)

—I know. It's just that I don't like to depend on others even though sometimes I need their help. But yeah, okay, I will accept your kind offer to pay for my dog's medical bills, but only because my dog is so important to me.

—I already knew how you felt. The other day, I read what you wrote for your English class. "Americans give me money for my education, but I feel nervous about that, asking them to bail me out."

---You read that?

---Yes, your notebook was lying open on the kitchen counter. You also wrote that Americans are uptight. You were talking about me obviously. Anyway, it wasn't anything I didn't know before. I always keep telling you that we all depend on each other, but you don't seem to understand that. That is the way life is. None of us would be alive without other people. Like you, I prefer to be as independent as I can, and I have set up my life to be so, but there are always limits to that. For example, if the electricity goes out right now and the grocery stores close, we all would need the help of each other around us. If my air conditioning stops working, I can't fix it myself.

—That is true.

—The money I would be giving you isn't for you anyway, if you want to think of it that way. And it would help you save your money for other necessary expenses.

—Okay, thanks again, Socrates.

—I know how stressful it can be when your dog is sick. When Rafie didn't feel good, I became quiet and just wanted to be close to *mi bebe hermoso* (my beautiful baby). Anyway, don't worry about responding to my texts. Just read them when you have a moment and respond when you feel able to.

—Okay. I haven't responded because I don't feel good. I feel pressured. I'm not thinking clearly, so I'm taking medicine to sleep.

—Oh my gosh, it must be serious. You never have sleeping problems.

—Last night, I suffered a nervous breakdown in the middle of a dance rehearsal at *La Casa de la Cultura* (House of Culture). I couldn't deal with it anymore and I started to cry.

—Oh no. That must have been super embarrassing, especially since you don't like to show your emotions in front of others.

—Yes, it was. I'm going to take more pills. My head hurts.

—Rafa, do you want me to call you to talk about it?

—No, not yet anyway. I don't want to think about it.

—Well, I'm here if you need me.

—I know. Thanks.

—Maybe consider taking a walk in your neighborhood. Distract yourself in a healthy way. Listen to your favorite music. When I'm in San Diego and need to clear my mind, I like to go to the beach and smell the ocean air.

—I wish there was a beach here.

—Just being outside and walking around sometimes is helpful. What about going to see a psychologist?

—Hmmm, I've never seen one.

—What's specifically wrong with Lillie?

—Her uterus has been bleeding.

Rafa took my advice and decided to walk for a few hours. As he walked home, he texted me.

—Do you have time to talk? I need to tell you the reasons I broke down yesterday.

—Yes, I do.

—Okay, Socrates, let me put on my sandals first.

We spoke for an hour. I tried my best to be a good listener and be empathetic towards his problems. He had a laundry list of stressors he was dealing with. Besides his dog's health issues, he also had a fight with his boyfriend, was worried about paying bills and family issues. After our talk was over, I texted him.

—It was nice talking to you. I hope it helped.

—Yes, it really did. Thank you, Socrates.

—I'm happy to help.

—You know Socre, I should focus on what I do have. I don't have much money, but I have enough food. I have what I need, so I can't complain. There are people who spend days without eating. There are children here who leave school to go sell candy in the heat of summer to help their parents. I've learned that I don't need expensive things to be happy. I was taught that as a child. But of course, I should ask more from life. But for now, I need to focus on my priorities. For example, I need to buy a new cell phone, but I haven't because I have other more important priorities.

—That's a good point. I'm glad that the walk helped you clear your head a little. And changing one's perspective in a positive way is always helpful in dealing with life's important issues.

—Yes, you are totally right.

—Maybe see this moment in time as a low point where you turned things around for yourself.

—Good idea. Unfortunately, here in Latin America, many people don't fight to improve their lives. Life's problems are too much for them and they give up. They become conformists and believe where they are in life is fine, but then they spend their lives complaining. They are too lazy to fight for their dreams. I learned from my father. He always had an entrepreneur's mindset.

—I have a lot of empathy for your fellow Mexicans, Rafa. Life here in Monterrey and in many parts of the country can be exasperating sometimes. But, yes, if it helps you, use your dad's memory to inspire you.

25 LILLIE'S PASSING AND A MASSAGE

few weeks passed and Lillie wasn't getting any better. The medications didn't seem to stop her bleeding, but the veterinarian wanted to give them more time to work before doing any type of surgery. Today, Rafa's exasperation over Lillie's lack of progress reached a tipping point. We were at his mom's house when he suddenly began to scream at and violently shake his dog for not wanting to take her medications.

---*¡Tómalo!* (Take it!)

---Hey, Rafa, stop it. I know you are frustrated and angry about Lillie not getting well, but don't take it out on her, please.

---She needs to take her medication. *Pinchi gorda.* (Fucking fat dog.)

---Calm down. Why don't you take a break and try again in a few minutes?

Later, after Rafa had calmed down, he tried again and this time, Lillie swallowed her medication. We decided to stay at his house and spend the rest of the afternoon and evening hanging out in his bedroom. Laying together in his bed among piles of clothes, we watched cartoons and played with his cats. After a few hours passed, it was getting late, and we still hadn't had any dinner, so we decided to walk down the street to a hotdog and taco stand in front of a neighbor's house.

When we arrived, my mouth immediately began to water. The air around the stand was permeated with the smell of sizzling meats, chiles and onions frying in a pair of vats. Various salsas, chopped cilantro, radishes, carrots soaked in vinegar and lime wedges sat out in small containers. Rafa and I looked on as the jovial cook was busy flipping over pieces of meat, all the while conversing and laughing with his customers. Juices were splatting onto his apron, adding to the abstract painting of grease and food stains on the garment. At his side, his wife heated up the freshly made corn tortillas on a griddle and prepared the tacos and hotdogs.

While we placed our order, seemingly out of nowhere, Rafa morphed into a version of himself that I barely recognized. Just a few minutes before in his bedroom, Rafa was conversing with me in clear and proper Spanish. Now, as Rafa stood with me and his neighbors, he was using a radically different Spanish street vernacular and inflection. His demeanor became more assertive. The introverted Rafa told jokes to the other customers. Despite trying hard, I couldn't understand even one of them.

I guess I shouldn't have been too surprised, since we all speak differently, according to who we are hanging around with. I knew this was due, in part, to our desire to make others feel more comfortable or to hide our true selves in order to be accepted by our peers. I could see now that Rafa had a great talent for easily switching gears. I imagined how useful this talent might be for his future acting career. After we filled up on tacos, Rafa invited me to stay the night at his place. We took off the next morning and went back to the apartment.

A few days later, I was invited to spend another Saturday with Rafa's family, while he was with his boyfriends, the married couple. I texted Rafa from his mom's house.

—Hey, I'm here with Lillie and she looks very sick. Despite being disoriented, she came over to me and we spent a half hour hanging out together. She's in the side yard now, resting. I think you should come over right away. Your mom thinks Lillie is close to dying and I think so too.

—*Mi gorda* (My fat one) is just dehydrated. My mom exaggerates things.

—Well, I don't think she is this time, Rafa.

I sent a video of Lillie to show him the state she was in, but still he refused to come over. While I sat with his family and friends, a daughter of one of the friends asked why I didn't look happy. Lola answered for me.

——*Está triste porque el perro anda mal.* (He's sad because the dog isn't well.)

The rest of the family didn't seem too concerned about Lillie. They partied as if nothing was wrong. It wasn't a surprise when Rafa texted me on Monday, saying his Lillie, the stray Rafa had taken in a year and a half ago, had died early Sunday morning, a few hours after I had left. I texted him back immediately.

—I'm so sorry. She was such a beautiful and sweet dog.

—Thank you. I really mean it. I'm obviously not happy right now and need to be alone. If I don't answer your text messages, don't feel bad.

—I understand. I love you, Rafa, I send you lots of hugs. I was lucky to be able to say goodbye to her on Saturday.

—I didn't get a chance to say goodbye. That is why I am so depressed. As you know, I told Lillie so many things that I couldn't say to others.

—I can imagine. But Rafa, you were often away from her living your life. You must be able to live your life too, but maybe because of that, you shouldn't have accepted the responsibility of being a dog owner. Of course, without your help, Lillie could have starved on the street, too. Try focusing on the fun times and how you made her life more enjoyable.

What shocked me was his mother's response to the death of Lillie. Not only did Lola wait until Monday to tell Rafa that Lillie had died, but she also put the dog's carcass into a bag and threw her into an empty lot. It was upsetting to me that she denied Rafa the opportunity to formally bury Lillie, so he could say goodbye to her. She was undoubtedly upset that he frequently left the dog for her to take care of. I left Rafa to be alone with his thoughts for a few days before texting him again.

—Hey's what's up? Feeling any better?

—Yes, I'm okay. I'll be coming over soon.

After he arrived, we talked about Lillie a little more, but he appeared to want to move on or at least not discuss it. He walked over to the refrigerator, where there was a list taped to it with the total debt Rafa owed me. He looked at the list and then made me a surprising offer.

---Hey, to pay down what I owe you, how about me giving you a massage?

---Okay, sounds good to me.

After the initial shock of what he said passed, I went to my room. I nervously removed my clothes, put on a jockstrap, and laid down on my back on my bed. Rafa walked in, took off his shirt and began to squirt the massage oil on his hands.

—Socrates, I only give massages to guys lying on their stomachs.

—Well, I'm not one of your clients. I want a massage on the front and back.

—I don't know how to do a massage on the front.

—Really? Just start rubbing me. 1 will instruct you how to do it.

—Well, okay. As you wish, your majesty.

—Finally, you addressed me correctly.

The massage began with a light touch.

—Can you please rub me harder, Rafa? A little more aggressively.

—Do you like it rough?

—Yes, I do. Pull my fucking hair. Oh, maybe not. My hair is too short to pull.

—Okay. Instead of pulling your hair, I will put lice and ticks in it.

As Rafa massaged me harder, I groaned a little.

—That's better, Rafa. I'm enjoying this.

—I can tell.

—I will try not to get a hard on.

—Thank you.

—I will try to imagine my grandmother so I don't get hard, but I can't promise anything.

—No sex. Anyway, you already sucked my cock last year.

—Yes. Maybe you forgot, but I did more than that.

—Oh. Well, as I said before, I wouldn't mind you doing it again sometime.

---Okay, I'll put sleep sex down on my calendar for next week.

We both laughed.

Obviously, I felt good being touched by Rafa. I was enjoying the stress being rubbed out of my body. He did get me excited but the tight pouch of the jockstrap holding my "package" prevented it from growing too big and turning it into sex. As the massage was ending, Rafa slapped my butt a few times.

—Thanks, Rafa. I especially liked the spanking at the end.

—I could see that you were getting excited.

—Yeah, the thinking of my grandma idea wasn't working too well. Not sure why, but you always excite me, even when all you do is touch or hug me.

I showered and then we hung out in the living room, watching videos on our phones and chatting occasionally. While Rafa looked at his phone, he was doing seated leg stretches. Then he made one of his typical, out of the blue suggestions.

---You know what, Socrates? I want to do a photo session in the apartment, with your help. I was thinking about buying a large black cloth to tape on the wall. I want to use it as a background while I pose naked, completely covered in body paint. I want you to take photos of me as an erotic, demonic figure. What do you think?

---Ooooh. I say let's go for it.

---Great.

---I wouldn't mind joining you, Rafa, if I could wear a mask.

---Hmmm…maybe. But then who would take the photos?

---True.

—We can plan it out later. What videos are you watching, Socre?

—*The Big Bang Theory*. They make me laugh so much.

—Hey, can you guess which one of the characters I'd like to date?

—Let's see. Hmm…Leonard?

—No.

—Don't tell me Sheldon? Jim Parsons?

—Yes. I wonder if he'd go out with me?

—Well, number one, he's married. Although apparently that isn't a problem for you, I imagine for him, it is. And number two, you are a prostitute.

—Yeah, I suppose. Hey, guess what?

—What?

—I'm going to shave my head soon.

—Really? You mean like when you were a Hare Krishna?

—I was a Jehova's Witness, *pendejo* (stupid). I still have my suit and ties that I wore. I have many ties.

—¿*Pendejo*? Awww…You called me stupid. That must mean we are getting closer.

We both laughed. I continued.

---I'd love to see you dressed up like that again someday. After the erotic demon photos, let's take some formal photos of you all dressed up.

---Sounds good.

Later, after Rafa left the apartment to his boyfriend's house, I had an urge to text Rafa, but I held off, remembering his request to stop my relentless and often superfluous texting. Despite his plea, I was at times unsuccessful at restraining myself, but I was getting better. I also needed to take into account that he undoubtedly had other friends texting him.

Later the next afternoon, Rafa texted me, saying that he had injured himself. Drama seemed to follow the young man everywhere he went, like a tenacious pit bull biting on his pant leg. No matter how hard he tried to shake it off, he could never quite do it.

—Socrates, I have suffered a slight muscle tear in my leg.

—Oh no. Does it hurt much?

—Only when I do certain movements.

—Did you cry?

—Yes, I cried a lot last night.
—Really? How did it happen? Due to another acrobatic sex move? Hahahaha.
—Hahahaha. No, silly. It was when I was dancing at the university.
—Well, no need to panic. Ice it, rest up for a few days and see how it responds to that. You seem to recover quickly from whatever happens to you.
—True. Thanks for always being my positive, supportive friend.
—Of course. What would you do without me? Hahahaha.
When Rafa didn't respond, I texted him again.
—You were supposed to respond by saying I would be lost without you. Let's start again. What would you do without me?
—I would be lost without you. I'd probably be sleeping on the sidewalk. Hahahaha.
—You'd be a prostitute standing in a sleazy part of downtown, asking for men to take you to their house.
—No, I wouldn't. I'd rather die from hunger.
—Changing the subject, hey, guess what? They are replacing the bathroom mirror in the apartment with a new one.
—Nice. Socrates, can you do me a favor and save the old mirror? I'd like to take it to my mom's house if they are going to throw it away. As you know, there is just a small piece of a mirror in the bathroom.
---Okay, hold on.
A few minutes passed.
---I just asked and the good news is yes, they saved it, and your mom can have it.
—Thank you so much!
—Anything for my Rafael. Now you can look at yourself all day like you've always wanted to.
—Hahahaha!
—Eventually everything I have will be yours. Hahahaha.
—Your bed also?
—Greedy! Hahahaha.
—It's just that your bed is great, Socre. So comfortable. It's almost like the Hilton Monterrey Hotel bed.
—You've said that before. And yes, I loved that hotel's bed too. I'll keep you in mind.

26 ANOTHER UNIVERSITY DETOUR

As I woke up today, I checked my phone and saw Rafa had changed his WhatsApp profile photo to a pensive, rather depressing graphic. It was common for him to post cryptic or sarcastic messages and graphics. He had said they were just jokes that didn't pertain to him, but more often than not, they did. The message he most often would attempt to convey was that he is depressed or sad, but instead of directly telling his friends, he would post messages as a riddle for us to solve.

—Hi Rafa. What's up with *The Simpsons* Millhouse graphic contemplating life on top of a jungle gym?

—It reflects how I feel right now. I learned that very few students paid their enrollment fees for the dance school at the university, so they might close it. They are probably going to return my money.

—Oh no. I can't believe it. What does it take for you to attend that damn university?! They are really putting you through the wringer. That means they are really making you suffer.

—I know. I was feeling upset yesterday, thinking about all this.

—You've really made such a great effort to get this far. You passed the entrance exam, only to be told that you wouldn't be accepted because the university wouldn't wait for you to obtain your high school equivalency certificate, which was delayed. Then you pass it again, only to be told this.

—I told Salvador that if they close the school, I'm not going to try to enroll again. I feel that everything was in vain. Oh well. I guess I'll try to study something else, somewhere else. Maybe computer science.

—What about applying for acting school?

—There is no acting school at this university. If there was, I would need to take the entrance exam again to be able to apply for it.

—What? That is crazy. In the U.S., once you are accepted into a university, you can major in anything. I love Mexico so much, but sometimes it's confounding. It doesn't seem fair.

—I know.

—I am upset for you.

—I was upset. Now I am just starving.

—Okay, well go eat something. I'm so sorry.

After a month had passed, there was some good news for Rafa. The dance school was successfully started. He was finally a University of Monterrey student. A few months into the school year, he said he was doing well in his classes. Meanwhile, I was trying to meet some new friends and get to know the city. One weekend evening, I texted Rafa after a long walk around my neighborhood.

—Rafa, I have hardly seen any gringos here in Monterrey since I moved here. I suppose no one is as crazy as me.

—Totally.

—I'm trying to figure out something to do. What do you do on the weekends with your boyfriend?

—We talk, laugh, kiss, have sex, eat, sleep and then sex again. Although we really don't have sex much anymore. It seems strange for me to say, being an escort, but I often prefer to watch others have sex. Although, I rarely, if ever, get to do that in person.

—Your routine sounds kind of robotic.

—Hey, I want to ask you something. Someone posted a fake TikTok account pretending to be me. Did you do it?

—No. I don't even have a TikTok account. Gee, I thought I was the only one stalking you. I wonder who my competition is. Hahahaha. I know you don't trust me anymore after the *Grindr* thing.

—It was only a question, Socrates.

—It has happened to me too. Someone used my Facebook account once to post naked photos of people, so I had to apologize to my friends. I was so embarrassed. I hope you reported it.

—I did, thanks.

—Hey, Rafa, I wanted to tell you not to come to the apartment for a few days. I got sick from something, and it hit me hard. And one of my eyes got infected.

—Wow, I've never met someone so delicate as you.

—Well, maybe take a look in the mirror. Hahaha!

—You're right. And guess what? I'm sick too. I have a fever, a tonsil infection, and a cough. I've been in bed since yesterday.

—Wow, you must really be sick if you didn't go to your rehearsal. We always seem to get sick at the same time. It's like we synchronize our illnesses.

I texted Rafa the following day.

—How are you feeling, No Bones? I think I'm a little better.

—I still feel bad.

—I'm sorry. Well, if you are going to die, I want the earbuds I gave you.

—Those are going with me.

—Hahahaha. I'll be looking over your dead body in your casket and trying to explain to your mother why you have earbuds, your cell phone, a mannequin of Lady Gaga, and your favorite Clif energy bars.

—Hahahaha.

——-You'll probably leave a note for everyone, saying you loved your dogs and cats and your mom and that you were faking your love for the rest of us.

—Hahahaha. You know me so well.

—When I die, my tombstone will read "Like everyone else, I tried to make Rafa happy and failed."

—Hahahahahahahaha. It's hard for me to laugh now, since I have a headache, dizziness and lots of diarrhea. I just spent 1,300 pesos on medicines. My mom gave me a penicillin injection, so hopefully that helps.

—I hope it helps you, too. I guess when you are back to being bitchy and grumpy, that's when I'll know that you are feeling better.

—Hahahaha.

27 HOLIDAY DANCING AND RAFA'S ABSENCE

After a week had passed, we both had recovered from our illnesses. The holiday season had arrived, which I knew Rafa didn't celebrate or did so half-heartedly, in part because of his personal beliefs and due to past experiences of Christmas' spent with family. He did, however, celebrate earning money. Christmas time was always a chance for him to help others enjoy its celebration in exchange for obtaining some extra pesos dancing.

I met up with him at three different events. The first was on a dirt lot next to a busy highway where Christmas trees were being sold. A makeshift stage of construction scaffolding was set up for Rafa and three other performers to dance to Christmas music wearing holiday attire. Rafa and the other male dancer were dressed in light red business suits, black pants and green bow ties, while the two women on stage were decked out in green dresses with red ruffles. As the first of several performances began, wind gusts blew up dust while noisy big rig trucks and cars drove by, often drowning out the music that blared from the speakers. The group performed all day. As the hours passed, maybe a total of a dozen people stopped to watch the performances. My job, now as his friend only, was to take photos and videos. It was glaringly obvious that Rafa was the most skilled dancer of the four and that this venue was beneath him.

At the end of the day, he had achieved his goal: he pocketed 500 pesos. As the shows came to an end, he and I, along with the other dancers, piled into a small Honda and headed off to a community theatre. After we arrived, Rafa and I started walking home to the apartment, but we first stopped for tacos at *El Huarachon*, one of his favorite tacos stands. After we received our order, a disheveled Rafa slouched at the counter in his untucked dress shirt, chowed down on one of his beef tacos. After finishing it, he glanced over at me and let out a sigh.

---What do you think, Socre? This is my life.

---It's not that bad. And neither was today's performance. Okay, so maybe hardly anyone was watching you guys. I thought you were cute in that colorful, frumpy suit. And I'm sure when you post the photos and videos that I took to your Instagram page, your friends will hardly notice the truck stop atmosphere.

---I guess. I'm too tired and depressed to think about it.

---Rafa, life isn't always about incredible performances. Sometimes it's about an honest day's work. It's often about finding pleasure in the mundane, getting through the day and paying the rent. Or in your case, paying for cigarettes.

Rafa smiled wryly and replied to my comment.

---And sometimes life is about your friend being philosophical and snarky at the same time.

I laughed.

---True. Sometimes I like to multitask.

As we finished eating, Rafa mentioned to me that next up for him would be a ballet performance, a bit of a switch for him. He told me that a few weeks ago, a local dance director saw him performing and offered him the lead male dancer role in the Christmas story The Nutcracker, the classical fairy tale ballet about a family's Christmas Eve celebration.

---I'm curious, Rafa. Why ballet now after so much time doing contemporary dance?

---Well, I love ballet as well. As you know, for a long time now, I have very much adored The Nutcracker. Now is my chance to perform it, so I plan to make the most of it.

---Cool. Will this be your first official ballet performance?

---No, I performed in a ballet performance in the form of a competition a few years ago.

---Okay. My only connection to ballet was when I was working as a reporter years ago, I was sent to do a review of a ballet performance by the U.S. International University at Tijuana's Cultural Center. It was the first ballet performance I'd witnessed in person and honestly, I was out of my league. I had no idea what I was reviewing, but somehow, I pulled it off.

---Interesting.

---Today, I'm almost as lost. Maybe you can give me a brief explanation of what I should be looking for.

---Just enjoy the beauty of dance.

---Of course I will, but I'm also interested in learning more details, such as some of the ballet terminology, what you work on in practice, etc. I'm familiar with one commonly known term---the pirouette, a controlled turn on one leg. What else should I know?

---I won't go into all of them, but here are two of them. One is allegro. It refers to fast, lively steps, jumps and turns. It requires me to perform with speed, precision, agility and lightness, all without falling on my ass. I really enjoy the high jumps.

---You are incredible with your high jumps, Rafa!

---Thanks. Another, adagio, refers to the opposite of allegro---slow-paced, graceful movements. It allows me to demonstrate my control, balance and expressive qualities. It's the part I most enjoy performing.

---I can see that. I just now googled other ballet movement terms. Allow me to read them to you. There is épaulement, which involves the correct placement of the head and shoulders and even beyond that to include arms and head tilt; plie, the bending of the knees; the tendu, the stretching of the foot across the floor; the fondu, the lowering of the body done by bending the knee of the supporting leg; and the arabesque, a pose where the dancer stands on one leg and extends the other straight behind him.

---That's correct. There are others, but those are most of the main movements.

---Thanks. This will be helpful for me when we talk about your ballet performances. I won't feel so ignorant. Is there a movement that gives you the most problems?

---That would be the fondu. Not due to the movement itself, but because of the burning or slight pain I feel while doing it repeatedly.

---I imagine that becomes easier over time. Speaking of easier, synchronizing your movements with the other dancers must be easier in ballet than in contemporary dance, since you aren't inventing anything new.

---True. Although, if you watch closely, whether it is contemporary dance or ballet, I will perform each presentation a little differently, while maintaining the same overall concept. My dance directors don't like it, but I get bored doing the same thing over and over.

---Yeah, I noticed that Salvador sometimes complains that he'd choreograph a scene for your dance group, but when you all got together to do it, many of you would just go off and invent your own movements, oblivious to what he directed you all to do.

Rafa laughed as he nodded his head in agreement. I continued.

---Regardless, you know I always enjoy watching you perform. And now you'll be wearing leotards. So sexy.

Rafa laughed some more. I continued with the conversation.

---You know me, Rafa. I obsess over the details. Like how you enhance the gracefulness of certain movements with the length of your inhalation or exhalation of breath. I like the way you show off every angle of your body, your finesse, the positions that you hold, your gestures, your strength, and the spring in your jumps. It's so impressive how you can tell a story with only your body movements, without words.

---You never stop with your obsessive, overly descriptive observations, do you? But yeah, that's why I love to dance. It's so much fun to expressively use my body, and to learn and show off learned skills. It's a lot of hard work. Even one of us being a little out of rhythm can mess it all up. But hopefully with enough practice, it becomes second nature. I am lacking a bit in the strength area. That's why I plan on going to the gym during this break in school. Being overly muscular doesn't work with well dancing, but some definition is needed.

With the weekend over, Rafa began the last week of ballet rehearsals before his much-anticipated performance. He was nice enough to invite me to one of them, enabling me to get an insider's glimpse of what was to come. Attending his rehearsal also gave me a chance to observe Rafa's work ethic. As I sat sipping my water bottle on the side of the dance floor, he spent a half an hour performing a potpourri of stretches before rehearsal began.

I'd never met anyone who took stretching so seriously, did it as much, or loved it as much as Rafa. Nor did I know anyone who was as knowledgeable of its anatomy and physiology. Before I met him, I already knew about the many of the benefits of stretching---improved flexibility, stamina, muscle strength and muscle and joint movement; reduction of muscle soreness and injury; and improved body alignment and posture. But being a constant witness to these benefits was now having a tremendous impact on me. Stretching now became a larger part of my daily routine.

I patiently watched as he performed all the different types of stretching---ballistic (bouncing movements), passive, static (the most common, extending muscles until a tension or discomfort is felt and then holding it for 15 to 60 seconds) and dynamic (swinging and jumping held for less than three seconds).

He stretched almost every body part that could be stretched---feet, calves, knees, thighs, hips, lower trunk, abdomen, arms, wrists, hands, shoulders, back, chest and neck. Without a rest in-between, he seamlessly transitioned from one stretch to the next. A few of these exercises included stretching his legs on a railing; laying on his back, side and stomach while using a resistance band while moving his legs upward; balancing on his toes while sitting in a crouched position; lying face down, locking his arms behind his head while lifting his upper torso several times; leaning forward as he stretched both of his legs; and seated lower trunk movements. Now sufficiently limber, he came over to me to grab some water.

---Very thoroughly done, Rafa. What's up with your ballet shoes? There are holes in both.

---Yeah, I know.

---Why don't you replace them?

---They aren't cheap, at least for me, and they don't last very long.

---That's understandable. No wonder your feet hurt so much.

With his warmup over, he joined his fellow dancers at the rehearsal. His usual casual attitude exhibited in past rehearsals was nowhere to be found. Instead, he was beaming with joy as he practiced each movement. I could hardly wait to see the final product.

The holiday performance was to be held on a dance stage in front of a large and beautifully decorated Christmas tree at *Galerías Monterrey*, an upscale shopping center. When the day of the performance day arrived, Rafa texted me that he was ready to give it his all. When I arrived and sat down in my seat, I noticed immediately that the ambiance felt very uplifting. There was a nice-sized crowd in attendance, and their energy was palpable. They were abuzz with holiday cheer.

As the ballet presentation began, Rafa's body language showed how much he was cherishing the moment. The performance of the holiday classic was very beautiful and came off without a hitch. Rafa performed a few spectacular jumps that amazed the spectators. However, I came away slightly disappointed. Apart from the allegro movements, his participation appeared to be rather menial, made up of a considerable amount of posing while the principal ballerina did the majority of the skilled dance moves.

His last holiday performance of the year was presented on one of several small stages at the annual Monterrey Holiday Festival. It was basically a large county fair decorated with holiday decorations, which

I very much enjoyed. I wish I could have said the same thing about Rafa's performance. He danced an abbreviated performance of a previously done playful skit involving French children. It was completed as planned, but this time around it seemed labored and mechanical. It was the first time I'd seen one of his performances that seemed lackluster and hardly worth watching. It was like his heart wasn't into it. After it was over, Rafa's nonchalant attitude seemed to confirm my view of what had just transpired. We spent the rest of the evening walking around the festival eating churros.

With his holiday dance season finished, Rafa was eager for some alone time. His boyfriends were going to be out of town visiting their families, so he'd have their ranch home all to himself. Before he went off to hibernate, I thought I would surprise him. I knew Rafa's past Christmas' were experienced with little to no gift exchanges, so I went to the University of Monterrey store, Liverpool and Sears and purchased several items that I knew he would love. After wrapping them up in the apartment, I set them next to a poinsettia plant and some candles on a red placemat, on top of a small table in the living room.

The day before he was to go on holiday vacation, I asked him to come by the apartment to say goodbye and he obliged. After greeting me, he distractedly walked straight to his room to set down his backpack, then he quickly grabbed some food and a large bottle of *Coca Cola* to pour into a glass.

—Are you ready to be surprised, Rafa?

—Sure. Let me check my phone first.

I patiently waited for him, seated on the couch in the living room. When he was finally done checking his messages on his main phone and his Lu escort phone, he sat down with me.

—What is all this, Socrates?

—What does it look like? I bought some Christmas gifts. There might even be one for you.

—Really?!!

—Yes.

—I don't believe you.

—Each of the gifts has a tag on them with the receiver's name. Go check them out.

He walked over to a small pile of gifts.

—Oh wow. This one has my name on it.

—Yeah, it does. Check out the others.

—This one too. Let's see. This one too.

—They are all for you.

—*¿En serio?* (¿Really?)

—*En serio*. When you are ready, go ahead and start opening your gifts. Let's see. How about you open that small one first?

Rafa picked up the gift, felt it, then grabbed some scissors on the coffee table and carefully opened it. He was the slowest, most careful gift opener I'd ever seen.

—You know, Rafa, you can rip open the wrapping paper if you want.

—I know, but the wrapping is so pretty. Wow! Some slippers. They look comfortable.

—Try them on.

—Aww. They feel great. Thanks, Socrates.

—I know you needed some, especially since it's so cold walking on the floor. Okay, open this one now.

Rafa opened the next gift.

—Wow, a university hoodie. Let me try it on. It fits perfectly. Thank you. What else is here? Oh nice. A university coffee cup and notebook. I love them all!

He continued opening more gifts. The next one was a black fitted compression t-shirt. During the entire time, he had a big grin on his face. I'd never seen him smiling and so happy for so long. He opened another gift.

—Wow, a scarf. It's beautiful!

Rafa tried it on, smiling from ear to ear.

—Rafa, when I tried it on at the store, I loved how it felt. It's so soft. Maybe you'll let me borrow it sometime.

—No, it's mine!

I laughed and continued.

—You have one more gift to open. That big one. Hold on a minute.

I went to get my cell phone and turned on its camara. I let him know that I was ready to videotape him.

---It's recording. Go ahead. Let me know if you like it.

—I haven't opened it yet, but I love it already.

After a minute of carefully removing the bow and wrapping paper, he opened the box and finally saw his gift, a heavy black, hooded jacket with gray sleeves, made of leather and wool. It was a practical gift choice, given that he was very sensitive to cold weather and his hoodies didn't provide enough protection from the elements.

—Oh my gosh! I love, love, love it!

—What are you waiting for? Try it on.

—Rafa proudly put the jacket on, posing for me while I took a photo of him.

—This must have cost you a lot.

—The cost is irrelevant. It's all been worth it just to see you happy. You really looked like a child opening each of your gifts. This moment brings me back to my youth at Christmas time.

—I feel like a child right now. You knew exactly what to get me. You really did. I truly love each and every gift. I could see that you put a lot of thought into each one.

—Do you really like all the gifts, Rafa? Tell me the truth.

——Yes, really. I don't know what to say. Thank you so much, Sorce. Come here.

As I stood up, Rafa walked over to me and gave me a big, long hug, followed by a quick kiss on the lips.

—You are very welcome, No Bones. I know you haven't experienced a Christmas with many gifts, and I wanted you to have that experience, at least once in your life.

Rafa was all smiles as he left the apartment an hour or so later. We continued texting each other during his time off. Eventually his university classes began, consuming much of his time. He also got a job as a youth dance instructor at a local dance school. His daily routine was now set--- school classes, dance instruction and dance rehearsal with his dance company, with a little escort work thrown in. He did his homework at the apartment and at his boyfriend's house, where he was now living permanently. The weekends were rehearsals, performances, homework, sleeping and hanging out with his men. A busy life for sure. As the winter months passed, our moments together were less and less. He kept texting me, saying he hadn't forgotten me, that one day he would come over and see me. When he did finally come over to the apartment, it was after I had gone back to San Diego for a few weeks. Upon my return, I noticed the emergency cash I had left him was all gone.

—Hey, Rafa, I saw you took all the money I had left. Did something happen to you? Are you okay?

—No, I'm not.

—What happened?

—I was waiting for the bus late last night to go to Enrique's house and two guys attacked me. They beat the crap out of me and stole all my belongings.

—Oh my gosh. That's horrible. How are you doing right now?

—My face is a mess. I have cuts over one eye and my lower lip is swollen badly.

—Where are you now? Did you have to go to the hospital?

—No, no hospital visit. I'm recovering at Enrique's house now.

—You poor guy.

Rafa sent me a photo.

—Socre, you are the only one who knows this happened to me, besides Enrique. Please don't tell anyone in my family. I don't want them to worry.

—Okay, I won't.

—Thanks.

—The important thing is that you are okay now. How traumatizing. Did you cry?

—Yes, I did. I'm trying to forget it happened, but my lip and eye won't let me. They hurt a lot.

—Rafa, maybe you should go to the hospital, just in case. Did you report the incident to the police?

—No, they never do anything.

—Did they take your wallet?

—Yeah, it was the one you bought me in Rosarito. I've lost all my identification information and my money, so that is why I took the emergency money you left. The bastards ripped my jeans too.

—Don't worry about that. Money and material items can be replaced, but you can't. Be grateful that they didn't hurt you more than they did.

—True. And thanks, Socrates.

—I'll let you recuperate. If you need anything else from me, please let me know. I worry about you taking a bus so late at night.

—I know you do.

—The next time you must do that, come over to the apartment here first and I'll give you money for the Didi so you can be dropped off at Enrique's house safely.

—Okay. thanks. I will.

—I love you, No Bones. Please take care of yourself.

—I will.

Rafa came over to the apartment a day later. I noticed that the swelling on his lip had gone down a little. While he was slowly recovering from the physical trauma, I wondered about the mental effect on him. He didn't seem too fazed by it when we talked, but he was very good at hiding pain. Maybe he was chalking it up as part of the price for living as a poor young man in Monterrey, but I wasn't entirely convinced of that. Some traumas are more difficult to recover from than others.

Rafa continued to act like the assault had never happened when I met up with him for coffee the following day. He told me he made up a story for his dance company director and dance instruction class administrator about his messed-up lip and face, saying he'd fallen off a ladder. This was proof again that he'd go to great lengths to hide his personal life and any embarrassing information about himself from others.

Sure enough, Rafa began to show signs that his mental wounds were not healing. He stopped texting me, his family and almost everyone else as well. I texted him for several days, telling him I was here if he needed me. Eventually though, I gave up. I had been ghosted. I dealt with the burden of his disappearance by telling myself that he would contact me when he was ready. I wanted to go visit him, but I didn't even know where his boyfriend lived. Even if I managed to figure out where they lived, I might not have been allowed in the house. I waited patiently, continuing to believe in our special bond and was hopeful we would be back together soon, enjoying our lives. I told myself that this wasn't about me, that he needed his personal space.

With or without Rafa, I was now staying in Monterrey for longer and longer periods, with only a few trips back to San Diego. With more time on my hands, I spent it working out each day, writing my book and painting. I was focusing more and more on my life and projects, and less on Rafa, although he was always on my mind.

When negative events happen to me, whether it's the loss of my dog or distancing of a close friend, I tend to go through a down period of withdrawal. This lull in my friendship with Rafa gave me time to reflect on why I was putting so much effort into helping him. He certainly didn't have much time for me and despite glimpses, didn't seem to care for me with the same passion that I did for him.

I also began to question whether what I was going through with Rafa was some form of limerence. Was I intensely and irrationally involved in a one-sided love affair? Was I spending too much time ruminating about memories of us together and imagining future interactions? Was I spending too much time longing for him? Was this longing now an addiction? Could I instead be doing more productive activities? After a period of reflection, my conclusion was yes to all of these questions.

Three more months passed. I kept busy painting, working out and writing. On a whim, I decided one night to break out of my rut and go see *La Consistencia del Agua* (Water Consistency), a presentation by *La Terraza* at the *Teatro de la Ciudad* (City Theater). I didn't want to bother Rafa, but I missed seeing his presentations. After witnessing the performance, I paused for a few minutes to send some photos of the theater to a few friends before I walked out onto the main square area. It was there that, from a distance, I heard a familiar voice yell out my name.

---Socrates!

I turned around and there was Rafa. He came running over to me, wardrobe in hand, with some of his character's make-up still on him. He spoke to me as he was trying to catch his breath.

---Hey there. How are you? Did you enjoy the presentation?

---I did. It was well done as usual.

---Thanks. I'm glad you came. Look, I'm sorry I haven't texted. I've needed some alone time to reflect on my life. Hey, I know this is kind of sudden, but would you like to go out for a drink with me?

---Thanks for the offer, Rafa, but no thanks. It's late and just want to go to sleep. I already requested a Didi. Oh, there it is now. I've got to go. Take care.

As I walked over to the ride share and as I opened the door, Rafa shouted out to me.

---Sweet dreams, Socre!

During the ride over to my apartment, a wave of sadness hit me. Usually, I'd jump at the chance to spend time with Rafa, but not now. The time apart from him had changed me. I couldn't do this anymore. Hanging around Rafa while in love with him without his reciprocation had become too painful. My time with Rafa was a nice chapter in my life, but it was now time to turn the page and move on.

28 MY TRANSFORMATION

I woke up the next morning feeling reinvigorated. I refocused on my reasons for leaving my job in San Diego. Previously, I had begun to research and discover how to best go beyond my limitations, but I hadn't gotten very far. When I told Rafa that I was leaving my job, I said I wanted to use my new freedom to transform myself, to study how to be a better human being. Now, with him out of the picture, at least temporarily, I told myself that this would be a great opportunity to dedicate more time to accomplishing these goals. My ideal transformation would enhance my physical, mental and emotional states. I envisioned myself as a sculptor, reinventing my body, mind and soul.

I was grateful for the experiences I've had with Rafa. We had developed a shared history that I had enjoyed immensely, but I didn't need to be with him to be happy. Now was an opportunity to take the archeological work I did, digging deep into his soul, and apply that work to myself.

My thought process was that we as humans are constantly changing, so, if possible, why not enhance this change in a positive way, rather than sit and watch a slow deterioration? While I have gained increased wisdom with age, not being able to function as well as I once did, no matter how I or others tried to spin it, never appealed much to me. If my physical decline was, indeed, inevitable, at least I would take steps to slow its arrival.

My idea was to use the knowledge acquired by humanity while putting my own unique stamp on it. This was my opportunity to come up with a comprehensive plan to allow myself to explore all the possibilities of self-transformation. Was I following the beaten path of many who foolishly attempted to recapture a part of themselves that was now long gone? Was I just another guy coming to grips with his fear of growing older? I didn't look at it that way. For me personally, this was nothing new. I had always reassessed myself during various stages of my life. The only difference was now I had 100 percent of my time available to do it.

To begin my quest, I attempted to shut out as many distractions as possible. My research involved many internet searches and listening to podcasts on a wide range of subjects pertaining to my objective. I also headed off to the *Biblioteca Central del Estado* (The Central State Library), as well as the *Biblioteca Universitaria de Monterrey* (The University of Monterrey Library), to check out books on a wide range of subjects. From this, I developed a plan for how to maximize my energy and transform myself into a new person.

I began my transformation with the most obvious of actions: I did aerobic exercise, lifted weights, and changed my diet, as well as my sleep patterns. I also continued with my stretching routine I began after meeting Rafa, which proved invaluable. I noticed that after a while, several aspects of my body and mind changed. I felt knots of tension loosen, releasing pent up emotions. My flexibility improved. Muscle soreness was lessened. Blood flow increased. My posture improved. Tension, stress and mood swings were lessened. And my balance and coordination were better.

I developed a skin care routine involving the standard exfoliation, cleansing and hydration process. This routine focused not only on my face, but my body as well. Although the skin is our largest organ, it is often the most neglected. Probably because there is so much of it to care for.

I focused on changing my breathing patterns to increase energy levels and improve my health. I learned that most of us breathe too rapidly and shallowly. I focused on making my breathing slow and steady, especially when exhaling. The benefits I reaped included a lower heart rate, lower blood pressure, reduced stress hormones, reduced lactic acid build up, improved immune system functioning, increased physical energy, and balanced levels of oxygen and carbon dioxide in the blood.

Another aspect of my transformation involved doing daily sessions of meditation. Controlled breathing and meditation were a powerful combination for enhancing my wellbeing. I found that after only a few weeks, my meditation sessions in the early mornings and late evenings began to have a positive impact. My stress and anxiety were reduced, my sleep improved, and both my blood pressure and inflammation levels lowered. My feeling of peace increased, as waves of calming energy filled my being. The more I meditated, the longer these waves lasted after I finished.

Meditation also helped me to slow down and pay more attention to my state of mind. Often during my life, I rushed out of the apartment with a nervous energy that would affect my mood in a negative way. After each of my meditation sessions, I became more aware of the need to focus on the energy I was giving out to the world, as well as the energy around me.

Other mental tools I used were visualizations and affirmations. I recorded affirmations in my own voice, designed to improve my mental outlook and see my physical self differently. I listened to these messages night and day until they had sunken deep into my subconscious. By focusing on these messages, negative thoughts about my abilities began to be slowly pushed out and replaced by positive ones. To aid my visualizations, I picked out photos of a younger version of myself and stared intensely at them each day, imagining that I was feeling the changes in my mind and body.

Next, I read books that provided great insight into unleashing the transformational changes I was seeking. These included those on miracle recoveries from illness and the mind-body connection. What I took away from these books was how to best use my beliefs to influence how my body worked.

As I absorbed this information, I began to realize that often my expectations were needlessly negative. My mental blocks didn't just appear in one day. They were built up over time and were often deeply buried into my subconscious. It would take time to change my way of thinking.

The aforementioned undertaken actions prepared me for the next and final step in my transformation process---attempting to alter the activity of my genes, in order to speed up the anti-aging process. Since I wasn't a scientist nor did I have a vast knowledge of how genes functioned, I had to glean what I could from science books. What I learned was the following:

- A gene is a sequence of nucleotides in DNA that provides the cell with instructions to make proteins, which carry out specific functions in the body.
- Genes are found in every one of the 37 trillion cells that make up our body.

- There are an estimated 20,000-25,000 genes in the human genome.
- Every person has two copies of each gene, one inherited from each parent.
- Of all these genes, there are an estimated 500 that can slow the aging of groups of cells in our body.

We as humans can't change our genes, but we can change their activity. That is where I concentrated my efforts. What could I possibly do to change the activity of these 500 cells for my benefit? I decided to focus on actions that are believed to improve gene activity. First, I stayed active. When our muscles are moving, they activate anti-aging genes that keep immune cells energized so they can bounce on invading viruses or bacteria. Second, I ate more fruits, vegetables, seeds and nuts. Third, I took a few minutes of each day to think of wishing friends and loved ones well. Thinking positive, caring thoughts activates a gene named OXTR that slows aging of tissues and organs, plus it strengthens one's immune system. Fourth, I called and texted family and friends on a daily basis. Emerging research shows that changes in the expression of hundreds of genes can occur as a result of the social environment we inhabit. These genes can be affected by our subjective perceptions of those conditions.

Now that I had reached a point where the framework for reaching my goal was built, I began to focus on the pivotal action that would most affect my gene activity---the use of the mental imagery. To accomplish this, I needed to learn the following. It was the preparation process before my mental "surgery" could begin.

- The anatomy and physiology of my body. I spent many days looking at photos and drawings of the insides of the human body. I read about how it functions, as well as how body parts were interconnected. Despite having achieved a university degree, I only had a vague idea of how my body worked. My body was mostly a stranger to me.
- Mental imagery can be used to clean areas of the body. It can heal the body from inflammation and create an environment for change. This cleaning affected corresponding areas of my body as well.
- Imagine motion. It was the optimal way to use mental imagery.
- Tell myself that the actions I had taken had been accomplished. No doubts.
- Repeat mental imagery daily to create a solid imprint in my mind.
- Use a disposal process after cleaning the area. Bury or drain out the unwanted materials.

My daily mental imagery involved the following: I first closed my eyes and breathed out three times with long exhalations. After those breaths, I took a light with me in my mind and entered my body through my mouth. As I made my way through to my bronchial tree, I visualized grabbing a syringe to suck up the mucus around me. After putting the mucus into a container, I sprayed water and white light all around me to enhance the cleansing process. Next, I used white light to expand and contract my lungs. I imagined that this process was forcing out carbon dioxide. I saw the carbon dioxide leave my body in a dark colored stream. I visualized grabbing my lungs to squeeze out what remained.

Next, I pulled out a wand and sprinkled the remaining areas of my body with white light. Once this process of cleaning was done, I swam deep down inside my body to see my chromosomes, long strands of DNA, which look like a twisted ladder. I saw my genes as a series of letters strung along each edge of this ladder. I imagined taking a kitchen tong out of my pocket and using it to remove the letters from the ladder that cause detrimental effects on my health. I put them into my container for disposal. Next, I visualized seeing the letters on the ladder representing the genes that had anti-aging effects. I tended to those genes with two spray bottles---one of water and another of white light, spritzing them with each. I imagined that these anti-aging genes were growing larger, spreading energy and vitality with each spritz. Next, using a flashlight, I left my body with the container in my hand. I finally imagined that I was burying its contents underground.

That was it. I continued doing this mental imagery exercise and all the other activities on a daily basis for four months. Despite feeling and looking better, I was seeing little to no progress in my effort to transform my body into a more youthful one. Despite this lack of results, I remained patient, persistent, and confident in the process.

Eventually, I began to notice a small difference in the texture of my skin. I'd been wanting to see some tangible improvement for some time now, so when I finally did, I wondered if I was fooling myself. So, I ignored it and continued with my routine, especially focusing on the mental imagery. As the weeks passed, little by little, more external and internal changes began to occur. Three months later, the changes were too astonishing to say it was just my imagination. I started to embrace the new me, even though some parts of the old me were still intact. My feet seemed the same, although my toenails looked better. While my body was more youthful, I still had the same body frame. But mostly, I only recognized myself by looking at photos of myself from 15 years ago. There were even parts of the new me that I didn't ever remember having, such as a different jawline.

I was now, indeed, a new man. My rough, leathery skin tone on my face and body had changed to smooth. Skin spots and spider veins were gone. The texture of my hair was thicker and oilier. The bags under my eyes were gone. It took me less time to stretch out my body when I woke up. My early morning cough with its accompanying mucus build up was gone. My butt was perky. My muscle to fat ratio had changed. And after I shaved my face and neck, the thick shadows were no longer there. The inner aches and pains had disappeared. My energy levels were back to being stable again.

I also now required less preparation to leave the apartment. Less skin moisturizer was needed. The arthritis in the fold under my left leg was gone, so no more applying arthritis cream. Also gone were the wrinkles on the side of my eyes when I squinted. There were no more creases on the sides of my lips. I stopped applying retinol and hyaluronic acid serum to my face. My eyes weren't as dry, so eye drops weren't needed as much.

I was very much enjoying the new me. I wasn't invisible anymore as I walked the streets. Both women and men would stare at me more often, like they did when I was in my twenties. While the new me was mostly a positive experience, lost in the excitement were problems I didn't quite think out. Like would my friends and family recognize me as changed or would they see me as a stranger? And what about my passport? Could I cross the border now? I told myself I would deal with those problems later.

29 ERIC MEETS RAFA

My transformation was now so thorough that I looked even younger than Rafa. Several months had passed since I'd last seen him at the theater. Even though I had moved on from him, circumstances had changed. I now had a glimmer of hope that Rafa might be attracted to the new me. The last thing in the world I wanted to do was to deceive Rafa again, but I also thought it would be too much of a shock to tell him I was Socrates. I was caught in a tough spot. Reluctantly, I went ahead and invented an online persona with a new name, Eric Peters. After posting my new profiles and photos on various social media platforms, I then requested to be friends with Rafa on each of them. There was no immediate response from him, but by the evening, he had added me as a friend to all of them. He liked several of my photos, especially those without my shirt on. I sent him a text message via one of the accounts.

—Hi.

—Hi. How are you?

—I'm fine. I'm Eric. And you?

—I'm Rafa.

—Nice to meet you, Rafa. Well, electronically anyway.

—Same here.

—How was your day?

—I'm tired from a rehearsal I had tonight.

—A rehearsal? A dance rehearsal?

---Yes.

---Okay, cool. Your profile caught my attention, Rafa. You are very handsome.

—Thanks. You are much more handsome than me.

—Thanks.

—You are welcome.

—I know this is sort of fast, but I was wondering if you were free to meet up and have coffee tomorrow. What do you say Rafa?

—Hmmm. Yes, I guess so.

—Great. I was thinking about Cafe Emma's at 9:30 a.m. The one near the University of Monterrey.

—I know where that cafe is. I used to go there all the time with a gringo friend of mine.

—I'm a gringo too, from Phoenix. What are the odds of knowing two gringos in Monterrey?

—I guess I attract you guys to me. Okay, then. See you there tomorrow.

When I stopped texting Rafa, I began to feel strange. Part of me wanted to excitedly say I'm Socrates! It's me who you think is handsome. It was, however, nice to be texting Rafa again after such a long break. I wondered now if he would be perceptive enough to figure out who I really was when we did meet. While I now looked different, my voice was mostly the same as before, except for maybe that I could sing a little better. I walked over to the bathroom mirror and started to practice a deeper, gruffer voice. I also practiced portraying a less enthusiastic, more stoic guy. I would try not to be so talkative. Rafa seemed to be more attracted to the boring guys who don't say much.

The next day couldn't arrive soon enough. I suffered through a restless night's sleep, tossing and turning in my bed. When the morning finally came, the new me jumped out of bed and quickly shaved and showered. When I walked over to my closet to figure out what to wear, I suddenly panicked. Oh shit, I thought, my clothes might give me away. Rafa is very familiar with my entire wardrobe since he used to wear half of my clothes. It was, however, too late to buy a new shirt and jacket. I'd just have to make do. After much indecision, I decided on a black jacket, gray shirt with black stripes and jogging pants. I was dressed casually, but clean looking. After putting on my clothes, I sat on the couch, taking deep, cleansing breaths, attempting to relax and imagine a fun meeting with Rafa. As I walked out the door, I was calm, but still wondering whether or not I would be able to pull this off.

I was the first one to arrive at the coffeehouse. Rafa texted me, saying he was on his way, and asked if could go ahead and order a large Frappuccino for him. When he arrived, he found me sitting on a couch outside on the café patio, looking at my cell phone, waiting for our orders to be completed.

—Eric?

—Hi. Yes, it's me. Please sit down.

Rafa was wearing slim fit jeans with a tight, black sleeveless shirt, despite it being a cold day. Wow, I thought, he's really going all out to look sexy. That shirt is what he usually wears when he does his escort work or when he goes out on the town to a party. To my relief, at least initially, he didn't recognize Socrates' part of me. As his Frappuccino and my vanilla latte were delivered, an excitement began to build inside of me. I started to think I might actually be able to pull this off.

—Nice jacket, Eric. A friend of mine owns the same one.

—Thanks. Yeah, I guess it's popular in *gringolandia.* Thanks for coming to meet me.

—The pleasure is mine.

—So Rafa, can you tell me a little about yourself?

—I was born and raised here in Monterrey, in a simple house just a few kilometers from where we are sitting, in *Colonia Aurora* (Aurora neighborhood). I loved growing up there. I have lots of fun memories. As you probably figured out by now, I'm a dancer. I attend the university across the street, work as a dance instructor and belong to a dance company.

—Wow, that is a lot on your plate. You must be a good juggler.

—My plate? And what's a juggler?

—Oh sorry. 'A lot on your plate' means you have a lot going on. I think a juggler is a *malabarista* in Spanish. I was using it figuratively to say that since you seem to have so many activities that you are involved in, you are similar to a juggler, with them all in the air.

—Okay. Yeah, that's me.

—So, what do you have planned for today, Rafa?

—Nothing. I usually try to do as little as possible since I'm so busy during the week. Lately, I've been rehearsing on the weekends for my dance company's next presentation, but I have this weekend off.

—Very cool. So, do I look different from my photos?

—You look better than your photos.

—Thanks. Rafa. Do you mind telling me what your relationship status is?

—I have a boyfriend, well boyfriends, but it isn't going so well. I'm usually hanging with them now.

—What's going wrong, if you don't mind me asking? Did you say boyfriends?

—Yes. One is my primary boyfriend. He is married to the other one. And he's focusing more and more of his attention on his husband. I'm not home that much either. And he isn't much into dancing or art, which is fine, but I at least expected him to support me regarding my goals in life. I just feel ignored sometimes.

—I see. Wow, so you are a boytoy for a married couple.

—Yeah. I know it's unusual. We are trying to work out our problems.

—And how's that going?

—I don't know. I'm here flirting with a handsome stranger. That should tell you something.

—I don't know what to say. I'm sorry it's not going well. Maybe we should just be friends. I don't want to cause you problems.

—It's okay, Eric. After all, he is married to someone else.

—What type of guy is...?

—Enrique? He's quiet, grumpy, even rude to people. Anti-social. He prefers to be away from people.

—And you find that type of guy appealing?"

—He is who he is. I don't want to change him. His personality was intriguing to me when I met him. I still love him. But I feel like I'm changing now. I'm not satisfied.

—Sometimes once the initial excitement is gone, there's a bit of a cooling off period. That's natural.

—Very true, but I've been with them for a while now.

—For me, I don't mind a quiet guy like that. But there must be more to the guy for me to be interested in him. You know what I mean, Rafa? If he is calm on the surface, he needs to be energetic underneath. I wouldn't mind the challenge of getting him to open up to me. But he needs to also be someone who has a sense of fun, a modest amount of ambition, someone who is audacious and curious. I'm looking for a guy to make me smarter, stronger and braver. Someone who works with me to help achieve my goals.

—Wow, you ask for a lot. Very little of what you said describes him.

—Is he at least as sexy as I am?

We both laughed. I continued.

---You know, to make up for his deficiencies.

—You are funny. I'm liking you already, Eric. But to answer your question, I do find him sexy, but we aren't having much sex anymore.

—I wish you good luck with that. And thanks for being honest with me.

—No problem.

—So, what type of guy are you into, Rafa?

—Someone who looks like you for sure. You are hot.

—Wow. You are direct. I like that.

—Why not be direct?

—Well, direct isn't always best. Sometimes you need to be considerate of a person's feelings. It's important to be empathetic.

—I suppose.

—Do you have any best friends? Maybe someone that fills in the areas your boyfriend can't.

—No, I don't. Well........I did.

—Really? What happened?

—I have a childhood girlfriend who I consider a best friend, but I don't talk to her much anymore. And the gringo I mentioned earlier was a good friend. We kind of went our own ways several months ago.

—I see. So, you were both just friends?

—Yes, just good friends, but I'm realizing now that I miss him. He made me feel important and admired. He helped me with my career and schooling. He took an interest in me and truly believed in me. He was or maybe still is in love with me, maybe even obsessed with me, but I don't feel the same. At least I don't think I do. I do have feelings for him. I just needed a break. His intensity can be a bit too much to handle. For example, sometimes I'd feel some unusual vibe and then look up and he'd be staring at me. I doubt I ever will meet someone like him again. Most people in this world don't give a shit about others and instead focus on their own needs. I'm sort of that way too. Not him.

—Wow, he sounds like he was a real friend. A special friend to support you.

—Yeah.

—How's your Frappuccino?

—It's really good. I usually go to 7-11 for coffee because they are so expensive here. Socrates always paid for my drinks when I came here.

—Socrates?

—He's the gringo friend I was just talking about.

—Oh, okay.

—So, Eric, what are you doing here in Monterrey?

—I'm a manager at a *maquiladora* plant that makes tractor equipment.

—Cool.

—By the way, Rafa, thanks for speaking in English with me. Yours is really good. My Spanish is awful, except for a few simple words and phrases I memorized. I also learned some work equipment words in Spanish related to my job. I'm trying to learn more, but it's very hard.

—Thanks for saying that. My written English is much better, but in the last couple of years, my speaking has improved by just hanging out with

Socrates.

—Wow, this Socrates guy really seems like he made an impact on you.

—He did, but if you ever meet him, please don't tell him I admitted that.

—Why not? I'm sure he'd like to hear it.

—I don't know. That's sort of how I controlled him. I didn't want him to think he was important to me. Because he is so obsessive, I wanted to keep him at a distance.

—That's kind of narcissistic and cruel, don't you think?

—No one is perfect.

—Hmmm. Can I ask you a personal question?

—Sure.

—Do you have low self-esteem?

—Sometimes. Socrates told me once that if he could buy me for what I think I am worth and then sell me for my true value, he'd be the richest man in Monterrey.

—Interesting. Can I ask why you guys aren't friends now?

—I'm not sure why. I am a busy guy. I suppose I don't really have the time to spend with him or any friend, for that matter. I rarely see my family either.

—So why did you come to meet me if you don't have free time?

—Well, I don't know for sure. If you want to know the truth, I think it was my dick that convinced me to meet up with you.

We both laughed.

—Well, I don't want to get your boyfriend mad at me. Isn't he wondering where you are right now?

—Maybe, but I don't care. Are you free after this or later tonight?

—No, I'm not, but maybe we can meet up during the week. How does that sound?

—Sounds good. Hey, I want to go to Oxxo to get something to eat.

—Okay, I'll go with you.

We got up together and took the short walk to the convenience store. We said our goodbyes at the entrance, and I headed back to the apartment. On my way back, I was all smiles, as I thought our meeting went well. As I got closer to my apartment, Socrates got a text from Rafa.

—Hey there Socrates. What's up?

—Oh my gosh, it's you.

—Yeah, how have you been?

—Do you really care? I haven't heard from you for so many months.

—I've missed you. Really.

—I don't believe you, Rafa.

—It's true. I started thinking about you right now, for some reason.

—You started thinking about how great a guy I am, right?

—No, that wasn't it. Hahahahaha.

—I see you haven't changed much at all. Truthfully, I've missed you too, Rafa.

—I want to tell you that I'm sorry. I'm a bad friend for waiting all this time to contact you. I will make it up to you. And I have a lot to talk to you about. I also have something to confess to you. I don't know if you have heard of the saying in Spanish *"Un gran amigo vale más que mil amores."* (A great friend is worth more than a thousand lovers.) That is how I feel about you, Socrates.

---Aww…thank you, but again, I don't believe you. You never talk to me like that. You must be drunk. Anyway, I hope you have been well.

---It sounds cheesy, I know. But it's the truth, and I am not drunk. I'm better now. Right after I last saw you at the theater, I began to suffer from various health problems.

---Oh no. I'm so sorry. Why didn't you text me?

---You know me. I hide my personal issues from everyone, but it reached a point that I couldn't hide them anymore. People started commenting on how skinny I looked. And you know how thin I already am. I went from weighing 67 kilograms to 57. I never really worried about my looks before, but I could see my ribs. My skin looked pale. I didn't want to eat. I was tired all the time. I had muscle aches and pains. When it started to affect my work and school, I finally went to a doctor.

---How horrible. What did the doctor say was wrong with you?

---I had some bumps in my groin area which at first, I ignored. Then they started to spread. The first diagnosis was that it might be cancer. After hearing that, I was an emotional wreck. After doing more tests, I was relieved to find out it wasn't cancer. It was some type of extreme inflammatory response that would require medical treatment, rest and a change of diet. It's been a long recovery, but now I'm mostly back to normal. I am not contagious in any way. I am still taking medicine for it, but lately, I finally have more energy and am gaining weight again. I'm back to my normal routine of school, dance instruction and doing dance presentations. I have even been working out at the gym. And most importantly, I feel better emotionally.

---I'm so happy that you are better. I know you are a determined guy. That must have helped with your recovery. It sounds like what you have or had is or was similar to molluscum. It's caused by a virus, and it's usually transmitted sexually. I assume by one of your clients.

---It could be that. The doctors weren't sure.

---Hey, Rafa, I have to go. I'll text you later, okay?

---Okay.

Several days passed without hearing from Rafa. So as Eric, I texted him and asked him if he was available to see a movie tonight. He said he would be free after his dance instruction class ended. When the time of our date got closer, I took a Didi over to *Cinepolis Galerías Monterrey* (a local movie theater). When I arrived, it was still early, so it gave me a chance to practice my deeper, non-Socrates voice. While I was talking to myself, a couple passed by me, giving me a strange look. A few minutes later, I saw him from a short distance, looking around for me.

—Hey Rafa, over here.

—Hi there. Wow, you look very handsome, Eric. I like those warmup pants. I used to wear those same ones. I like how they stretch to fit my body.

—Yes, they are very comfortable. So, what type of movie do you want to see? I'm guessing a horror movie.

—How did you know I liked horror movies?

—It was a lucky guess.

—And you?

—Something non-violent.

—Socrates was the same. He couldn't watch them without being overly affected by them.

—How about a comedy, Rafa?

—I love those too.

As we sat together in the theatre watching the film, I saw Rafa glance at me with puppy-dog eyes.

---Are you enjoying the movie, Eric?

---Yes, I am.

In fact, I laughed several times during the movie, often by myself. The Hollywood-made movie was full of American cultural jokes that the Mexican audience didn't quite understand. Rafa said very little, as usual. After the movie ended, we both were starving, so we decided to go to the Chinese restaurant Howah, on the outskirts of downtown. After being seated and choosing what we wanted to order from the menu, I looked up and saw Rafa nervously fidgeting in his seat. He had accidentally dropped his napkin on the floor. After picking it up, he sheepishly stared up at me. It was a Rafa that I hardly recognized. Our roles were now reversed. He was swooning over me, extremely compliant, hanging on my every word. He ignored his cell phone as it vibrated in his pants pocket. The waiter finally returned.

—*¿Están listos para ordenar?* (Are you guys ready to order?)
Rafa nodded in the affirmative, so I ordered first.
—*Estamos listos. Voy a pedir Chow Mein con verduras y para tomar, una Coca.* (Yes, we are. I'll have the vegetable Chow Mein and to drink, a Coke.)
—*Gracias. ¿Y para ti, joven?* (Thank you. And for you, young man?)
—*Quiero el pollo Kung Pao y una Coca también.* (I'll have the Kung Pao chicken and a Coke too.)
—*Una selección excelente. Vuelvo enseguida con sus bebidas.* (Excellent choice. I'll be right back with your drinks.)
We both smiled at each other. After a long pause, I broke the silence.
—The waiter said your selection was an excellent choice. Why did he say that? Was my choice not excellent too?
Rafa laughed.
---True.
—And am I not young too, Rafa?
—I am always mistaken for a teenager.
—So, what did you think of the movie?
—I enjoyed it.
—I noticed that there were even some dancers in it for you.
—True. And they had great legs, my favorite part of the body.
—I know...err...I mean...why is that Rafa?
—I don't know. Maybe because they are connected to the longest and strongest bone in the body, the femur.
—I'm out with a handsome guy and I learned something new today. It can't get any better than this.
—Yeah. It goes from the pelvis to the top of the knee joint. And it has numerous muscle attachments. All together, they are key to many dance movements. As a dancer, it's necessary to know how the body functions, and how all the body parts are interconnected.
—I've always been fascinated with the inner workings of the body.
Just then we paused our conversation as our drinks arrived. After we took a few sips, I took up where we left off.
—Rafa, I love how you know so much about body parts and how they work. This may sound strange, but I often do mental imagery exercises, pretending to explore my body.
—Socrates likes that mental imagery stuff, too. He is obsessed with it, as well as everything he does in his life. For me, I don't have the patience for it or to be honest, the interest.
---You talk about this Socrates guy a lot. Are you sure it isn't you who is obsessed with him?
---I'm sorry. That is rude of me. We can talk about something else.

---It's okay. And yeah, I get that any of us can overdo stuff.

—I guess it's just that I'm not accustomed to people like that. Socrates totally overdoes it. At least for my taste. He really thinks about things, arriving at unusual conclusions. His paintings are bizarre. He loses me. I don't understand half of the things he says or the ideas he comes up with.

—Wow, he paints. Nice. He sounds like a true renaissance man.

---What is that?

---It's someone knowledgeable about a wide variety of subjects, like writing, painting and speaking different languages. That kind of guy.

---Thanks for explaining it. Yeah, I suppose. He does have a big imagination.

---I imagine that it is probably hard for him to be accepted by others.

---Maybe. Despite being strange, I must admit that he became someone I could trust. Well usually. And he trusted me. Maybe he trusted me too much. I mean, he even described his dreams to me. Sexual dreams. He could remember the smallest details. He often texted me these long descriptions. I don't miss that. I just realized that I'm describing him like he is dead, in the past tense.

—Well, you did say he was your friend before. Or is he still a friend?

Before Rafa could answer the question, we were interrupted as our food had arrived. Rafa then continued.

—Yeah, I suppose he still is a friend. I should be more accepting of how he is. And even if it seems too much for me to deal with, I'm never bored with him. He usually makes sure I am happy, even when I'm too busy to pay attention to him. Which, I suppose, is most of the time.

—Nice. So how do I make you happy right now?

Rafa laughed.

---I'm happy just being in your presence, Eric.

—Thanks. How about you teaching me about other parts of the anatomy dealing with dancing?

—Like what?

—Maybe this isn't acceptable dinner talk, but I'm going to ask you anyway. How do I stretch my anus for "dancing" in the bed?

Rafa nervously laughed as he shook his head. He took a bite of his Kung Pao chicken before he spoke.

—You do know that there are limits to what professors teach us in dance school, right?

—I'm sure. But sometimes professors who go beyond the normal curriculum are the best ones. For example, my college Spanish teacher taught us some street Spanish. To understand and to communicate well, it's important to learn those words or phrases, too, don't you think?

—Good point. I do have to say, you really move fast. It's only our second date and you smoothly transitioned into sex talk.

—Sorry, Rafa. I need to be more of a gentleman.

—Yes, you do, but I'm okay with that. Maybe just wait until after we are finished with our meals.

—I understand. The sex talk is more appropriate for the dessert portion of the meal, right? The cherry on top of the sundae.

Rafa laughed.

---You are crazy, Eric. By the way, my cherry is still on top of my sundae.

I laughed.

—I am crazy. And I really doubt that about your cherry.

—You are correct.

—About what? I completely forgot about what I asked you.

—You are correct to assume I know something about anal stretching.

—Oh good. I'm a versatile top, but I'd like to try bottoming more, but it hurts too much sometimes.

—I can give you some tips or pointers, if you want, Eric.

—Wow, excellent pun! I'd love to receive your pointer. I mean pointers.

Rafa laughed and continued.

—First, it's important to learn how to relax the anal sphincter muscles. The sphincter muscle has two functions: contracting and relaxing. To stretch anal muscles, it helps to know how they work.

—Teach me Professor Coria. I'm "open" to learning new things.

—Touché. Nice return pun, Eric. A bit corny, though. Good anal sex for the receiver involves learning how to control the contracting, pulling, pushing and squeezing. Stretching the anus out involves repetition. It can become too tight as well. And not everyone's experience is the same.

—I'd like to start out slow and work my way up.

—Okay. Maybe start with inserting a small butt plug or other sex toy. You may feel discomfort at first, but that is normal. But stop if you feel a lot of pain. To enjoy bottoming, it's important to be able to enjoy a little discomfort. The anus is an erogenous zone of the body, so it can be pleasure mixed in with a little pain.

—Cool. I need to get better at enjoying the discomfort.

—To prepare for it, if it isn't obvious, it's important to have a bowel movement before and clean yourself out in the shower with warm or hot water, preferably with an anal wash object.

—Okay, so once that is done, what's next, Rafa? What's the best position for a beginner?

—Positioning is more about what feels comfortable for you. Try using a dildo, going in and out with it, until you meet resistance. When your anus stretches, the ring of the muscle, the sphincter, opens. It can tear, even causing bleeding if it stretches further than it is used to. You want to stretch the anus enough to maintain it optimally tight without overdoing it and making it too loose. Butt plugs are good to use before sex to help relax the muscle.

—I suppose like everything, you need to reach a sweet spot, a balance.

—Yeah. When I'm not having sex, I stretch my anus by relaxing my ab muscles, then tightening my pelvic muscles. I repeat it during the day. Doing consistent squats and other gluteal work in the gym is helpful too. You can have too much anal sex, which can result in a loss of function. People with this issue tend to like bigger toys or penises or engage in fisting.

—I don't think I have to worry about that, Rafa. If anything, I am too tight.

—Most likely.

—Thanks so much for the quick class.

---You are welcome, Eric. By the way, how was your Chow Mein? My chicken was tasty.

---It was also delicious. How about some dessert?

---Oh no. I'm too full.

---Rafa, the dessert I am referring to is some "hands on" instruction from what you were teaching me. You know, to help us better digest our food. Are you up for that tonight?

—I am.

—Great. If it is okay with you, I'll reserve a room for us now.

—Sounds good to me.

I proceeded to make reservations for the Marriott Hotel near the *Club Campestre* (Country Club). I wanted our first official experience together to be as memorable as possible and the Marriott seemed very nice. Although making it memorable for Rafa might be a challenge, since sex and hotels were his work and workspace. As our Didi approached the elegant 14-floor hotel, I looked out the window to admire the full moon lighting the sky above it. When we arrived, two young hotel attendants wearing tight black dress shirts and pants opened the double door to let us in. We were greeted by a friendly woman at the check-in desk, who confirmed our reservation and provided us with the electronic door key for our 10th floor room. After settling into our room, Rafa and I decided to partake in the complimentary wine included with it. The moment I'd been dreaming about for so long was about to become a reality.

After finishing our wine, Rafa showered first. I was next. I was hoping that the hot water raining down onto my body would calm my nerves. When I got out and dried off, I saw that Rafa was propped up in bed, looking at his cell phone, and wearing a black tank top and tight black underwear. If Rafa was nervous, he didn't show it. I walked over to the bed with only a white towel draped around my waist and snuggled up close to him. Before setting down his phone, he turned on some music with a rhythmic Latin beat. I recognized the music from one of porn videos on his escort website. We both smiled as we held each other.

---I love how tall you are, Eric.

---I guess six-foot two inches is tall in Mexico.

---Definitely. You have such a smooth, sexy body, slender yet muscular. I love your back and shoulders, but especially your legs. They are so long and strong.

---Thanks, Rafa. It's mainly due to lots of hard work at the gym.

---Your chest is huge. I could suck on those nipples of yours all night.

---I'm all yours. Suck anything you want.

As we looked into each other's eyes, the expression on Rafa's face changed to one of intense desire. I felt the passion in me begin to rise as well. I leaned in and slowly kissed his tender, full lips. His sensuous lips kissed me back in a way that got the attention of my penis, which was now pressing hard against my towel. The musty smell of his smooth body engulfed my senses. Our unchoreographed sexual dance had begun.

Moments of tenderness and aggression ensued. I attempted to keep pace with the ever so flexible Rafa, as he contorted into different positions. As he twisted his body, I bent down to lightly bite Rafa's butt. Next, I teased his tight hole with my wet tongue, as he moaned in delight. When it seemed like Rafa's euphoria had reached its peak, I dove my face into his sweaty butthole. I did this with as much vigor and lust as the winner of a County fair pie eating contest. Before I knew it, Rafa had flipped me over and he was inside me. The seemingly interminable thrusts of his long, smoothly knobbed cock plowing into me sent waves of ecstasy all over my body. Rafa instinctively knew how to build up the moment before orgasm. Each time he pulled back, I urged him not to stop, while he asked me how badly I wanted it. His stopping and starting culminated with one last thrust of Rafa's, a penetration so deep that felt as if he touched my soul. We both came at the same time. In that brief, glorious moment, I felt like one with Rafa. As his moist body collapsed on top of mine, I hoped he felt the same. But I couldn't help but wonder if he could separate the escort sex and the date sex. He rolled off me and we laid together, in contented silence. After several minutes had passed, Rafa finally spoke.

—Eric, do you have some medical issues?

—Not that I know of. Why?

—Well, your lips swelled up when you were kissing me. As I was penetrating you, your butt seemed to expand, and I felt a tightness inside of you that I'd never felt with anyone before. It was a unique experience.

—Wow, I had no idea. I guess maybe you got me really excited.

—I think it was more than that. It was incredible, but maybe you ought to have yourself checked out by a doctor.

—Okay, thanks for letting me know.

Rafa's comments about my body made me realize that my transformation was most likely still in progress. I wondered what else could be happening to me. We spent the post-sex part of the evening cuddling, laughing and enjoying each other's company. After using the bathroom, I came back to find Rafa sitting out on the balcony, staring out into the night, smoking a cigarette and drinking wine. As I opened the sliding glass door and leaned closer to him, I recognized the look on his face and his body language. In a matter of minutes, he changed from being full of energy, happy and playful to being disconsolate and lost in thought.

—Beautiful night, isn't it, Rafa?

—Oh hey. Um, yeah, it is.

Several minutes passed without Rafa saying another word as he gazed out into the distance. I decided to break the silence.

—What's on your mind, Rafa?

—Not much. Just thinking.

—Did you enjoy the evening with me?

—I did. I really did. The dinner, the conversation and the sex were amazing. You know, you are very beautiful. You could probably have anyone, and you are with me.

—I'm glad. I did too. Thanks for the compliment, Rafa. I guess I contributed something to my outer beauty—exercising, eating, sleeping well and dealing with stress. But much of outer beauty is also an accident of nature. And incredible sex only goes so far. I view external beauty like a book cover. An attractive or appealing cover may draw you in, but you must read all the contents inside to know if is really any good. Many people get too enthralled with the cover. You know what I mean?

—Yeah, I do. Your point is well taken. Did I say that correctly? Your point is well taken about people focusing too much on outside appearance. I'm totally guilty of that. Maybe that is why I thought I would feel more excited after I met you. As I said before, you are very handsome, Eric. And you've said all the right things. But there is something missing. I can't exactly say what. If you don't mind me being direct, I don't feel a connection with you.

—Well, give me a chance. We just met.

—True. But I feel empty. It's not your fault. My schooling and dancing are really taking a lot out of me. Maybe I am searching for someone who doesn't really exist, but I really need the support of someone who truly gets me. Don't get me wrong. You seem like a great guy. But understanding me takes a lot of time and work.

—I understand. You're also a good guy. You'll be okay.

—Everyone says I'm going to be okay. I'm not so sure. Sometimes I have no confidence in myself. I often feel alone in the world. Like no one really understands me. Well, almost no one. I want to do a lot in my life, yet here I am, still in Monterrey, tired and confused. I'm sorry to be boring you with my problems. This night should be fun. If you don't mind, I'd like to be alone for a few moments more to gather my thoughts. I'll go back inside to sleep with you in a few minutes.

—No problem.

—Thanks.

While I sat in bed, waiting for Rafa to return, I thought about all the work I'd done to transform myself into this new person. When I told a few friends, in vague terms, about the planning of my transformation, their response was that I should just accept myself as I am. I responded by saying that my desire to transform myself wasn't out of vanity. I wanted to improve both my physical and inner self. To me, it was worth the time and effort. Now I look good and feel more confident. I am proud of my efforts and would do it all over again.

When I set out to do this transformation, my idea was to do it only for myself. At least I thought I did. But if I'm honest with myself, maybe unconsciously, I did it to make myself more attractive to Rafa. I figured that who I was on the inside was enough for him, but not on the outside. Now that I improved my outward appearance, it seemingly wasn't enough to win Rafa over. The lesson I am learning now is quite humbling. There are intangible, often unexplainable aspects of who we all are that win others over that none of us can control. Who and why we fall in love with someone often doesn't make sense at all. Beyond that, it also includes the day-to-day history of spending time together, of helping each other and loving each other. And frankly, it involves work, lots of it. It involves sharing mundane tasks with someone, as well as giving up a part of one's life to help the other. I did that for Rafa. Well, the Socrates part of me did. But I can't force it. There's a lot of wisdom in the phrase "hang on loosely, but don't let go." But maybe, just maybe, it was time to let go. As I was deep in thought, I heard my phone buzz. It was a text message from Rafa, sent to Socrates.

—*Hola Socrates. ¿Cómo estás?* (Hi Socrates. How are you?)

—I'm good, thanks. And you?

—I could be better.

—What's wrong, Rafa?

—Nothing in particular. Hey, I miss you.

—Really? Again?

—Yes, I'm serious. Again.

—Okay. Can I ask why?

—I'm realizing now that I have been too careless with you. You always supported me, no matter what.

—Well, of course I supported you. There were few strings attached for my help, other than appreciate me and don't ignore me. I've been glad to be another person in your life that has helped you on the way to where you are going.

---That's just it. I have ignored you too much. And I haven't appreciated you as much as I should have. Look, I have to go now. I will text you later, okay? Sweet dreams.

—Sweet dreams to you too, Rafa. Hey, one more thing.

---What?

---I love you.

---I love you too, Socrates.

Rafa finally came in from the balcony and got into bed with me.

—Good night, Eric.

—Good night.

Before laying down, I sat up in bed, thinking over this entire situation. I wished Rafa knew that his Socrates was in bed right next to him. I thought about revealing who I really was right here and now, but I'm sure it would be too difficult to believe. I didn't want to witness another one of his explosions. But what other option did I have? I couldn't go back to how I was before.

—Rafa?

—Yeah?

—*Te tengo una pregunta. ¿Quieres verme otra vez?* (I have a question for you. Do you want to see me again?)

—*Sí, pero solamente en plan de amigos. ¿Está bien?* (Yes, but as friends only. Is that okay?)

—Fine.

Rafa turned his back to me and went to sleep. No cuddling, no more affection. After a sound night of sleep, I was awakened in the early morning by Rafa bustling about, hurriedly preparing for his departure. My eyes squinted to block the recessed lighting above him, as I propped myself up in the bed.

—Oh, sorry about waking you up, Eric. Thanks again for the dinner and hanging out with me. Stay here and take your time getting up. I have things to do.

—Okay. Thank you too. Hey, I know this will sound odd, but before you go, can you do me a favor and ask me a question about you that you think I don't know.

—Why?

—No reason. Just ask, please.

—Okay, what's my mother's name?

—Lola.

—Wow! How did you know that?

—Ask me another.

—What day is my birthday?

—May 4.

—Correct. Okay, what is the name of the club I used to work at?

—768 Downtown Club.

—You must have known all this from my social media posts. Okay, let me think. Here's a question where the answer isn't on my social media posts. What type of food do I most hate?

—Fish, except for maybe tuna.

—What? OMG. But how? I don't understand. Have you been stalking me? No one knows those things about me, except for a few people.

—I will tell you later.

—No, tell me now. I rarely talk about the personal details of my life.

—It's that I am really Soc....I mean, I'm psychic.

—What?

—I have special psychic powers.

—I don't believe you. Well, thanks again, Eric. Bye.

With an upset and confused look on his face, Rafa hurriedly opened the door of the hotel room and left. I lost the courage to tell him who I really was. The next day, Rafa texted Socrates.

—Hey, I'm nearby. Can I come over?

—No, I'm busy. Sorry, Rafa.

—Okay, how about this weekend?

—I will let you know.

---Okay, thanks.

30 MISTAKEN IDENTITIES

When Saturday morning arrived, I was anticipating to spend a quiet, relaxing day finishing up a painting I had been working on for more than a week. But sometimes it is on the quietest of days that life decides to surprise you and throw you off keel. As I ventured into the kitchen to wash the dishes, I looked out of the window and saw Rafa had walked through the open garage door. He spotted me before I could duck down and hide. My hair stood on end as a sudden sensation of panic came over me. As Rafa got a better look at me through the window, his eyes opened wider, and he grimaced. I opened the door.

—Eric?

—Hi Rafa.

—What are you doing here? I came to see Socrates. Where is he?

—The Socrates you knew and loved isn't here anymore. Well, at least the physical part of him. Come on in, if you want.

—What does that mean? How do you know Socrates?

—Sit down and let me explain.

Rafa walked past me and sat down on the couch he loved so much. Instead of pulling out his cell phone like he usually did, he sat straight up on the end of the sofa cushion. I had his full attention.

—Okay, I'm listening. What's going on?

—I'm just going to say it straight out. I'm Socrates.

—What? No, you aren't.

—Remember when I knew all those aspects about your life at the hotel? It was because I am Socrates.

—I can't believe Socrates told you all that information about me. I'm going to kill him.

—No, he didn't. I am him.

—Look, I don't know what weird game you are playing with me but...
I interrupted Rafa.

—It's not a game. If you don't believe me, ask me more questions that
only Socrates would know.

—Why did he tell you stuff about me? Did you get him to tell you
things about me to impress me?

—I know this is hard to believe. I wouldn't believe it if I were you,
either.

Rafa pulled out his phone and immediately sent the text "Where are
you!!!???" to Socrates. My phone vibrated. Rafa's voice got louder.

—You have Socrates' phone??!

—I have my phone. Text Eric something.

Rafa texted "What did you do with Socrates?" to Eric. My phone
buzzed again. I showed him both messages.

—Rafa, I transformed myself during the time I was away from you into
a younger, better-looking version of myself. I made up the Eric
personality because I knew this would be too much of a shock for you
to handle. I wanted you to be attracted to me. And it worked. Well,
almost worked.

—You must have done something to steal Socrates' text messages and
receive them yourself.

—I know it's a shock, Rafa. Maybe you should just go home to think
it over.

—I am not going home until I see Socrates.

—Well, you are going to be waiting a long time, because the Socrates
you knew isn't coming home.

—What have you done with him??!!!

—Nothing. Nothing at all. Let me explain a little more. Please be
patient.

—I'm listening.

—First of all, doesn't my voice sound like Socrates?

—Well, yeah, but that doesn't prove anything. You could be one of
those people who can fake others' voices.

—This is my real voice. As I said before, I decided to transform myself
in an attempt to win you over.

—I'm not buying it. You are Eric. You didn't do anything.

—Eric is made up. I'm not him. I'm Socrates. When I answered those
personal questions about you at the hotel, I told you that I was psychic
because I knew you would react like this if I told you the truth. I am

the Socrates that knows you love Lady Gaga, that knows you hate Christmas songs. I know you got accepted at the University of Monterrey only to not be allowed to enter due to a delay in the delivery of your general education-high school equivalent degree. I know your brother stole your money. I even know you are an escort.

Rafa began glaring at me. His voice now became even more agitated and loud.

—You must have stolen the identity of Socrates and his phone and read our text messages!!

—Calm down. No, I didn't. Honestly, I didn't. Can't you see I did this to get closer to you?

—No! I don't know you. All I see is someone who is mostly a stranger to me, sitting in my friend's house, telling me he isn't coming home!

Rafa took a few moments to let what he just said sink in. I watched as his anger turned to fear. He immediately got up from the couch, opened the door and left. I watched as he ran down the street.

At first, it didn't dawn on me, but I now realized that I might be in trouble. I didn't have time to sit around and wonder if Rafa was going to call the police or not, so I decided to start gathering my important documents and reserved a bus ticket to Tijuana. I quickly stuffed my backpack with a few belongings. Just as I was heading out the door, two Monterrey policeman pulled up in a patrol car. I opened the door and walked over to them to find out what they wanted. They said they'd like to ask me a few questions regarding the reported disappearance of a Socrates Chamberlain. I explained to them that I was him, but when I showed them my California driver's license, SENTRI and my passport, the photos on these identification documents obviously didn't look like me anymore.

After a lengthy period of interrogation, the police finally got tired of asking me who I really was and why I wasn't showing them my real identification information. After a brief search of my apartment, they could not find any paperwork to identify who I was, so they asked to speak to the apartment building manager, Alicia Lopez. I escorted them over to her next-door apartment and knocked on the door. After a long delay, she finally opened it. One of the policemen began to speak.

---*Perdón Señora, buenas tardes. ¿Usted conoce este joven? Estamos buscando Socrates Chamberlain. ¿Es él?)* (Excuse me ma'am, good afternoon. Do you know this young man? We are looking for Socrates Chamberlain. Is this him?)

Alicia looked at me up and down and then responded.

---*Buenas tardes. No, no lo conozco.* (Good afternoon. No, I don't know him.)

The other policemen answered.

---*Gracias. Muy amable. Es todo.* (Thank you, kindly. That is all.)

Before I could argue my case with Alicia, she shut the door. It was at that moment that my heart sank into my stomach. I was taken back to my apartment, where I was immediately handcuffed and taken to a detention facility. When I arrived, I was sent to a holding cell, where the questioning by the authorities continued. Where is Socrates Chamberlain? What is my real name? Why was I at Socrates Chamberlain's apartment? Why did I have his cell phone? I continued to respond by saying that I am Socrates, and that I had undergone a makeover and that's why I looked different. While it was helpful that I could communicate to them in Spanish, they continued to be skeptical of my answers and refused to release me.

Obviously, at this point, I was very nervous. The police told me that until they had further information, they could not release me. They stopped their questioning and directed the detention facility personnel to move me to a different location. A guard escorted me to a cell. He unlocked the cell door and introduced me to my two new cellmates.

—*Oye Chato y Hernandez, tienen ya un nuevo compañero de cuarto. Trata de comportarse bien. ¿Okey?* (Listen up Chato and Hernandez, you guys now have a new roommate. Try to behave yourselves, okay?)

"Chato" and "Hernandez" were lying in their beds, looking at me. Neither got up to introduce themselves. Both had tattoos covering their arms. Chato was slender, unshaven, with a long nose. He was the older of the two, maybe in his mid-30s. He gave me a suspicious look, then went back to staring at his crotch. The guy named Hernandez, apparently just known by his last name, appeared to be in his 20s. He had a robust build and a darker, more mestizo skin tone. He seemed to be the friendlier of my two cellmates. He acknowledged my presence with a head nod and smile. I cleared my throat as I introduced myself.

—*Hola. Soy Socrates. No puedo decirles que es un gusto estar aquí. Para mí, es una pesadilla. Pero es un gusto conocer ustedes.* (Hi. I'm Socrates. I can't say it is a pleasure to be here. For me, it is a nightmare. But it is a pleasure to meet you guys.)

My politeness kicked in, even in jail. Neither jail inmate responded to my comments, so I forced a smile. Upon entering the cell, I walked over to the unoccupied bunk bed and sat down. I stared at the floor, incredulous as to where I was. After a few minutes had passed, I lifted up my head to scan my surroundings. The cell's light green paint on its walls had mostly peeled off. I noticed a heart with initials had been etched onto the wall between the beds. The paint of the steel frames of each of the bunk beds was mostly all chipped off. My mattress had seen better days. It was thin, with yellow stains, lumpy, with several springs missing. An open urinal was located between the four beds. Other than that, the cell was relatively clean. The only smell I noticed was that of the body odor of my cellmates. In another setting, their body odor might have aroused me, but not now. All I felt now was desperation and depression.

Previously, I'd read about the overcrowding, violence, corruption and lack of resources in Mexican prisons. I'd also read about prison environments that were more relaxed, where families often visited, bringing in food each day to their relatives. I wasn't sure what awaited me. Later, we were released from our cell to wander about and get some food. I stood in line waiting my turn to grab a bowl and a plate and be served the choices for today's meal, which were fried chicken and beans and tortillas. After I ate, I mingled among the other inmates but said nothing. Some stared quizzically at me, the lone gringo, but I was mostly ignored. I eventually sat down on a small stool off in a corner and watched a card game. While I observed the game and the others loitering around, I began to feel some strange sensations in my body. I tried my best to ignore them. Eventually nighttime had arrived, and my new reality began to sink in.

When the clock hit 9 p.m., those of us still in the common area were ordered back to our cells. As I entered mine, I noticed that my roommates were already asleep, one snoring softly. As I crawled into bed, my intestines were churning, and the top of my head had begun to throb. My arms and legs were now tingling as well. The veins in my body began to twitch, and my legs ached. I thought about calling over to the guard on duty to ask for medical help, but decided not to, at least for now. I assumed what I was feeling was typical for a first night in prison. Somehow, despite all the weird sensations, aches and pains, I was able to fall asleep. At one point in the night, I jumped up from my bed, my body sweating profusely, after a bad dream. Across the room, I could see Chato moving under his bed covers, apparently jerking off. At least he wasn't looking at me while doing it. It was enough for me to be Rafa's bitch. I had no intention of being anyone else's, if this indeed was going to be my home for a while. Chato soon finished his business, and I was able to drift off to sleep again.

A few hours later, I awoke again due to cramping in various parts of my body. My torso now felt numb. I continued to rationalize my pain, attributing it to some weird anxiety reaction to incarceration.

Anxiety issues have been a long-time, unwelcome friend of mine. Back to sleep I went, dreaming of the old me with Rafa, cuddling together on the couch. The sweet dream was a temporary respite from my new reality. When I woke up, the previous strange sensations of the long night and early morning were gone. Other than being slightly disoriented as to where I was, I felt relatively well, ready to face whatever came my way. I couldn't help but notice that my roommates, who all but ignored me yesterday, were now both sitting up on their beds, staring at me. The guy named Hernandez finally spoke.

—*Güero. ¿Qué te pasó, wey?* (White guy. What happened to you, dude?)

—*Buenos días. Ya sé, me veo horrible. No dormí bien.* (Good morning. I know. I look horrible. I didn't sleep well.)

—*Usted necesita mirarse en el espejo. Se ve mal.* (You need to look in a mirror. You look bad.)

Chato then chimed in.

—*No se ve mal, Nacho. Se ve mayor. Parece que este wey es otra persona ahora, con la misma voz.* (He doesn't look bad, Nacho. He looks old. It appears that this guy is another person now, with the same voice.)

Nacho Hernadez then spoke of a previous experience he had.

—*Si tienes razón. Recuerdo hace años, cuando tomaba psicodélicos, las personas a mi alrededor cambiaban su apariencia frecuentemente. Pero no estoy tomando nada ahora. Gringo, le falta ir al doctor.* (Yes, you are right. I remember years ago when I was taking psychedelics, people around me would change their appearance frequently. But I'm not taking anything now. American guy, you need to go to the doctor.)

I smiled and nodded at them. I understood what they were saying, but I didn't pay much attention to their comments. Me looking horrible after a bad night of anxiety symptoms and lack of sleep was nothing new. But as I casually glanced at my hands, arms and then my legs, my eyes bugged out in shock. I blinked my eyes a few times and looked down at myself again. It appeared that I had reverted to my old self. When the guard unlocked the cell door to let us all out to eat, I quickly headed to the bathroom to look at myself in the mirror. Standing in front of it, I removed my shirt and stared at myself in disbelief. I'd mostly converted back to how I was before. I've had some bad nights in my life, but to have aged 15 years was a new first for me.

It was a bittersweet moment. All the hard work I put into transforming myself was now all for naught. After getting over the initial shock, I became excited. Regressing back to my old self could be my get out of jail free card. Instead of lining up at the chow line, I walked over to the guard to request a talk with one of the administrators. While I was waiting, I requested and was granted one phone call to anyone I chose. I called Rafa, hoping he would answer. Unfortunately, he didn't. I then called my apartment manager. She answered.

—*¿Bueno?* (Hello?)

—*Buenos días, Alicia. Soy Sócrates.* (Good morning, Alicia. I am Sócrates.)

—*¿Dónde usted ha estado? Rafa y la policía le han estado buscando.* (Where have you been? Rafa and the police have been looking for you.)

—*Ya lo sé. Estoy en la cárcel preventiva en el centro. Mira, necesito pedirle un gran favor. ¿Usted puede venir por acá para identificarme? La policía me ha confundido con otra persona y necesito que usted me identifique para aclararlo. Puedo darle los detalles más tarde.* (I already know. I'm at the downtown state correctional center. Look, I need to ask you for a big favor. Can you please come down here to identify me? The police have confused me for another person, and I need you to identify me to clear it up. I can fill you in later on the details.)

—*Está bien. Puedo venir esta tarde.* (That's fine. I can come this afternoon.)

By the time my apartment manager had arrived, I had already spoken with the administrator and tried to explain to him that I was the missing person they were looking for, and that I was mistakenly taken in. I asked him to look again at the allegedly stolen identification papers of Socrates Chamberlain. He pulled up my driver's license, U.S. passport, and SENTRI card and could see that the photos on each now appeared to be of me. After conversing with his superiors, he said he couldn't release me yet. They needed to do an internal investigation. Oh great, I thought. How long is that going to take? That afternoon, he and a few of the jail staff interviewed my cellmates and couldn't believe what they were telling them about my transformation from a young man to an older one. The security guard confirmed nothing unusual had happened and that I had never left my cell. The principal administrator pulled up my booking photo and compared it to what I looked like now. He couldn't quite believe it.

When Alicia finally arrived, I was asked to go to a holding cell and hang tight. After what seemed like an eternity, there was a knock on the door. Alicia appeared, along with the administrator and a security guard. The administrator asked Alicia a question.

—*¿Él es Socrates Chamberlain, su inquilino?* (Is he Socrates Chamberlain, your renter?)

—*Sí.* (Yes.)

—*Gracias, Señora. Señor Chamberlain, también contactamos al caballero que lo acusó de secuestro y entrar el departamento sin permiso. Él necesita identificar usted para liberarlo de los cargos. Francisco, favor de dejarlo entrar.* (Thank you, Ma'am. Mr. Chamberlain, we also contacted the gentleman who accused you of kidnapping and breaking into the apartment. He needs to identify you in order to release you from the charges. Francisco, please let him in.)

The door opened and emerging from the shadows, there he was, my Rafa. When he walked into the room, his facial expression changed from serious to excited. He shouted out.

—*¡Socrates, eres tù!* (Socrates, it's you!)

Rafa ran forward to hug me, but the security guard grabbed his arm to hold him back. The administrator nodded to the security guard to release him. As he did, Rafa walked forward and gave me the biggest hug I'd ever received from him in my life. As he held me tight, he whispered into my ear.

—I thought I'd lost you.

Now that Rafa had confirmed that I was indeed Socrates, the charges were dropped, and I was free to go. After the signing of a few documents, my release was finalized, and my belongings returned. As I walked into the lobby of the detention center, I saw Alicia and Rafa sitting down on a bench, looking at their phones. As I approached them, Rafa looked up, jumped to his feet and hugged me again. After we pulled apart from each other, I thanked Alicia and Rafa for coming.

As we walked out the main door to exit, the bright Monterrey sun broke free from behind a cloud, shining down on us. Overcome with a mix of joy and relief over what had just transpired, a feeling of lightheadedness overtook me. I stopped for a moment to steady myself, as Rafa and Alicia continued walking towards Alicia's minivan. What came out of my mouth next can only be described as over exuberance. Invoking the famous civil rights activist and church leader Martin Luther King, I belted out my emotions to no one in particular.

---Free at last! Free at last! Thank God Almighty, I am free at last!

Rafa and Alicia, both already having reached the van, turned to look back, wondering what all the fuss was about. Rafa then yelled out to me.

---*¡Vámonos gringo loco! ¡Rayos! Tanto escándalo por solamente unas horas en el bote.* (Let's go you crazy American! Good heavens! Making such a big deal about only a few hours in jail.)

I ran over to catch up with them. As I opened the front passenger door, Alicia interjected.

—*Tengo mucha basura en el asiento delantero. ¿Por qué ustedes no se sientan en los asientos atrás?* (I've got a lot of junk in the front seat. Why don't you two sit in the back?)

After climbing into the back of the vehicle and seating ourselves, Rafa conducted himself in a way the Socrates version of me had rarely seen. Ignoring his cell phone, Rafa's brown eyes were fixated on me as he reached for my hand and held it. Next, without saying a word, he smiled and leaned his head on my shoulder. The sweet and tender moment was fleeting, interrupted by comments from Alicia.

---*Me alegro de que estés libre, Sócrates, pero estoy confundida. La policía se presentó ayer en mi puerta, preguntándome si un tipo que no conocía era un inquilino de nuestro edificio. Vi que lo llevaban en la patrulla. Ahora hoy, Usted me llama, diciendo que fue identificado erróneamente.* (I'm happy that you are free, Socrates, but I'm confused. The police showed up at my door yesterday asking me if some guy I didn't know was a renter in our building. I saw them take the guy away in their patrol car. Now today, you call me, saying you were mistakenly identified.)

I responded.

---*Es una larga historia, Alicia.* (It's a long story, Alicia.)

Rafa lifted his head off my shoulder and spoke up.

---*También estoy confundido. Reporté tu secuestro. Entonces, si encontraron a Eric, ¿por qué te detuvieron también?* (I am also confused. I reported you kidnapped. So, if they found Eric, why were you detained as well?)

---*La policía también me detuvo hasta que pudieron aclarar quién era yo y qué había pasado. Eric no me secuestró. Estaba usando mi pasaporte, SENTRI y licencia de conducir.* (The police held me too until they could clarify who I was and what had happened. Eric didn't kidnap me. He was using my passport, SENTRI and driver's license.)

Rafa followed up with another question.

---*Pero ¿cómo se conocieron y cómo obtuvo tu información de identificación?* (But how do you know each other and how did he get your identification information?)

---*Estoy exhausto. Te lo voy a explicar todo más tarde en el departamento.* (I'm exhausted. I'll explain it all later at the apartment.)

31 GIFTS OF LOVE

When we arrived at the apartment building, I again thanked Alicia for taking time out of her busy day to help me out. As I unlocked the door and let Rafa and myself in, I breathed a sigh of relief that the stressful ordeal was finally over. At least part of it was. I still owed Rafa a more detailed explanation about what really had happened. For the moment though, we said nothing. Rafa and I both crashed on the couches in an attempt to reenergize. Eventually, Rafa broke the silence.

—Socrates, when you are ready, please explain more in detail what happened between you and Eric. Did he steal your identification and cell phone? I didn't even know you guys knew each other.

As I prepared to speak, I took a deep breath. Rafa continued.

---You know what the weirdest thing was? When I found him here in your apartment, he said he was you. How absurd, right? He said something about transforming himself into a different person. And he knew all this stuff about me. I don't know how. I figured he read our text messages.

—Rafa, instead of me explaining what happened, maybe it would be better if you read the copy of the police report.

I handed Rafa the report. While reading it, an expression of incredulity appeared on his face. The report confirmed what I, as Eric, tried to explain to Rafa, that Socrates and Eric were indeed the same person. The same person who Rafa had arrested and charged with kidnapping. The police report stated that several witnesses, including my cellmates Chato, Nacho and a prison guard, attested to the fact that something unexplainable regarding my appearance had happened in my jail cell, returning me back to my former self.

After Rafa finished reading the report, he set it down on the coffee table, turned away from me and stared out the living room window. When Rafa finally turned back around to look at me, his built-up indignation sent me tumbling backwards, sending a shiver down my spine. He yelled out.

---No, no, no!

Rafa immediately stood up, grabbed his pack of cigarettes and headed out to the patio for a smoke. I nervously waited for what seemed like an eternity for his return to the living room. After about 10 minutes or so, he reappeared with a much calmer disposition. After a long silence, he finally spoke.

—This is a lot to take in, Socrates. Your obsession with me. Your deception. And how you were able to change your appearance. I don't know what to think about it all.

—Rafa, Look...

—I've got to go.

As Rafa let himself out of the apartment, I sat quietly on the sofa, pondering not only what had just happened, but also all my time spent with the young man. For much of the afternoon and evening, I drank from a bottle of wine in an attempt to drown my sorrows, while listening to my favorite classical music and a few hauntingly sad songs. At that moment, I felt like a dam in disrepair, as it strained to support the heavy weight of the water. I held the water back as long as I could until the dam burst wide open. As my tears flowed freely, memories of my time with Rafa flooded my memory bank. I scrolled through photos from my cell phone of Rafa and I together, having fun on the beach in Rosarito. After the bottle was empty, I managed to fall asleep in a drunken stupor.

The next morning, I awoke with a bad headache, but my storm of emotions had come and gone. I slowly started back into my daily routine of painting, exercising and writing. I patiently waited a couple of days before texting Rafa, asking him for forgiveness, but unfortunately, there was no response. This was not a big surprise to me, given my experience with post-Rafa rage. Whether he understood or not why I had transformed myself, Rafa now knew the lengths I would go to being close to him. Despite my good intentions, I did feel ashamed of my actions. I assumed that he was probably tired of me by now. I was just tired, period. Tired of chasing after someone who was seemingly always just beyond my grasp. I was still very much in love with Rafa, but I was forced to accept the reality that my style of giving everything I have in my relationships was too much to handle for most people.

As more days passed, I'd mostly given up on seeing Rafa ever again, figuring the damage done was too much to repair. It was time to refocus on other priorities. Today, as I went out to water my plants on the patio, I saw a green and orange colored hummingbird. It was the first time I'd ever seen a hummingbird in Monterrey. As I went from plant to plant with my watering pot, it followed me, as if it was attempting to tell me something. This small bird brightened my spirits.

My next task for the day was to figure out where to hang a large acrylic painting I made of Rafa. I planned to give it to him before being sent to jail. It was a collage I created with painstaking detail of his different facial expressions, from anguish to ecstasy. After thinking about it for a while, I decided not to hang the painting anywhere. Instead, I'd put it away in my bedroom closet. Maybe I'll try to sell it, I told myself. I figured that maybe, just maybe, it was time for me to put away this obsession of mine once and for all.

My next priority was replenishing my food supply. I put on my black hoodie and headed out from my apartment to the Soriana supermarket, as thunder rumbled from storm clouds gathering in the distance. Once I arrived, reminders of Rafa were all around me. I found myself reminiscing about my previous shopping experiences, almost always focused on buying specific food items that I would cook for him. Soon, I found myself muttering Rafa's name. That is when I shouted out loud to myself.

---Stop this! Time to move on.

My loud shout didn't go unnoticed, A startled woman in the same aisle stared at me. I sheepishly smiled at her and turned away to continue my shopping. After paying for my items, I exited the store. Instead of requesting a Didi, I decided to test my luck and walk back home, despite the ominous dark gray storm clouds overhead. My luck ran out a couple of blocks from my apartment, as the clouds suddenly burst open, with sheets of rain pouring down on me. I began a half sprint, head down, groceries bags in hand, towards the apartment. As I arrived at the door of my apartment building and pulled out the key from my pants pocket, I looked up and there he was. Head down, crouched over while sitting on the curb next to the garage entrance door sat Rafa, seemingly oblivious to the rain pelting down upon him.

He looked up at me, he grabbed the plastic bag he brought with him, stood up and greeted me.

—*Hola.* (Hi)

—Hey there, Rafa. What are you doing here?

—Can we talk for a few minutes?

—Um, okay, sure.

After opening the door, I took off my shoes and asked Rafa to wait in the doorway until I could bring us towels to dry off. After we both were sufficiently dry, I brought dry clothes for both of us to change into. Once changed, he sat down on the couch. I told him I'd be with him in a minute, as I hurriedly put away the food items I'd purchased. Rafa was squirming around on the couch, unsettled. He seemed to be searching for something to say. Just then, I pulled out a bottle of wine from one of the bags, which gave Rafa an opening to start a conversation.

—Oh, I see that you bought our favorite wine.

---What?

---*Riunite Lambrusco.*

—Oh yeah, I did. Old habits die hard, I guess.

—Nice.

—Look Rafa, before you say why you came, I want to apologize. I told myself after what I did on *Grindr* that I'd never pretend to be someone else to you again. I broke my promise to myself and to you. It was wrong and I'm sorry. I'm always getting carried away. You were right all along. I am obsessed with you.

—It's okay, Socre.

—No, it isn't. You need your space, and I haven't given it to you. I need to be more aware of how others perceive me. My craziness reminds me of an interview I recently saw with Oprah Winfrey, the talk show host. The interviewer asked her what the most common characteristic was of all the successful people she interviewed in her life.

---What did she say?

---She said their common characteristic was they knew where they wanted to go. She said most people don't know. And after these successful people decided where they wanted to go, every choice they made after that was to move them in the direction of their vision. And when they did that, the forces of life rose up to achieve it. That's exactly what I've strived to do. I put all my focus on what I want. But regarding us, I now see that maybe I should have scaled back my enthusiasm. I should have considered who you are, what your style of doing things is, and where you are in your life. We work best as a team if both our needs are met.

—Socrates, you think I don't understand how you are by now? I'll admit that it took me a while to figure you out and make sense of your style. At times, I was overwhelmed by you. Sometimes I still am. But that is also what makes you unique. You are exactly like those successful people Oprah mentioned. I have always admired how you are always learning, growing, and inspiring me and others.

—Thanks. Again, I apologize and am deeply sorry for my actions. I messed up again.

—Thanks, but this time was different from the Grindr deception. This time you did try to tell me the truth and it was I who wouldn't accept it. I should apologize to you for not believing you.

—Oh please. No one would be expected to believe that I had transformed into a different physical self. That's why I pretended to be someone else. I was eventually going to tell you. You just forced it out of me when you arrived here unannounced.

—So okay, maybe we both messed up a little. Let's just call it a tie.

—Sounds good to me.

—You must tell me something, Socrates. How did you transform yourself? You must have some special powers.

—I'm not sure myself. It was a mix of alchemy and hard work. I uncovered latent abilities that I believe we all have and learned how to harness them in a way that few people have done. I used several methods to achieve it, such as mental imagery, repetitive recordings and meditation. It didn't happen simultaneously. It took months.

—Wow. You worked for months to perfect yourself just to be my boyfriend. You are amazing. I will never doubt you again. I'm still in shock.

—Don't get carried away. I didn't do it for you. Well, maybe some of it was for you. I mostly did it for self-improvement. I am disappointed that my efforts were only temporary, but frankly, I'm just relieved that I'm no longer in prison. I was beginning to think that I would be there for years. By the way, thanks for reporting me to the police, bitch.

Rafa laughed nervously.

—I'm sorry, Socre. I did it for Socrates' part of you. I was afraid Eric had kidnapped him or worse.

—I'll forgive you this time.

—Thank you. So, what are you making for lunch today?

—I was thinking about spinach and cheese raviolis with potatoes and broccoli.

—One of my favorites. I miss that dish.

—Well, it isn't hard to make. You could make it yourself.

—Yeah, I guess if I was forced to, because you know I don't like cooking. But even if I tried, I couldn't make it like you do.

—What do you mean?

—When you made meals for me, you made them with a lot of care and love. I'd look up from doing my homework and see food, pots, pans and utensils everywhere, with you in the middle of them, chopping, sauteing and simmering. You made sure every detail of the meal was to my liking, so that it was both visually appealing and delicious. Socrates, your artistry isn't limited to painting and writing. Your life is art.

—I do enjoy having someone to cook for. Well, I did. I did everything I could to make you happy.

—You made me feel at home. Thank you for that.

—I tried my best. So anyway, I'm still waiting to hear why you came here to visit me.

—I came to tell you that I decided, as of today, that I will be retiring as an escort.

—What? I thought you enjoyed being an escort. Is that really the reason you came over? To tell me that?

—Well, that is partly why I'm here.

---Can you even do that? It seemed like it fulfilled the sex addict part of you. You've said before that you were quitting only to return to being an escort.

---I know, but this time I really mean it. I'm tired of it. It's time for me to grow up and focus on what I really want to be.

---Okay.

---I'm also here to apologize for running out on you the other day. I know I don't apologize much at all to you because of my pride and ego. After I read the police report, I was confused. You know me by now. I explode. That's my thing. My defect. Well, one of them. I didn't tell you, but I've been seeing a psychologist friend of mine who is giving me a few free sessions. We are working on why I explode so much and other issues. She's really been helpful. Anyway, I wanted to see you to clear the air.

—Send your psychologist over to me when you are done with her. I need help too.

We both smiled. I continued.

---Okay, well, you've seen me now. You can go now, if you want. I know you are always busy, and I have more errands to run.

—Not so fast. Wait. I'm here for another reason. An important one.

—Let me guess. You are here to tell me that you are acting in a movie now. Or you're moving to Germany. Or maybe you found a third boyfriend. You know whatever it is, I'm happy for you. You deserve it. You are achieving your dreams by yourself, just like you always wanted to. I'm just happy to have been a part of it.

Rafa laughed.

—A third boyfriend. I could barely deal with the two I had. Anyway, I've decided to end my relationship with Enrique and Abraham. I still love them, but I decided that it is best to let them focus on each other. And you know it's important for me to be independent, to not be controlled or feel trapped in any way.

---Yes, I know that.

---After some soul searching, I've come to realize that, as hard as I have worked to get where I am now, it is also true that being completely independent was a lie I told myself. I could never have done it all by myself, especially these last couple of years. I always had support from others. But mostly, I always had you, Socrates. You always came to the rescue when I needed help. When I was falling, you were there to pick me up. You helped me even when I showed disinterest or even disdain towards you, which was far too often that I care to admit. You were right. I took you for granted. But instead of saying 'I'm out of here,' you never went away. Most people would have said to themselves that this guy is too reckless and messed up.

Upon hearing Rafa's frank words, I tightened my lips to avoid getting too emotional. I barely got out my next words.

—Yes, you always did have me.

—This week-plus time away from you allowed me to reflect on us. When I thought that I had lost you, when I thought Eric had kidnapped or killed you, I went crazy. Only then was I able to realize everything you've meant to me. I was flooded with emotions that I didn't know I had and didn't know what to do with. When I sat down with my psychologist friend to sort them all out, your name kept popping up. Finally, she asked me who Socrates was. Later, she asked me various questions. Who do I most learn from? Who challenges me? Whom can I trust? Who brings me joy? It wasn't easy for me to admit, but the answers to those questions were Socrates, Socrates, Socrates and Socrates.

---I've tried my best to bring out the best in you.

---I know you have. I thought about all that you have done for me and have kept doing. I've taken more from you than I ever gave back to you. You never stopped believing in me. I thought about what you sacrificed to be with me. You gave up a comfortable living situation, moved to another country and joined my struggle. I was basically a stranger when we met, an uneducated, young, unstable guy, and you trusted me. And you did it for almost nothing in return.

---It wasn't for nothing. I got to see you happy and improving your life. Anyway, you are wrong. Lots of people bring you joy. I'm just one of many. You always told me that, especially when I began to think I was an important person to you or even your best friend.

---I never told you that you were my best friend because if I admitted how important you really were to me, I thought you might become even more intense with me, if that is possible. You know me. I'm afraid of anyone knowing too much about me and you know a lot.

---Well, I didn't force that information out of you.

---I know you didn't. But you did force me to see the not so good side of me, the bruises, the messy side, the part I try to hide from everyone, even myself. You exposed me, entering my soul so easily without me even realizing you did it. I allowed you to do so because I'm so comfortable with you. You also have shown a bright light on my attributes in an attempt to lift me up. And you have succeeded. I'm a better person because of it. I now trust you even more than my own family.

---And yet, after all my efforts, you ghosted me. I knew nothing about you for half a year.

---I know I did. I needed my space. And time to reflect and mature. I'm still somewhat of a wreck, a work in progress. But I am sure of one thing. It took almost losing you to realize how happy I am with you. I sat alone in my room and asked myself "Who would ever do all this for me?" And I thought about what you always told me about us all being energy and that good looks are just accidents of nature. You said what counts is who we are inside, who inspires us, who gets us, who pushes us, who is there day after day, who will do anything to make us happy, especially if we are unhappy. You are still inside my soul, Socre, despite my attempts to remove you. That's quite an achievement. If I was a video game, you'd be the top scorer. You've made it to a level even I didn't know existed. I can't ignore that, even if I wanted to.

—That's nice to know, Rafa. I know how hard it is for you to say all this. If this is your way of saying thank you for all that I've done for you, you are welcome. It's nice to know I've had some impact on you while you were constantly distracted on your cell phone, looking at *Instagram*, *TikTok*, *YouTube* music videos, posting porn videos to your hidden *X* accounts, texting clients of Rocco and Lu and guys on *Grindr*.

Well, I've got stuff to do. If that is all you came for, you can....
Rafa interrupted me.
—Hold on. I'm not finished. Stop rushing me. I just thought about another reason why I enjoy being with you, Socrates.
---Why?
---It's something rather simple. I remember when I first met you, you told me how observative you are. At the time I thought, who cares. But now that I've been apart from you, I really missed it when we'd walk down the street together. You'd point out trivial aspects of our surroundings. The beauty of cracks in the street. Shoes hanging on a telephone wire. A gum wrapper lodged into an empty soda bottle. You have the mind and eye of a painter, an artist. You'd make the ordinary seem extraordinary. I get more out of life by just being by your side. You have taught me to appreciate aspects of life that I usually miss. I know you think I am too distracted to notice, but when I look up from my cell phone, sometimes I do pay attention.
—That's impressive that you noticed that about me. You never stop surprising me.

As I was getting up to go to the kitchen, Rafa quickly stood up and stepped in front of me, grabbing my wrist, then my hand.
—Hey, remember how I always tell you that I'm going to buy you a gift for your birthday or Christmas, and then I never do it, because I don't have much money, or I forget? Well, believe it or not, I have a gift for you now. Are you ready for it?
—Really? I'll believe it when I see it. And it's not Christmas or my birthday.

Rafa grabbed his cell phone and set it up to play one of my favorite classical music pieces from the movie *The Pianist–Op. 22: Andante spianato in G major*. It's a very light piece of music that I often played to quiet my mind. He next pulled rope out of the bag he brought with him to the apartment.
—Socrates, can you please loosely tie the rope around my wrists, then turn on the music? Thanks.

After I followed his instructions and the music began playing, Rafa stripped off his clothes down to his black underwear. Then he laid down on the tile floor, crunched up like a ball. A few seconds later, he began to unfurl his slender body, while loudly grunting and screaming in anguish, contorting it in unusual ways, with his hands still tied together. After a minute or so of struggle, he opened his hands. He began moving frantically, as he attempted to break free from the rope. As he finally unleashed the rope, the bonds that restrained him, he thrusted his body upward. Now, his facial expression had changed from anguish to joy. He was now glowing as he performed slow, light movements with his arms, hands and body. He glided about the living room, in rhythm with the music, then turned and swiftly ran down the hallway. He performed high and strong jumps, aerial splits and twirls. Upon his return, he turned to face the opposite direction of me as he turned with his leg extended, bent his back over, until his face was upside down, his eyes fixated on mine.

The grand finale of the dance was flawless brilliance. Slow, flowing movements increased in speed, ending in a long spin and splits. Rafa suddenly stood up from the splits position and fell to his knees, looking upward at me, arms stretched out, grabbing my legs, as the music ended. There was silence for a few seconds afterwards, as he was breathing hard. He continued to look at me as he finally caught his breath. He smiled broadly, then spoke.

—What did you think, Socrates?

---It was beautiful, very expressive and emotional. Thank you. It was pure you, your rawest self, expressing your unique talent, style, technique and theatrical mastery.

---I choreographed it just for you, Socre. It is my special gift to you. It represents me breaking free from all my bonds, my troubles and internal struggles. It's also representative of our special bond, a bond that I never want to break free from.

—Wow. I don't know what to say, except thank you so much.

---You are welcome.

Rafa's gift of dance inspired me to give him a gift in return.

---Okay, Rafa, it's my turn to give you a gift as well.

---No, absolutely not. You've given me too many gifts already. I don't deserve another one. Look at the list of money I owe you on the refrigerator.

---Please, just one more. But if you don't like it, you have to say so, okay?

---Well, okay, I promise.

---Close your eyes and wait a second while I go get it.

As Rafa stood near the kitchen counter in his underwear, with his eyes closed, I went to my bedroom closet to retrieve my painting of him.

---Ready?

---Yes, I am.

I put my hands on Rafa's waist and guided his body over to another part of the living room.

---Okay, you can open your eyes now.

Rafa's opened his eyes, then opened them even wider while letting out a gasp, putting his hand over his mouth. He stared directly at the huge painting I'd made for him.

---This is over the top incredible, Socrates. I love, love, love it! The details, the colors, the skin texture, my different faces. You held nothing back. How in the world did you come up with this? It's like you…you…you reached deep inside of me. I do have one question, though. What is that abstract area mixed into the center?

---You can't figure it out? Look again.

---Wait, don't tell me. Wait, wait…oh my gosh, it looks you painted yourself amongst my faces, with your hand reaching for something. Are you reaching for my soul?

Rafa looked at me as I nodded affirmatively. He continued.

---Wow! So amazingly beautiful. Such a unique interpretation. I don't know what to say. I…I…

What I witnessed next was unprecedented---a facial expression that I didn't include in Rafa's painting. I decided not to include it in the painting because it was a face I'd never seen in person. As Rafa continued to absorb the contents of the painting, he stood in awe, motionless and expressionless. I saw his brown eyes begin to well up with tears. One of them dribbled down his face. A few seconds later, an uncontrollable onslaught of tears came streaming down his cheeks. He bowed his head down and began to sob uncontrollably. A minute or so passed as the waterworks continued to flow and primordial sounds echoed from deep inside of his bowels.

I walked over to him to make sure he was okay. With his head still down, he saw me closing in on him out of the corner of his eye. He stuck out his hand, waving me off, signally to me to stop where I was. He began to compose himself, sniffling while he dried his face off.

---Are you happy now, Socrates? You've finally seen me cry in person. I now lay bare for you to see. I don't know how you do it. I absolutely hate you because of it.

---Do what?

---You have this unique ability to…unleash feelings trapped deep inside of me.

---Look Rafa…

Rafa interrupted me.

---It's okay. You know what else? Seeing this beautiful painting and your extraordinary talent made me realize something. All this time, you've been propping me up, promoting me, saying how talented I am, doing what you can to make me the best I can be. Meanwhile, I've ignored what you bring to the table. Your gifts and skills. I feel ashamed.

---It's okay. I forgive you.

---No, it's not okay. Thanks to my psychologist, I've come to realize how unappreciative I have been. Like you said, I am very narcissistic and thought that's how I should lead my life. Always me first. As you know, I am so busy with projects, leading a distracted life. That was my excuse for not thanking you enough. I haven't been a good friend. I never really have asked much about you and your goals. I know you said this to me before about how I am, but I had to discover this myself, on my own timeline.

---You are now older and wiser.

---I think I am. Hey, I have one more surprise for you. Another gift. Well, it's a gift for us both.

—Another one? I don't know if I can take another one. What are you up to now?

Rafa reached into his pocket and pulled out a passport.

---I got my Mexican passport with a visa to go to the U.S.

---Wow! Finally. Congratulations!

---I haven't used it yet. I want the first time crossing to be with you. To go to San Diego with you, like we always talked about.

---Rafa, I will be more than happy to show you San Diego.

---I have another surprise for you, Socre.

---No more, please. I'm exhausted.

---Please. Just trust me. You've touched my soul with your painting and with everything else you've done for me. Now it's my turn to return the favor. I'm going to try to do it. It's your turn to close your eyes. Don't open them until I say so, okay?

—Okay but hurry up. I've got things to do.

After nothing happened for several seconds. I became impatient. Then I felt Rafa grab my hand and hold it.

—Rafa, what is it? What are you doing?

The next thing I felt was Rafa's breath on my face. What happened next was completely unexpected. His large, smooth lips were tenderly touching mine. They were touching Socrates' lips, not Eric's. The subtly soft, sweetness of his lips, combined with his strong musty scent, engulfed me once more. My first reaction was to wonder if I was dreaming. My knees began to buckle. The long, seemingly eternal kiss was like kryptonite for me, gradually weakening me as I took it in. If I was breathing at this moment, I don't recall, so spellbound was I by his intimate gift. As he slowly pulled away, I finally opened my eyes. There he was, his face smiling, still moist from his fallen tears. Just when I thought the spell he had cast was lifting, he doused me with more passionate kisses which I tried my best to match. He then pulled away, grabbing my arms and putting them around his waist. Rafa smiled at me again. At least it looked like a smile. I was so mesmerized by the moment, so overwhelmed by my new reality, that for a second or two, I wasn't sure about what I was experiencing or even where I was. I began to smile back at him but then I stopped, as the logical part of my brain slowly began to kick in. I tried to let go of him, but Rafa refused.

—Look, Rafa, if this is some game or just some momentary weakness on your part. If it's some...

Rafa interrupted me.

—Shush. Stop overthinking. Just relax and enjoy the moment. There's no need to transform yourself anymore. If there is someone in this world who I truly love, who truly understands me, it's you, Socrates. My long search for the meaning of true love is over. It was right in front of me, and I refused to see it. My eyes are wide open now. The rain and my tears are now gone. *Te amo, Socre. De verdad, te amo. No solamente para hoy. Para siempre.* (I love you, Socre. Truthfully, I love you. Not just today. For forever.)

I began to tremble with joy as his words resonated inside of me. It was my turn to cry. As happy tears began to stream down my face, Rafa wiped each one of them off with his lips. Despite my being overcome with emotion, I somehow managed to muster up the ability to speak.

—I love you too, *puto* (whore). Are you saying that I am now, finally, officially, your bitch?

—Socrates, you always were. You always were.

We both laughed as we embraced each other once more.

THE END

ABOUT THE AUTHOR

Coming Up for Air Inside the Soul of a Mexican Dancer is author Bruce Even's first book. He is a former journalist and employee for the County of San Diego Health and Human Services Agency, Public Health Services. He has a Bachelor of Arts degree in Journalism from San Diego State University. Mr. Even currently resides in San Diego, California.